Books are to be returned on or before
the last date below.

**Political Women
1800–1850**

Political Women
1800–1850

EDITED BY RUTH AND EDMUND FROW

Introduction by Julia Swindells

PLUTO  PRESS

London • Winchester, Mass

First published 1989 by Pluto Press
345 Archway Road
London N6 5AA
and 8 Winchester Place, Winchester
MA 01890, USA

Cover illustrations (from left to right): Mary Anne Tocker, Eliza
Sharples, Anna Wheeler; (below) Peterloo Medal

British Library Cataloguing in Publication Data

Political women 1800–1850
   1. Great Britain. Politics. Role of women,
1800–1850
   I. Frow, Ruth II. Frow, Edmund, *1922*–
323.3'4'0941

   ISBN 1-85305-053-9

Library of Congress Cataloging-in-Publication Data

Political women, 1800–1850/ edited by Ruth and Edmund Frow:
introduction by Julia Swindells.
   p.   cm.
   Includes bibliographies.
   ISBN 1-85305-053-9
1. Women in politics – Great Britain – History 19th century.
2. Women social reformers – Great Britain – History 19th century.
3. Women in trade-unions – Great Britain – History 19th century.
4. Working class women – Great Britain – History 19th century.
5. Women's rights – Great Britain – History 19th century. I. Frow,
Ruth. II. Frow, Edmund.
HQ1236.5.G7P65 1989
305.4'0941–dc20   89–8708
                                         CIP

Printed in Great Britain by Billing and Sons Ltd, Worcester

Contents

Introduction

JULIA SWINDELLS

Betty Harris, age 37: I was married at 23, and went into a colliery when I was married. I used to weave when about 12 years old; can neither read nor write. I work for Andrew Knowles, of Little Bolton (Lancs), and make sometimes 7s a week, sometimes not so much. I am a drawer, and work from 6 in the morning to 6 at night. Stop about an hour at noon to eat my dinner; have bread and butter for dinner; I get no drink. I have two children, but they are too young to work. I worked at drawing when I was in the family way. I know a woman who has gone home and washed herself, taken to her bed, been delivered of a child, and gone to work again under the week.

I have a belt round my waist, and a chain passing between my legs, and I go on my hands and feet. The road is very steep, and we have to hold by a rope; and when there is no rope, by anything we can catch hold of. There are six women and about six boys and girls in the pit I work in; it is very hard work for a woman. The pit is very wet where I work, and the water comes over our clog-tops always, and I have seen it up to my thighs; it rains in at the roof terribly. My clothes are wet through almost all day long. I never was ill in my life, but when I was lying in.

My cousin looks after my children in the day time. I am very tired when I get home at night; I fall asleep sometimes before I get washed. I am not so strong as I was, and cannot stand my work so well as I used to. I have drawn till I have had the skin off me; the belt and chain is worse when we are in the family way. My feller [husband] has beaten me many a time for not being ready. I were not used to it at first, and he had little patience.

I have known many a man beat his drawer. I have known men take liberties with the drawers, and some of the women have bastards.[1]

Children's Employment Commission – Mines, 1842, p. 84

Women in History

History, and in particular the history of work, has been written almost exclusively from the male perspective. In this collection, Ruth and Edmund Frow contribute forcefully to the growing body of women's and working-class history which is undergoing the slow and painstaking process of correcting this perspective. Until surprisingly recently, early nineteenth-century British history was presented to us in terms of the achievements of prominent industrialists and politicians. E.P. Thompson intervened into this account making the irresistible claim to show us 'the making of the English working class' in this period. Subsequently, radical historians have built on this model and women historians have begun to challenge the stereotypes about women which persist even in much history of the working class. Betty Harris, whose oral account of working in a mine prefaces this Introduction, gives a testimony all too frequently lost to the actual experience of women's work, particularly work outside of the home. We know that women worked in mines and factories, but the accounts we have of mining and factory-work tend to yield an image of male labour. Betty Harris speaks to us from a perspective rarely shared with the reader of history of a *woman's* work in the mines and shows that general relationship of work and domesticity so frequently invisible in the male-authored historical record.

This collection shows up the perspective of *women* in the period, consolidating and clarifying our understanding of working-class experience as a whole.[2] It shows women and their experiences particularly in that area of 'the public sphere' where there is least documentation of women's lives, except of a few notable individuals. The power of the collection is not only that it takes as its basis the woman-authored perspective, but also that it gives us overwhelming evidence of women's involvement in political struggle and in effecting political change. The history of unionism and electoral reform, again so frequently shown as a history by men and of men, is here challenged with a panorama of female agency and activism. Look in the reform movements, and the women are there. Look at early union organisation, and the women are there, and not merely as crowds and bystanders or supporters of men, but as prominent thinkers and doers.

Sheila Rowbotham and other women historians have commented on the amnesia which seems to beset many prevailing historical accounts.[3] As recently as the 1984 miners' strike, women's part was predominantly represented to us as something unusual. Women were shown actively engaged in the strike as if this was an exceptional feature of industrial action. It is against these classic models of agency and militancy that the history of women has to work. Built into the classic model, as Bea Campbell and others have shown, is a particular valuing of male manual labour, which confers dignity on the male miner, but leaves the woman miner out of account.[4] What is more, this act of conferring dignity comes not from the male miner himself, but from those who seek to be philanthropic towards him, in other words, those in a position of dominance over him. Women workers, in this process, are left stranded on isolated islands in the sea of history, either without a representation of their experience, or with one that fails to integrate them into the general account. We literally forget or, as Sally Alexander has put it, 'delete' them from historical continuity.[5]

The collection in this volume shows that women's involvement in the struggle for workers' rights has a continuous history. In the period chosen women are shown playing a significant part in a period of intense struggle when workers were becoming increasingly aware of their identity as a class. Women as well as men took up commanding roles and made sacrifices to 'the cause'.

Historically, much of the relative status of women vis-a-vis work – a relative status which, as we are seeing, puts women in and out of the account without systematic integration – can be explained in relation to 'the family wage'. In the fourteenth-century Guilds, work was literally subcontracted to the family unit through the leading man of the household. He then 'employed' his wife and children. These property and employment relations persisted in the nineteenth century in the form of 'the family wage', as Marx showed us. This persistence of 'subcontraction' was, of course, divisive both within the family and in the workplace outside of the home. The common argument was that the introduction of machinery enabled women to enter sectors of employment occupied previously solely by men, and because of their relative status in the labour market, they could be employed at a lower rate of pay. But despite divisions, the Frow collection shows that women fought for improvements in conditions of employment both in separate benefit societies or clubs of their own, or by organising with men. As early as 1747, women and men joined the Small-ware Weavers' Association in Manchester. They paid the same dues and received the same strike pay. When the Combination Acts made trade unions illegal, women lacemakers in Loughborough combined 'to dictate to their employers and to raise the price of their wages'.[6] They sent organisers to other towns to generate further unions. When the Luddite movement protested against the implications of the introduction of new machinery, the Leicester hand-spinners' women's union, numbering 18,500, fuelled the movement.

Women's Working Conditions

The population employed in the cotton factories rises at five o'clock in the morning, works in the mills from six till eight o'clock, and returns home for half an hour or forty minutes to breakfast. This meal generally consists of tea or coffee, with a little bread. Oatmeal porridge is sometimes, but of late rarely used, and chiefly by the men; but the stimulus of tea is preferred, and especially by the women. The tea is almost always of a bad, and sometimes of a deleterious quality; the infusion is weak, and little or no milk is added. The operatives return to the mills and workshops until twelve o'clock, when an hour is allowed for dinner. Amongst those who obtain the lower rates of wages this meal generally consists of boiled potatoes. The mess of potatoes is put into one large dish; melted lard and butter are poured upon them, and a few pieces of fried fat bacon are sometimes mingled with them, and but seldom a little meat. Those who obtain better wages, or families whose aggregate income is larger, add a greater proportion of animal food to this meal, at least three times in the week; but the quantity consumed by the labouring population is not great. The family sits round the table, and each rapidly appropriates his portion on a plate, or they all plunge their spoons into the dish, and with an animal eagerness satisfy the cravings of their appetite. At the expiration of the hour, they are all again employed in the workshops or mills, where they continue until seven o'clock.[7]

The first half of the nineteenth century saw significant advances in mechanisation and work techniques as well as changes in living standards and working conditions. But far from benefiting from these developments, most women experienced the double exploitation that was consolidated by advancing capitalism – at home and in paid work. This period which, as we see in the classic account of labour history, fermented working-class consciousness thereby required a strong and united political commitment from its activists, and as the Frow collection shows, women did not balk this commitment. To understand the contribution women made to the movement in its widest sense, it is necessary to remind ourselves of the difficulties that they were undergoing both at home and in paid work.

In their lifetimes, most women did one or more of the following five jobs: domestic servant, factory operative, needlewoman, agricultural worker, domestic industry worker. Very few women experienced any other type of work. By far the largest area of employment was in domestic service, but factory work was a growth area, with the number of women working in it increasing annually in this period. Mining only involved a small percentage of women workers, but the graphic experiences that we have seen delineated in Betty Harris's account were arguably not greatly bettered in factory work. While Isabel Hogg was arguing to a Royal Commission that women should be pulled out of the pits – 'tell Queen Victoria that we are good loyal subjects ... but [we] object to horse-work' – Elizabeth Taylor, a midwife attached to Manchester lying-in hospital, was finding that the children born of women factory workers were dangerously delicate and that factory women, like the mining woman cited in Betty Harris's account, took hardly any break before or after childbirth.[8]

Women factory workers experienced cruel difficulties both in paid work and at home. They worked amongst 'dust, dirt, stunning noises, unpleasant smells and close air', and were constantly in danger from industrial accidents (one out of every 87 inhabitants of Manchester was seriously wounded or injured every year).[9] They were housed in 'a dense urban area whose noxious defects provided spectacular material for the pioneer public health movement', among the mills, factories, yards and warehouses, without garden or tree.[10] Needlework was considered of slightly superior status to ordinary factory work, but lack of recognition of women's working conditions was as great in this area. When William IV died and there was a period of general mourning, needlewomen worked night and day to complete orders. One woman reported that she had no more than four hours' rest a night in three months, rising at four and going to bed between midnight and one. Neither was there any recognition of the need for childcare. The normal pattern was for mothers to work while the baby was minded by a young girl or elderly woman, hired for a few coppers.

The growth of factory work did not mean, either, that conditions were eased in agricultural work, nor that women escaped that context. Mary Rendalls of Exeter describes her day:

> When I was an apprentice, I got up as early as half-past two, three four or five to get cows in, feed them, milk them, and look after the pigs. I then had breakfast, and afterwards went into the fields. In the fields I used to drive the plough, pick stones, weed, pull turnips, when snow was lying about, sow corn, dig potatoes, hoe turnips and reap. I did everything that boys did. Master made me do everything. I took a pride to it, when I used to reap, to keep up with the men. My mistress was a very bad temper; when bad tempered she treated me very ill; she beat me very much; she would throw me on the ground, hold me by the ears, kneel upon me, and use me very ill ... when she was violent we had not enough to eat.[11]

It is difficult to gauge the extent of women's work in agriculture in this period as many did not register as farm workers when the Census was taken. As we have seen in other areas of work, employers relied upon 'the family wage' so that women were drawn unpaid into farm work alongside their husbands and fathers.

Political Activism – None but a Fool would set our Power at Naught

Who will presume to say, that the laws of this, or of any country, calling itself civilised, are just in their treatment of woman? The pretext assigned by man, for keeping absolute dominion himself, and allowing woman to have no share in framing the laws, is, I believe, the physical and mental superiority of himself to the other sex. But, if this were admitted, is it right that punishments for infraction of those laws should be as severe in the one case as in the other? Woman, 'the gentle race and dear', is recognised equally as strong in mind and body when the hour of trial and infliction arrives. The tender limbs, the weak muscle, or the feebler mind of woman have had no influence with man, when he has had to pronounce her condemnation! The torture, the stake, the axe, or the gibbet, have not spared *her*; until a very few years the lash numbered *her* as its victim. In fact, no species of punishment has been introduced, at all supporting the proposition of woman's inferiority in strength of body or of mind; each have ascribed to her an equal power of judging correctly; an equal strength in the endurance of physical suffering. Is it wrong to wish woman to have a share in framing the laws? Looking around, and seeing the vast amount of evils that poison each wholesome current, which should supply purity and peace throughout the whole frame-work of society, traceable, as we consider they are, to the defective state of our laws and institutions, are we deficient in thought, or in correct feeling, when we desire to have those laws new modelled, those institutions otherwise arranged?[12]

The first half of the nineteenth century was characterised by campaigns involving both women and men in attempting to change the conditions in which they lived and worked. The historical record of these campaigns has tended to be one which has shown working-class activism as a mindless, mob-led threat to stable government or, where it has been sympathetic to working people, has emphasised the heroism of the working man. The collection before us draws on that material least accessible to the historian, in particular on transient periodicals and journals, to give us the evidence of the involvement of working women. We hear voices and see writing of the most vital and arresting kind, showing a commitment and political passion which is difficult to capture without turning to the collection itself. Individual women and women in their tens and hundreds, in the case of at least one petition, address us in lectures, speeches, letters, and even, as with Mary Ann Tocker in the first chapter, conducting their own defence in court (and winning!).

As the evidence is put before us, the historical record is modified and corrected. We see women not only in the general movement, in the general challenge to oppressive working and living conditions, but also in those specific acts and at those specific moments which signal great or dramatic events in the history of the labour movement. We begin to see women where history *has* been written – in the Peterloo Massacre, in Chartism and other movements for parliamentary reform leading up to the 1832 Reform Act, overwhelmingly in the Owenite movement as lecturers and organisers as well as camp followers. And we see them where history has *not* been long written – in that widespread movement of working people towards education and knowledge, opposing government censorship and taxes on journals and newspapers, in that general opposition towards oppression and exploitation at work, accumulating in the organisation of trade unions and political associations. Above all, we see women *actively* involved, sometimes arguing and working *against* men where the interests of working people were put in conflict over such issues as 'the family wage', often arguing and working *with* men, but always alert to the oppression and exploitation which made life miserable for both their families and themselves. In a letter to Richard Carlile supporting his stance on press freedom (quoted in full in Chapter 3), 150 'female volunteers in Birmingham and its vicinity', made their own five-page declaration, their own impassioned appeal to 'the men of England' to recognise the cause of women. It begins:

We take the present opportunity of expressing to you our deep sympathy for your past sufferings, and at the same time our admiration of your unflinching conduct in the sacred cause of freedom. Some men may ask, why do women make it their business? Our reasons are two: first, because Englishmen have neglected theirs; and, secondly, because our interests are inseparably connected with the welfare of men: and, being so, we are bound to co-operate with them for the general good. Others may ask, what can women do? To such we would reply by asking, what have not women effected? None but a novice can doubt our ingenuity, and none but a fool would set our power at nought.

Julia Swindells
Cambridge, August 1989

Notes

1. *Children's Employment Commission – Mines*, 1842, p. 84.
2. Barbara Taylor, *Eve and the New Jerusalem, Socialism and Feminism in the Nineteenth Century*, Virago, London, 1983, for groundwork on perspectives of women in the period.
3. Sheila Rowbotham, *Dreams and Dilemmas*, Virago, London, 1983, with particular reference to Part 4, 'Memory and Consciousness'.
4. Bea Campbell, *Wigan Pier Revisited, Poverty and Politics in the 80s*, Virago, London, 1984. Also, first chapter of Lisa Jardine and Julia Swindells, *What's Left? Women in Culture and the Labour Movement*, in press with Routledge.
5. Sally Alexander, 'Women, Class and Sexual Differences in the 1830s and 1840s: Some Reflections on the Writing of a Feminist History', in *History Workshop*, 17, 1984.
6. Barbara Drake, *Women in Trade Unions*, Labour Research Department, p. 3.
7. James Phillips Kay, *The Moral and Physical Condition of the Working Classes*, 1832, p. 23.
8. *Children's Employment Commission*, p. 30.
9. J.G. Kohl, *England and Wales*, 1844, p. 126.
10. *Manchester and District Regional Survey Society, Housing Needs of Ancoats in Relation to the Greenwood Act*, Manchester, 1930, p. 30.
11. *Reports of Special Assistant Poor Law Commissioners on the Employment of Women and Children in Agriculture*, 1843, p. 112.
12. Catherine Isabella Barmby writing in the *New Moral World*: see here Chapter 6, note 22.

1

Radical Reform

'Why Stand you apart? Are you not of our number?'
'No' replied the group; 'You are of the people; we are a privileged class; we have laws, customs and rites peculiar to ourselves.'
  People: 'And what labour do you perform in society?'
  Privileged Class: 'None: We are not made to labour.'
  People: 'How then have you acquired your wealth?'
  PC: 'By taking the pains to govern you.'
  People: 'To govern us! And is this what you call governing? We toil, and you enjoy; we produce, and you dissipate; wealth flows from us, and you absorb it. Privileged men, class distinct from the people, form a nation apart and govern yourselves.'
  C.F. Volney, *The Ruins or a Survey of the Revolutions of Empires*, 1795.

Introduction

Much of the political activity of the early years of the nineteenth century centred around the need for a reform of parliament. The system of representation was more or less the same as it had been in Elizabethan times, being based on a feudal structure of society in which the landed aristocracy held the right to all positions of power. Only they had a vote and in their hands rested the nomination of the Member of Parliament. As the structure of society changed, more people worked and lived in towns; the wealth of the country accumulated in the hands of the owners of industry and the need for change became apparent.

There was an alliance of the forces wanting change. Influenced both by the American colonialists' struggle to be free from British rule and the French Revolution, organisations began to be formed with the object of reforming parliament. The campaign in support of these aims developed during the first 30 years of the century. After the Reform Act of 1832, which enfranchised property owners paying £10 a year rates and gave some larger towns such as Manchester and Birmingham a representative, the alliance that had worked for the changes split. The middle class had obtained its objective while the workers had been ignored.

Whilst much of the campaigning was undertaken within organisations which sprang up and declined over the years, occasionally one individual made a particularly effective contribution and was acclaimed throughout the radical movement.

Mary Ann Tocker was the sister of a solicitor, Henry Tocker, who practised in Plymouth. She was, therefore, well versed in legal matters.

So far as is known, Miss Tocker did not belong to any of the reform movements of the early nineteenth century, but she strongly disapproved of the corrupt practices of a local lawyer, Richard Gurney, and she said so forcefully in a letter to a newspaper, the *West Briton and Cornwall Advertiser.*

The substance of her objection to Gurney was that he was involved in purchasing votes by placing his friends and relations in jobs which carried suffrage. It was very much part of the campaign for the reform of parliament and an end to the system of 'Rotten Boroughs', where the appointment of a Member of Parliament rested in the power of the landowner even if there were no residents.

Because she was familiar with court procedure, Mary Ann Tocker conducted her own defence in the case for libel which Richard Gurney brought against her. In her letter under the pseudonym 'An Enemy to Corruption' Miss Tocker had accused Gurney of extorting money from clients. She was able to plead the truth of that statement in court and the jury acquitted her in spite of the direction of the judge, Mr Justice Burroughs.

The radical press was delighted and the trial received full coverage particularly in *Sherwin's Political Register* and the *Black Dwarf.* William Cobbett[1] was in New York whilst the trial was on and was delighted when he heard the result, because the same judge had handled him somewhat roughly in 1809. Cobbett reprinted the report of the trial as soon as it was received in America.

Apart from the reports in the press, Mary Ann's victory was acclaimed by radicals throughout the country, some of whom were even moved to record their pleasure in verse. Richard Carlile[2] commented on 'the lady's fame which shall remain unsullied, when the name of her oppressors shall be buried in oblivion'.[3] Unfortunately he did not reckon with the blanket which obscured women from history and Mary Ann Tocker's case has not received the attention which its historical importance deserves. At the time, the trial was circulated in numerous editions.

* * *

The Trial

The King v. Mary Ann Tocker

As soon as the cause was called, the Lady appeared in Court as her own Advocate, and was accommodated at the Barrister's Table.

The following Gentlemen were sworn as the Jury:

THOMAS TRELOAR,	JOHN WILTON,
JAMES MITCHELL,	JOHN STEVENS,
RICHARD ARTHUR,	JOHN EVANS,
NABOTH RANDALL,	EDWARD BLAKE,
BARNARD RUTHER,	HUDDY BRAY, and
HENRY COLLIER,	JOHN THOMAS.

Mr Wild opened the pleadings. This was an indictment against the Defendant, Mary Ann Tocker, for a libel published in a newspaper, called *The West Briton and Cornwall Advertiser*, upon the Plaintiff, Mr R. Gurney, Jun. Vice-Warden of the Stannary Court in the county of Devon; the defendant has pleaded not guilty.

Mr Sergeant Pell then stated the case, which he observed, consisted chiefly in a charge made against the Plaintiff of malversation in the discharge of a public office. He could not bring the merits of the question, which the jury was now about to try, more shortly under their review, than by reading the libel itself, as it appeared in a public journal. It was addressed in the form of a letter to the editor of the *West Briton*, and was in substance as follows:

Sir – The fact which I am about to communicate may, perhaps, appear more singular than important, although in times less calamitous than the present, the statement of any circumstance illustrative of the borough-mongering system, now universally execrated, must of itself excite an interest. It is something new in the history of this country that it should possess an outlawed Judge. It might be called an instance unparalleled in the annals of Europe, if a case had not recently occurred at Vienna, of a magistrate and a minister of justice being sentenced to the punishment of sweeping the streets. A gentleman of the name of Tonkin was some time past removed from the office of Vice-Warden, of the Stannary-Court, in order to make room for Mr R. Gurney, son of the Rev. R. Gurney, of electioneering notoriety. This last gentleman, not perfectly satisfied with two considerable benefices, the reward of former services on precuring this situation for his son, obtained at the same time a promise that the salary should be octupted – a promise which, to the honour of the patron has not been fulfilled. Soon after this promotion of Mr Gurney the younger, it unfortunately happened that he was obliged to leave the county in which he had been appointed to exercise judicial functions, and this necessity arose from pecuniary embarrassments. In consequence of this absence, a petition was presented to the Lord Warden, complaining of the neglect and delay of justice, occasioned by this conduct, and desiring the appointment of a new Vice-Warden, but no notice was taken, of this representation. After this statement it may be matter of wonder that he should still retain his place; and the fact can only be traced to the famous borough mongering system, and to political motives. Lord Yarmouth has lately purchased largely in the borough of Tregony, with a view of opposing the interest of the Earl of Darlington. Under this protection Mr Gurney found it convenient to go to the Continent, and was twice outlawed in the marketplaces of Plymouth and Dock, which outlawry has not been reversed. Instead of attending his court, he was therefore obliged to secrete himself. Now, Sir, after this statement, no one can be at a loss to conjecture what are the motives which operate in retaining this man, in a situation the duties of which he is unable to discharge. I forbear occupying too large a portion of your valuable and patriotic paper, or I could mention many anecdotes showing how Mr R. Gurney and his son have profited in the school of corruption. I shall only add, that he demanded various sums of money from the suitors over and above the fees of court, in the only two causes which he ever decided, viz. Lopes v. Doubtfree, and Whitehair v. Webb.

I am, Sir,

An Enemy to Corruption

It was impossible, he apprehended, that a more injurious or scandalous libel could be published against the character of any man. He should be able to prove the publication, not merely in the usual way, but by means of a subsequent letter addressed to the editor, in which the libellous matter was distinctly acknowledged. The brother of the defendant had been secretary to the vice-warden, and upon his informations she had ventured to charge Mr Gurney with bribery and corruption, and with the specific act of extorting 20 guineas from the parties in a cause which he refused to decide till the sum in question was paid. The worst part of the libel it still remained for him to state. It was contained in a subsequent letter, and must fill every well regulated mind with a sensation of disgust. The defendant thought proper to instruct the editor that Mr Gurney had been outlawed, that his outlawry had not been reversed, and that he was incapable of bringing an action. He was sorry to see a lady of understanding and talents so conspicuous in the situation of the present defendant; but he felt himself bound to say, that no slanderer had ever aimed a more deadly blow at the reputation and character of a gentleman. The Defendant, he understood would be her own advocate, and was a woman of no ordinary understanding. He had to lament that she did not make a better use of the faculties with which providence had been pleased to gift her; it was not too late to make atonement, although that atonement must follow a verdict of guilty. He would not dwell with any peculiar emphasis upon the nature of a newspaper publication, because he thought such publications most important and beneficial to society: but he would state, that in his opinion, the surest means of preserving that invaluable blessing, was, that the freedom which it involves should not be abused.

Mr E. Budd, the Editor of the *West Briton*, was then called, and deposed that the defendant had in conversation acknowledged the original statement to be her own. He received it by the post, but had subsequently seen her, and in talking upon the subject she had admitted the former writing to be her own. It had been submitted to him with a discretionary power of altering or omitting such passages as he might deem unfit for publication, and he had accordingly made considerable alterations. He had certainly received a pledge from Captain Woolridge of the Navy, the brother-in-law of the Defendant, that no prosecution should be instituted for any letter, except that which was printed in the *West Briton*.

The evidence for the prosecution being finished, Miss Tocker rose in her own defence.

My Lord and Gentlemen of the Jury,

I stand here with reverence, but without fear. Fear, indeed, is the inseparable concomitant of guilt, and of any offence in a moral view my conscience entirely acquits me. I do not appear here personally from any feeling of presumption, but from an inability to procure counsel. This inability has been caused by a debt due to my brother from Mr Gurney, which he has refused to pay, and from my own disinclination to encroach on the comforts of a widowed parent. I may be indiscreet, but I am not conscious of criminality. This is the first time that I have ever entered a Court of Justice, but no person can entertain a deeper sense than myself of the excellence of that enlightened system of jurisprudence which has been established in this country. I throw myself upon the indulgence of the Court, and hope any irrelevant matter I may bring forward, will be attributed to ignorance and not to intention. I come before you wholly ignorant of the equivocations of law; unpractised in the arrangement of argument, and destitute of the graces of oratory; possessing only the rude weapons of reason and the untutored eloquence of nature, to oppose tried talents and professional skill: I am not qualified to discuss the question but on the moral ground of right and wrong, and on this it must finally rest: the prosecutor, will, however, derive his chief advantage from my ignorance of the law, for I can only take the plain and simple ground of denying the falsehood and malice charged in the indictment. With the permission of the Court, I will now read a passage from Lord Ellenborough's address to the jury on the trial of William Cobbett.[4] [Here Miss Tocker read an extract from the reported speech of the Chief Justice, touching the license in discussing the character and conduct of men in public offices.] Gentlemen of the Jury. The main point on which I rest my defence is, that Mr Gurney is a public officer, and that I and every other subject are entitled to examine his conduct in that capacity. I am fully prepared to prove the truth of every statement contained in the published letter.

Mr Justice Burroughs – That, the law of the land will not allow you to do. I cannot allow you to make these statements; what had you to do with exposing his bribery and corruption? Why did you not state these facts to the Attorney General? You cannot be allowed to state the truth of the charges as a justification.

Miss Tocker – What am I to do, my Lord? Will you not allow me to defend myself in the best manner I can? I mean to shew that the publication is no libel, and I can do so in no other way. [Miss Tocker proceeded.]

The prosecutor is well aware of the advantage which this doctrine of truth being in no case a justification of a charge of libel gave him; for not long since he had observed with exultation, to a person who had said that I could prove all my charges: 'That will avail nothing, the greater the truth, the greater the libel.' Gentlemen of the Jury, I trust you will this day show you are of a contrary opinion. The sophistical assertion, that truth was a libel, astonished and confounded – as irreconcileable with the spirit of our laws, and subversive of all free discussion – opposed to the principles of the English constitution, and equally repugnant to religion and reason. Was it possible that our ancestors could have contemplated the law as thus expounded? No! It must have been perverted and misconstrued. How, otherwise, should such a dogma have found its way into a body of laws so tender in every point that regards the personal liberty of the subject, and the free expression of opinions? I will venture to assert, that such an interpretation was first pronounced by the cunning abettors of tyranny, ever watchful to enslave mankind. Is it possible that it should be the same thing to the accused and condemned? Yet this was the conclusion to which his doctrine would lead us. It is on this proposition: the greater the truth, the greater the libel, that the prosecutor rested his hope. Vengeance, not the vindication of character, was the unworthy and unmanly motive of the prosecutor; had he meant merely to vindicate his character, he would have brought his action for damages, and placed his cause on a broad denial of the truth of my statements. It was to suppress, not to elicit truth, that he had adopted the cowardly, ridiculous expedient of indicting a female for a libel, tending to a breach of the peace. [Miss Tocker then proceeded to comment on the allegations in the alledged libellous publication. The prosecutor was charged with being 'an outlawed Judge'.] In a letter of his, dated April 22nd 1817, is the following passage: 'I am rather in the clouds at this moment, as a rascal of a tailor has sued out a process of outlawry against me; but it will be speedily removed, as Snip already repents of his folly.' Had I been instigated by malice against the prosecutor, I would have made him appear as ridiculous as he had made himself by quoting his expressions; but instead of this, I have softened instead of heightened the description in my letter. The next paragraph reflected on the manner of Mr Tonkin's removal from the office of Vice-warden, and Mr Gurney's appointment to it. It is well known that Mr Gurney had the Vice-wardenship through the interest of Mr Holmes, a friend of Lord Yarmouth's, and the late member for Tregony; with a promise of an augmentation of the salary attached to the office, from £50 to £400. The next charge was, being obliged to leave this country to avoid his creditors. I can prove incontestibly, that at the close of 1815, the Vice-Warden of Devon was obliged to seek an asylum from his creditors, in France; and that in May, 1816, he was twice outlawed. The next charge related to the neglect of his official duties. I can prove from the Vice-Warden's own letters, dated April 22nd, 1817, that one of the suitors in this court wrote to the Lord-Warden, complaining of the stop that was put to the business of the Stannary Court, by the non-attendance of the Vice-Warden. I now come to the most serious part of the charge; his having demanded money from the suitors in his court. To speak correctly, I should have said, extorted; for that was the fact. That in the only two causes he had ever determined, namely, Whitehair v. Webb, and Lopez v. Doubtfree, he had done so could be proved; in the first instances, by a letter in his own hand writing, dated March 26, 1816; and in the second by the oath of a witness who had heard his admission of the fact. I can prove that the Vice-Warden has demanded and obtained from one of the parties twenty five guineas, and from the other twenty guineas, though he had himself admitted he was not entitled to as many shillings. I can not only prove that the Vice-Warden took this money, but that he actually delayed giving his decrees until he had received the sum he demanded. In bringing these instances of corruption before the public, I have, I trust, rendered a service to society, and shall always consider it as one of the most laudable actions of my life. Bribery in a Judge was once deemed so heinous a crime, that in the reign of Edward the Third, Chief Justice Thorp was hanged for the offence.

Mr Justice Burroughs interrupted the Defendant by telling her, that she was proceeding in a course that could only aggravate her offence; but as she appeared determined to go on her own way, or to stop altogether, he saw she was a tool in the hands of others, and should suffer her to proceed.

Miss Tocker continued. Was it not to be expected, that if this conduct had not been exposed, and the prosecutor had continued in office, his demands would have been proportioned to the importance of the causes he had to decide?

In that case, what might have been the price of a decree in a cause of equal magnitude with that of Crinnis Mine, where even delay might have been worth purchasing at an enormous price. Heaven only knew; for rapacity was only limited by possibility. It should also not be forgotten, that in the Vice-Warden's court there was no Jury; all was left to the decision of the Judge.

Miss Tocker – Gentlemen of the Jury. After your having heard this statement and the evidence I shall adduce in support of it; I have no fear for your decision.

Mr Justice Burroughs – You cannot bring forward any such evidence.

Miss Tocker proceeded – I contend, that the publication is not false, as I can prove its truth; it is not wicked, for I am satisfied that the effect of exposing corrupt practices must be beneficial; and as for malice I have none; and none can be proved; unless the disclosing of a crime, highly injurious to society, be a proof of malice.

The Prosecutor has published a statement, in which he has asserted that I had secreted myself, to avoid being brought to justice. This I deny. The prosecutor has done his utmost to involve me in expence, by the mode of proceeding he has adopted. I believe the ground of his malevolence against me, is for charging him with having confessed his having laid a plan, with two other persons nearly connected with him, to enforce payment of a note for a gaming debt, amounting to £10,000 given him by Mr R.B. C– nephew to Mr B– who had given the living of Tregony to his father. Had I, by any publication of mine, made Mr Gurney half so contemptible as he had himself, I might possibly deserve the appellation of libeller, on the ground of the greater the truth, the greater the offence. Mr Gurney has had the experience of six months imprisonment for assaulting Sir Robert Gifford the present Solicitor General, for having spoken freely of his father's conduct during the Tregony Election, before a committee of the House of Commons; and he had expressed his conviction, that I should be imprisoned for twelve months, and have to pay a fine of £500, which he well knew with his debt to my brother would be rendered equal to a sentence of imprisonment for life. But I trust and believe that you Gentlemen of the Jury will disappoint his malice. The statement which I sent to the Editor of the *West Briton* referred wholly to the official and public conduct of the prosecutor; and with great submission to the Court, I apprehend that the conduct of every person in a public station is open to public examination. This position, as I have before stated, I have the authority of Lord Ellenborough in maintaining.

Mr Justice Burroughs – Lord Ellenborough never could talk such nonsense, or assert that a man in a judicial office may be charged with bribery and corruption by any person who thinks proper to publish such a statement to the world. I am sorry to see you transgressing the law at every step, from a false notion of moral right. Many gentlemen at this bar would have been happy to assist you, and would, I am sure, have advised a very different sort of defence.

Miss Tocker continued, and begged leave to read a clause of the act of 32d of George the Third, by which the Jury, in a case of libel, are empowered to give a verdict on the whole matter, and on the general issue of guilty or not guilty.

Mr Justice Burroughs – This act was never construed to enable a defendant, upon an indictment, to justify by proving the truth of the libel.

Miss Tocker – The essence of the indictment consisted in the evil tendency of the publication. The tendency of this publication, I am prepared to show is good, and will contend that resentment might exist without malice. The celebrated Mr Locke[5] has quoted an expression from St Paul to this effect 'Be ye angry, but sin not.' If the law of libel really is what I have heard it interpreted to be; that the greater the truth the greater the libel, a new system of ethics ought to be affixed to it. No Lawyer or Legislator could intend to punish where there was no malicious motive or intentional provocation. The falsehood and malignity were all on the other side; and I hope that no legal sophistry will induce you, Gentlemen of the Jury to convict me for an offence where my object was meritorious.

Mr Justice Burroughs – I very much lament the injudicious course you have taken, and I am sure that had you possessed a friend in the world you would have been dissuaded from acting in so imprudent a manner; I plainly see that you are a tool in the hands of others.

Mr Wild observed that such was the case; she was the tool of a person who had been equally guilty with herself, but had been forgiven on expressing his contrition and asking pardon for the offence.

Miss Tocker proceeded – Gentlemen of the Jury, the law constitutes you the sole judges; you are to say whether you consider this publication a libel or not. Should you be bewildered by legal sophistry, and induced to return a verdict of guilty against me, in place of punishing the guilty and making restitution to the injured, you would see the oppressor triumph, and the oppressed overwhelmed with ruin. Pitiable is my situation even if acquitted: for the expences of this prosecution fall heavily on my family, even though I have resorted to this unusual, and perhaps ineligible mode of defence. Alas! Gentlemen, should you this day condemn me, you would date from it as from a melancholy epoch in your life. Perhaps at some future period, when recalling some event that the lapse of time had stolen from your memory, you would observe, 'it happened in that year, when my verdict sent to the solitude of a prison, a being who was both innocent and helpless.' But, Gentlemen, I look forward with confidence to a far different decision; feeling as I do, that there are on my part rectitude of intention, candour, and truth; and on that of my prosecutor, corruption, malice, and falsehood.

The defendant sat down overpowered by her feelings; but soon rose and desired that her sister, Miss Susan Tocker, might be sworn, which was done; but after she had put a few questions, the Judge stopped the examination, perceiving that she intended to substantiate the truth of the statements made in the alledged libel. The Defendant then offered the letters of the prosecutor as evidence for the same purpose; but these were also rejected by the court. Finding this ineffectual, she said, that as the prosecution was nominally at the suit of the crown, the real prosecutor might be examined, and she desired that he would come forward that she might compel him to admit of the facts. This, the Bench told her could not be allowed, and the Defendant immediately left the Court.

Mr Justice Burroughs proceeded to charge the Jury. He went over the various allegations in the publication, commenting on them as he proceeded, and pronouncing the whole an atrocious libel. He informed the Jury that the law did not allow of the Defendant giving in evidence the truth of the alleged libel in a criminal prosecution; because a libel was considered as tending to a breach of the peace. The truth or falsehood would come before the Court of King's Bench by affidavit: where all due weight would be given to what the defendant had to state. But with this the Jury had nothing to do. Formerly the opinion of the Court decided on the nature and tendency of the alleged libel; but by a late Act, the Jury were to look at the paper and say, whether it were a libel or not. This act required the Judge to give his opinion; and this he did most strongly, that the publication before them was libellous in the highest degree; as it charged, in the strongest way possible, a gentleman filling a high judicial situation with the grossest corruption. This was his opinion, and he believed it was that of the Jury; for he could not conceive that any Jury could lay their hand to their heart and say the publication was not a libel.

The papers were now handed to the Jury, who immediately desired to read them. This request was wholly unexpected: but after some time a room at an Inn opposite the Hall was provided, and the Judge withdrew, desiring them to bring their verdict to his lodgings. In about half an hour the Jury were introduced to his Lordship, when the Foreman produced a verdict of *not guilty*!

Address

We congratulate the Public on the result of this extraordinary and unprecedented trial. This Trial, although far removed from the fountain of corruption, may be fairly considered as a glorious victory over it, and the triumph of just resentment over its baneful and overwhelming influence. The pleasing idea of seeing one of our fair countrywomen standing forward to expose the abuses and corruptions of the horrid and diabolical system we live under, is a matter of exultation. What degree of baseness must that mind possess, that could so meanly betray its own corrupt motives, by compelling this Lady, unaided but by her own innocence and talents to justify in a Court of Justice (or rather Court of Law) the charges which she had advanced?

We rejoice at the result of this fair one's exertions, as we are not altogether strangers to the character and conduct of her Persecutor. We shall anxiously wait the meeting of Parliament to see whether an individual may be found amongst its members, honest enough to bring the conduct of this 'corrupt judge' before the House of Commons.

We cannot pass by the glaring and unfeeling conduct of the Judge who presided at this Trial, his repeated endeavours to thwart and interrupt the lady in the mode of defence; his quirks, quibbles, sophistries and contemptible jargon about the law of the land; his endeavour to influence the minds of the Jury by all that was unfair; his pronouncing the truth to be a most atrocious libel, must leave a stain of infamy and reproach on his character, which time cannot efface. Thanks to the honest Jury, that were not to be deluded by any legal sophistry or corrupt practice. These protectors of injured innocence have raised a monument to their own and the lady's fame, which shall remain unsullied, when the names of her oppressors shall be buried in oblivion, or only mentioned to be execrated.

When it is recollected that the Lady has never been present in a Court of Justice before, even as a spectator and that she went through the business without the slightest hesitation. How plain must have been the truth of her statement? How forcible the effect of that truth on the Jury that boldly and conscientiously acquitted her after a laboured charge from the Judge to find her guilty. 'The reader will not fail to contrast the simple eloquence, the pure ethics, the easy flow of unsophisticated feeling, the irresistible force of heavenly, unconquerable truth, which marked the words, and adorned the language of our fair countrywoman, the enlightened Defendant.' The reader will not fail to contrast this with the malign efforts of those who were arrayed against her. Well might the *Judge learned in the law* have said, that if the Lady had sought the assistance of any of the Gentlemen at the bar they would have advised a very different sort of defence.

To Miss M. A. Tocker

To The Patriotic Ladies of Great Britain
Shall Tocker pine for want and die
Who fought for truth and liberty?
Nor fought in vain, but gain'd her end,
And prov'd her country's zealous friend
Perish the thought that one so vile
Should E'er be found in Britain's isle,
Who would not offer some relief
To Virtue, overwhelm'd with grief,

From losses in her country's cause
Th' effect of gross-perverted laws
Alfred.

Black Dwarf, 4 November 1818.

Rights of Women

Sir,

I am a constant reader of your paper, and have often regretted you did not occasionally insert articles that might call the attention of our sex to a due sense of their own importance in the political world. I think, Sir, we might be valuable auxiliaries; or to speak more legitimately, valuable allies in the hallowed cause of rescuing our country from its present state of political degradation. If you will take the trouble of instructing us, you will, I believe, find us apt scholars. We do not wish to be fitted for orators, nor do we wish to claim a right to vote for representatives in the great council of the nation, though one of the wisest of men has said we ought to do. We wish to be instructed in what way the ascendancy we possess, and wish to retain over your sex, may be most beneficially exerted. The best works we have on education are lamentably deficient in the kind of information that might assist the mother in giving her children correct ideas on the nature of civil and religious liberty, and the rights of men generally. Ha! Mary Wolstencraft [sic]![6] How much cause have we to regret that thou didst not take the advantage of thy friendship with Dr Richard Price[7] to give us a work on the duties of women, in the training of their children. Thy talents, aided by the judicious counsels of that intrepid asserter of the rights of his species, if properly employed, might have made us thy debtors to the latest posterity! In a letter to your clerical friend, you have, Sir, taken the trouble of *ironing* us; and in a following number a correspondent flatters us. We do not wish for irony and flattery, we wish you to address our reason. We conceive that we discover in your writings generally much wit – sometimes eloquence, and we always feel the absence of those coarse metaphors so often used by some political writers. We entreat that a small portion of your paper be devoted to our service; and we think the consciousness that our sex look to you for instruction will sharpen your wit, and give additional elegance to your style: but while we wish to be pleased by the *manner*, it is the *matter* to which we would principally attend. I have spoken throughout this epistle in the plural number, because there are many mothers who, like myself, wish to rear patriot sons, but who are, like me, destitute of that knowledge which it is requisite for them to possess, to enable them to fulfill that important duty.

I am, Sir, yours respectfully

An Old Friend with a New Face
Black Dwarf, 7 October 1818.

Miss M.A. Tocker
Sir,

On reading the witty remarks of your correspondent J.M. on the Rights of Women, in the last week's *Dwarf*, I was led to hope that he would, for the honour of his fellow *lords of the creation*, have concluded his ingenious remarks with some substantial proposition for the benefit of that heroine, Mary Ann Tocker, to whose case he but very obscurely and flippantly alluded. The observations of your other correspondent, the Blue Dwarf, are a little more determinate and useful. He recalls to the recollection of the public what you so generously recommended in the *Black Dwarf* some weeks ago, that a subscription be immediately commenced. But unaccountable as it is, no further notice is taken of it. During the last six and twenty years many have been prosecuted and suffered for writing and publishing what was by the government called libel; that it almost became a matter of course that to accuse was to convict. To prove the truth of what they had written and published was not permitted, because, forsooth, the lawyers, down to the present day, one after another, have continued to repeat and tried to enforce the foolish doctrine which Lord Mansfield[8] rashly, and without either law or justice, asserted from the bench, upwards of fifty years ago, that 'the greater the truth, the greater the libel.' Subscriptions were, in those days and on those occasions, instantly opened for their support and renumeration. There was a right spirit manifested by good works, and I rejoice in it (observe that I am not an inexperienced giddy girl), but I am now much surprised when I view the apparent neglect of that same English Public to the superior claim to which Miss Tocker has to their gratitude. In her excellent defence on her late trial she displayed uncommon courage and talents, and having truth and virtue for her sword and shield, she completely exposed, and I hope forever destroyed, that absurd and abominable doctrine that 'truth is a libel.'

Why is it? What is the cause of such indifference to the interest of Miss Tocker? Is it because a female tyro, has encroached upon the exclusive privileges of the gentlemen of the long robe? Aye and advanced with success too. It is very true, I must confess, that a part of the British Public have been liberal in their praise of her; that, so far as it goes, is good; but there is more than that wanted, and expected, something more substantial, than fleeting applause. Well then, I have now Sir, the pleasure to inform you, and the friends of truth and justice, that a few ladies have considered her peculiar situation, and are interesting themselves in her behalf – and as they see that their *lords and masters* are so tardy, they have agreed to open a subscription immediately, and should this meet the eye of any of your female readers, for no doubt you have many, it is hoped they will add their mite to such a laudable undertaking.

I remain Sir, etc.

Maria Smith

Great Russel Street
3rd October 1818

Black Dwarf, 7 October 1818.

Notes

1. William Cobbett (1763–1835). One of the greatest popular journalists of all time. A Member of Parliament and author of many works. He edited the Political Register from 1802 to 1836.
2. Richard Carlile, writer, bookseller and lecturer who led the campaigns for the freedom of the press. Imprisoned in Dorchester Gaol 1819-25.
3. Richard Carlile, Address in *The Trial of Mary Ann Tocker*, 2nd edn, n.d. (*c.* 1818), p. 13.
4. Trial of William Cobbett for publishing a seditious libel, 15 June 1810 before Chief Justice Ellenborough and one of the government's Special Juries.
5. John Locke (1632–1704). Materialist philosopher, economist and political writer.
6. Mary Wollstonecraft was an early advocate of women's rights. She wrote *Vindication of the Rights of Woman*, published in 1792 and her work has often been used as a source by feminists ever since.
7. Richard Price (1723–91). Non-conformist Minister, writer on morals, politics and economics.
8. William Murray Mansfield (1707–96) in 1756 became Lord Chief Justice of the King's Bench with the title Baron Mansfield.

2

The Massacre of Peterloo

I met Murder on the way –
He had a mask like Castlereagh –
Very smooth he looked, yet grim;
Seven bloodhounds followed him:

All were fat; and well they might
Be in admirable plight,
For one by one, and two by two,
He tossed them human hearts to chew
Which from his wide cloak he drew.

P.B. Shelley, *The Mask of Anarchy*

Introduction

The cause of parliamentary reform gained steadily during the first two decades of the nineteenth century. Technological advance made the old domestic-based trades such as hand-loom weaving obsolete and the unemployment and depredations caused by the Napoleonic wars caused great distress. The traditional methods by which the people had taken grievances to the ear of the monarch in petitions had been shown to be ineffective. They had no representative in parliament and no way of obtaining relief from their desperate state.

In these circumstances, the connection between social distress and political representation became increasingly obvious and campaigning organisations calling for a reform of parliament began to proliferate. The meeting held in Manchester on 16 August, which became known as the 'Peterloo Massacre', was not an isolated incident. In 1818 there was a strike wave throughout Lancashire when trade depression had forced wages of hand-loom weavers down to as low as six shillings a week. Prices meanwhile stayed high in the aftermath of the war. Radical political unions were formed and demands formulated for annual parliaments, universal manhood suffrage and the repeal of the Corn Laws (which kept the price of bread high).

Radical reformers such as John Knight of Oldham[1] and William Fitton of Royton[2] were tireless in travelling around the growing towns of Lancashire raising the banner of reform. Such meetings became working-class social gatherings as well as political meetings. The Manchester meeting was planned to be the largest expression yet seen of determination to achieve parliamentary representation.

But before that, a significant development had taken place at Blackburn which was the first weaving community to have a mass meeting in the radical cause. It attracted large numbers and it was the first occasion at which a Female Reform Society played a prominent part. Samuel Bamford[3] reported that during the summer of 1818, when the movement was just beginning, he had insisted that women who were standing on the outskirts of the crowd which he was addressing, should have the right to participate in the meeting and in any vote which was taken. Following that episode, it was reported that a Female Reform Society had been formed at Blackburn.

The moving spirit behind this move was Alice Kitchin. She printed an address on behalf of the members of the Female Reform Society in the *Manchester Observer* in which a connection is drawn between the cause of parliamentary reform and the economic distress confronting the people of Lancashire. A call was made to women to instruct their children in democratic ideas so that such suffering would be avoided in the future. At the Blackburn meeting, the Female Reformers arrived in procession to present John Knight, the Chairman, with a 'most beautiful Cap of Liberty, made of scarlet silk or satin, lined with green, with a serpentine gold lace, terminating with a rich gold tassel'.[4] Participation by women in a like manner came to typify reform meetings in the succeeding months.

Following the example set by Blackburn, other Female Reform Societies were founded, in Manchester, Stockport, Royton and other Lancashire towns. A feature of these societies was the formation of schools, usually held in the rooms where the Union Societies met, at which children were taught a 'deep and rooted hatred of our corrupt and tyrannical rulers'. Women organised their own societies most efficiently. They issued pamphlets which clearly indicate that although they were not calling specifically for the right to vote, they were certainly not the passive followers of the men that some historians have tried to imply.

At the meeting held on Peter's Fields on the hot sultry 16 August 1819, women played a significant part. The meeting was planned as a peaceful demonstration. Processions converged on the field during the morning and a number of them were led by members of the female societies dressed in white and preceded by female bands. As each contingent reached the field, the women carrying the banners joined the other standard bearers round the farm carts that were acting as the platform.

Royton's banners read, 'The Royton Female Union' and 'Let Us Die Like Men and Not Be Sold Like Slaves', while those from Stockport called for 'Annual Parliaments', 'Universal Suffrage' and 'Vote By Ballot'.

Mrs Mary Fildes

Mrs Fildes was the President of Manchester Female Reformers. She was personally known to Mrs Linnaeus Banks[5] because her son, Henry Hunt Fildes, was employed by Mrs Banks' father.

As Henry Hunt approached Manchester in a carriage on his way to Peter's Fields on 16 August 1819, he was met by very large and enthusiastic crowds among whom were the members of the Manchester Female Reformers. The idea was that the ladies in their white dresses should precede the barouche on to the field, but the crush was so great that they had to walk behind and keep up as best they could. Mrs Fildes, who was supposed to lead the women, was taken on to the carriage at Hunt's suggestion and she sat beside the coachman carrying a white flag with the words 'Manchester Female Reformers' and a figure of justice on it.

Hunt described Mrs Fildes as being 'rather small' but with a 'remarkably good figure and well dressed'. He considered that she 'added much to the beauty of the scene'.[6]

On the platform, Mary Fildes joined the radicals and several reporters who had come especially for the meeting. When Joseph Nadin, the Deputy Constable, made his way through the terrible confusion caused by the charge of the Yeomanry Cavalry into the closely packed crowd to arrest Hunt and the others on the platform, Mrs Fildes was knocked and fell off the side where her dress caught on a nail. As she struggled to free herself, she was 'slashed across her exposed body by one of the brave cavalry'.[7]

It is possible that Mrs Fildes escaped arrest through this mishap because Mrs Elizabeth Gaunt, who had taken refuge in Hunt's carriage to escape the crowd, was arrested, possibly being mistaken for Mary Fildes. The magistrates, having made the mistake, kept poor Elizabeth Gaunt in solitary confinement for a week before releasing her. Mrs Fildes was not arrested.

Susanna Saxton

Among the members of the Hampden Club[8] in Manchester after its formation in October 1816 were a husband-and-wife team, John Thacker Saxton and his wife Susanna. He was a convinced and determined radical and his wife shared his views.

When the *Manchester Observer* was launched in 1818, he became its sub-editor. He had been connected with the cotton trade but had a talent for writing which he used in the radical cause. Mrs Saxton was also active and she became the Secretary of Manchester Female Reformers. On their behalf, she had intended to present Henry Hunt with an address but in the melée following the charge of the Yeomanry the opportunity did not arise.

Although John Saxton was arrested, he was not found guilty at the trial because he was able to plead that he had only been on the platform as a reporter. Susanna was not arrested. She may have been among the women round the platform when the Yeomanry advanced and thus been able to get away.

When Henry Hunt stood up to speak, the magistrates ordered his arrest. Joseph Nadin,[9] the Deputy Chief Constable of Manchester who represented the civil authority of the town, said that he would not be able to carry it out unless he was assisted by the military. An army had been assembled around Manchester and they were sent for by William Hulton,[10] the senior Magistrate. The first group to reach the field was the Manchester Yeomanry Cavalry,[11] young amateur soldiers who on that hot day had been waiting since early morning in a yard near the field. They had been drinking and found it difficult to mount their horses. They went on to the field brandishing their sabres, which had been sharpened in readiness for the occasion.

As the cavalry became entangled in the huge crowd of people, regular soldiers, men of the 15th Hussars, entered the field from the opposite side and pushed the people in front of them. In the melée, eleven lost their lives and many hundreds were wounded. Among the dead were two women, Martha Partington of Eccles, who was thrown into a cellar and killed on the spot, and Mary Hays of Manchester, who 'was rode over by the cavalry'.[12] That there were many women at the meeting is undisputed. Samuel Bamford estimated that the Rochdale/Middleton contingent had between 300 and 400 women marching. Among the lists of wounded published after the event, there were many women.

Mrs Elizabeth Gaunt

On the morning of the Peter's Fields meeting, Elizabeth Gaunt had made certain of a place near the platform, but because of the oppressive heat and the crush of the crowd, and the fact that she was far into pregnancy, she became faint. One of the men in Henry Hunt's carriage, possibly Hunt himself, saw her and suggested that she might be safer and more comfortable inside the carriage.

However, when the Yeomanry hacked their way through to the platform they hauled her out – in so doing inflicting cuts and bruises – and then arrested her.

Mrs Gaunt was kept in prison in the New Bailey, in spite of her condition, until the hearing before the magistrates on 26 August, ten days later. By that time she was so weak that she was only able to answer her name in a very feeble manner. Since there was only one witness willing to speak against her, and on the flimsiest evidence, the magistrates were asked to release her and 'had great pleasure in ordering her immediate discharge'.[13]

Elizabeth Gaunt retained her interest in the radical movement because she wrote to Jane Carlile[14] when she was imprisoned in Dorchester Gaol,[15] sending a small present that she had made with her own hands. Writing to Mrs Carlile on 22 April 1822, she said that she was certain her own work would be more acceptable than 'diamonds from a tyrant'.[16]

Another woman who was arrested was Mrs Ann Scott. So far as can be ascertained she was not an active member of the Reform Society, but was arrested during the evening of the massacre and accused of inciting people to commit an assault. She protested her innocence but in spite of attempts by her husband, a boatbuilder, to see her and obtain her release, she was held in prison for nine weeks.

Women continued to be active in the cause of parliamentary reform. The Female Reformers of Leeds presented Henry Hunt with a gold medal and chain after his trial at York and when he called for exclusive dealing – shopping only where the shopkeeper was sympathetic to the radical cause, it was women who supported him. The High Street branch of the Preston Female Association reported that they were carrying on exclusive dealing 'to the very letter, even of the mangle-man and baker'.[17] At Hunt's last appearance on a radical platform in 1833, he was presented with a silver cup from the Female Union of Preston 'for his unwearied exertions in advocating the cause of liberty and promoting the welfare of the Labouring classes of the community'.[18]

Throughout the campaigns for the reform of parliament women played an active and significant part. It is not yet clear – and further research may lift the veil – whether their participation was on behalf of their men or whether their own emancipation was implicit in their efforts.

* * *

Female Reformers of Blackburn

If we were to attempt any thing like a description of the numbers assembled, it would indeed appear to many of our readers a most preposterous account – we are well assured, that when we estimate them at between 30,000 and 40,000, that we are within compass; but from whence this mass of population sprung, it is utterly impossible for us to account, suffice it to say, that they were peaceable, though determined and firm to the important object upon which they had met. After they had ascended the hustings, one of the Requisitionists

proposed that Mr Knight be called to the chair, and after some observations on the necessity of a Radical Reform of the Commons House
of Parliament, he requested Mr Fitton to read the resolutions that had
been prepared to be submitted to the adoption of this meeting; after
they were read, a most interesting and enchanting scene here ensued,
subsequent to a base attempt that had in vain been made by the
agents of Government, to throw the meeting into confusion. The
Committee of the Blackburn Female reform society appeared at the
entrance to the ground, and were desirous of approaching the hustings – they were very neatly dressed for the occasion, and each wore a
green favour in her bonnet or cap. No sooner did our worthy
Chairman perceive the anxiety of the ladies to make their way
through the immense crowds, than he signified his wish that a road
might be opened for the accommodation of the Committee of the
female reform society; which was no sooner said, than the request was
instantly complied with. The ladies ascended the hustings amidst the
reiterated acclamations of the people, which continued for several
minutes before silence could be restored. The ladies then stepping
forward toward the chairman; one of them, with becoming diffidence
and respect, presented him with a most beautiful Cap of Liberty, made
of scarlet silk or satin, lined with green, with a serpentine gold lace,
terminating with a rich gold tassel.

No language can express the torrent of approbation that spontane-
ously burst from the people. 'LIBERTY or DEATH', was vociferated
from every mouth – the tear of welcome sympathy seemed to trickle
from every eye. *'God bless the women'*, was uttered from every tongue;
in fact, imagination can only do justice to this interesting scene.
Could the cannibal Castlereagh have witnessed this noble expression
of public sentiment, he must have had a heart of brass if it had not
struck him dead to the ground!

The presentation of the Cap of Liberty was accompanied with the
following short emphatic speech, delivered by Mrs Alice Kitchin.

Will you, Sir, accept this token of our respect to those brave men
who are nobly struggling for liberty and life; by placing it at the
head of your banner, you will confer a lasting obligation on the
Female Reformers of Blackburn. We shall esteem it as an additional
favor, if the address which I deliver into your hands be read to the
Meeting; it embraces a faint description of our woes, and may apolo-
gise for our interference in the politics of our country – (*very great
applause.*)

The banner was then lowered, crowned by the Cap of Liberty, and rehoisted amidst the continued shouts and huzzas of the Meeting.

Silence being again restored, the Chairman observed, that he held in his hand the address of the Female Reformers, which with their permission, he was desired to read.

To the Chairman and Friends to radical Reform, in the Representation of the Commons House of Parliament assembled at the Meeting, to consult of the best means of attaining their Rights and Liberties.

Mr Chairman and Brother,

The members of the Blackburn Female Reform Society, beg leave with the greatest diffidence and respect, to render into your hands the emblem that has ever been held sacred to the people, in the most enlightened ages of our history; and particularly to our ancestors, who contributed so much to the fame of our beloved country –
THE CAP of LIBERTY!

In presenting this Cap of Liberty, which we trust no ruffian banditti will be allowed to wrest from your hands but with the forfeiture of your existence, we hope it will not be deemed presumptuous to offer a faint sketch of the misery and sufferings we are doomed to endure; and which we are thoroughly convinced, arise entirely from the misrule of a profligate system of government.

Having shared with you, our fathers, our husbands, our brothers, our relatives and our friends, in the overwhelming misery of our country, and possessing as we do the hearts of sympathizing females, we deem it necessary to acquaint you that under the name of the Blackburn Female Reform Society, we have already come forward with the avowed determination, of instilling into the minds of their offspring a deep rooted abhorrence of tyranny, come in what shape it may; whether under the mask of civil or religious government, and particularly of the present borough-mongering and Jesuistical system, which has brought the best artizans, manufacturers, and labourers of this vast community, to a state of wretchedness and misery, and driven them to the very verge of beggary and ruin; for by the griping hand of the relentless taxgatherer, our aged parents, who once enjoyed a comfortable subsistence, some of them are reduced to a state of pauperism, whilst others have been sent to an untimely grave.

We appeal to you and our countrymen in general, this day, and wish to shew that were it possible to erect a standard on this ground, and call every labouring man there to it, there to make a full disclosure of his sufferings and wants – we do not hesitate to say, it would then be proved that the cup of each man's misery overflows, and for ourselves and our neighbours we can speak with unassuming confidence, that our houses which once bore ample testimony of our industry and cleanliness, and were fit for the reception of a prince, are now alas! robbed of all their ornaments, and our beds, that once afforded us cleanliness, health and sweet repose, are now torn away from us by the relentless hand of the unfeeling tax gatherer, to satisfy the greatest monsters of cruelty, the borough-mongering tyrants, who are reposing on beds of down, while nothing is left us to stretch our weary limbs upon but a sheaf of straw, laid on the cold ground, with insufficient covering to shelter us from the inclemency of the weather.

But above all, behold our innocent wretched children! Sweet emblems of our mutual love! How appalling are their cries for bread! We are daily cut to the heart to see them greedily devour the course food that some would scarcely give to their swine. Come then to our dwellings, ye inhabitants of the den of corruption, behold our misery, and see our rags! We cannot describe our wretchedness, for language cannot paint the feelings of a mother, when she beholds her naked children, and hears their inoffensive cries of hunger and approaching death.

We cannot boast much of female courage, though we are not without proof in history of women who have led armies to the field, and carried conquest before them; and we do assure you, that had it not been for the golden prize of reform held out to us, that weak and impotent as might be our strength, we should long ere this have sallied forth to demand our rights, and in the acquirement of those rights to have obtained that food and raiment for our children, which God and nature have ordained for every living creature; but which our oppressors and tyrannical rulers have withheld from us.

We, the Female Reformers of Blackburn, therefore earnestly entreat you and every man in England, in the most solemn manner, to come forward and join the general union, that by a determined and constitutional resistance to our oppressors, the people may obtain annual parliaments, universal suffrage, and election by ballot, which alone can save us from lingering misery and premature death. We look forward with horror to an approaching winter, when the necessity of food, clothing, and every requisite will increase double fold; and should you not come forward ere then to demand your rights as men, who knows but the same fate, though in a land of plenty, might befall our children, that befell the children at the Siege of Jerusalem, when mothers devoured their own offspring. God of nature avert the dreadful alternative! But who will believe that to this wretched state we are reduced, while it is a notorious fact that 2,344 persons receive yearly 2,474,805 for doing little or nothing.

To remove these evils, we are willing to render every assistance in our power, nor will we relax in our exertions till universal liberty is restored to this land.

We have the honour to subscribe ourselves,

The Members of the Female Reform Society,

in the Town and Neighbourhood of Blackburn.

July 5th, 1819.

Black Dwarf, 14 July 1819.

The Manchester Female Reformers' Address
To the Wives, Mothers, Sisters, and Daughters of the Higher and Middling Classes of Society

Dear Sisters of the Earth,

It is with a spirit of peaceful consideration and due respect that we are induced to address you, upon the causes that have compelled us to associate together in aid of our suffering children, our dying parents, and the miserable partners of our woes. Bereft, not only of that support, the calls of nature require for existence; but the balm of sweet repose hath long been a stranger to us. Our minds are filled with horror and despair, fearful, on each returning morn, the light of heaven should present to us the corpse of some of our famished offspring, or nearest kindred, which the more kind hand of death had released from the grasp of the oppressor. The Sabbath, which is set apart by the all-wise Creator for a day of rest, we are compelled to employ in repairing the tattered garments, to cover the nakedness of our forlorn and destitute families. Every succeeding night brings with it new terrors, so that we are sick of life, and weary of a world, where poverty, wretchedness, tyranny, and injustice, have so long been permitted to reign amongst men.

Dear Sisters, we feel justified in stating, that under the oppressive system of Government that we now live, the same fate that hath overtaken us, must speedily be the lot of many of you; for it is said in the word of God, 'Where the carcase is, there will the eagles be also'; and this we have proved to demonstration, that the lazy Boroughmongering Eagles of destruction have nearly picked bare the bones of those who labour. You may then fairly anticipate, that when we are mixed with the silent dust, you will become the next victims of the voracious Borough Tyrants, who will chase you, in your turn, to misery and death, till at length, the middle and useful class of society, is swept, by their relentless hands, from the face of the creation.

From very mature and deliberate consideration, we are thoroughly convinced, that under the present system, the day is near at hand, when nothing will be found in our unhappy country but luxury, idleness, dissipation, and tyranny, on the one hand; and abject poverty, slavery, wretchedness, misery, and death, on the other. To avert these dreaded evils, it is your duty therefore to unite with us as speedily as possible; and to exert your influence with your fathers, your husbands, your sons, your relatives, and your friends, to join the Male Union for constitutionally demanding a Reform in their own House, viz. The Commons' House of Parliament; for we are now thoroughly convinced, that for want of such timely Reform, the useful class of society has been reduced to its present degraded state – and that with such a reform, the English nation would not have been stamped with the indelible disgrace, of having been engaged in the late unjust, unnecessary, and destructive war, against the liberties of France, that closed its dreadful career on the crimson plains of Waterloo; where the blood of our fellow-creatures flowed in such mighty profusion, that the fertile earth seemed to blush at the outrage offered to the choicest works of heaven; and for a space of time was glutted with the polluted draught, till the Almighty, with a frown upon the aggressors, drew a veil over the dismal scene!

Let us now ask the cause of this dreadful carnage? Was it to gain immortal happiness for all mankind? Or, if possible, 'was it for a nobler purpose?' Alas, no! The simple story is this, that all this dreadful slaughter was, in cool blood, committed for the purpose of placing upon the Throne of France, contrary to the people's interest and inclination, the present contemptible Louis, a man who had been living for years in this country in idleness, and wandering from one corner of the island to the other in cowardly and vagabond slothfulness and contempt. Let it be remembered at the same time, that this war, to reinstate this man, has tended to raise landed property three-fold above its value, and to load our beloved country with such an insurmountable burden of Taxation, that is too intolerable to endure longer; it has nearly annihilated our once flourishing trade and commerce, and is now driving our merchants and manufacturers to poverty and degradation.

We call upon you therefore to join us with heart and hand, to exterminate tyranny and foul oppression from the face of our native country. It affords us pleasure to inform you, that numbers of your ranks have voluntarily mixed with us, who are fully determined, in defiance of the threats of the Boroughmongers,[19] to aid us in our just and constitutional career. Our enemies are resolved upon destroying the last vestige of the natural Rights of Man, and we are determined to establish it; for as well might they attempt to arrest the sun in the region of space, or stop the diurnal motion of the earth, as to impede the rapid progress of the enlightened friends to Liberty and Truth. The beam of angelic light that hath gone forth through the globe hath at length reached unto Man, and we are proud to say that the Female Reformers of Manchester have also caught its benign and heavenly influence; it is not possible therefore for us to submit to bear the ponderous weight of our chains any longer, but to use our endeavour to tear them asunder, and dash them in the face of our remorseless oppressors.

We can no longer bear to see numbers of our parents immured in workhouses – our fathers separated from our mothers, in direct contradiction to the laws of God and the laws of man; our sons degraded below human nature, our husbands and little ones clothed in rags, and pining on the face of the earth! Dear Sisters, how could you bear to see the infant at the breast, drawing from you the remnant of your last blood, instead of the nourishment which nature requires; the only subsistence for yourselves being a draught of cold water? It would be criminal in us to disguise any longer the dreadful truth; for, in the midst of all these privations, if we were to hold our peace, the very trees of the forest, and stones of the valley, would justly cry out!

These are a few of the consequences resulting from the mad career of the Boroughmongers' war, to say nothing of the thousands and tens of thousands that have been slain! The widows and orphans that have been left destitute and unprotected. The hyprocrital [sic] hireling will blasphemeously tell you that these things are of divine ordinance; but in vain does he publish this to reason and common sense – the great Author of nature makes no distinction of persons – the rich and the poor are all alike to him; and surely the forked lightning, the awful thunder, the terrible earthquakes, and the howling and flaming volcanoes, are sufficient to chastise the most obdurate, without man becoming the oppressor of man. We close the disgusting scene; for language would infinitely fall short in painting the portrait of our woes in all their horrible deformities.

In conclusion, we earnestly entreat you to come forward – posterity will bless the names they see enrolled under the banners of Reform. Remember, that all good men were reformers in every age of the world. Noah was a reformer; he warned the people of their danger, but they paid no attention to him; Lot did in like manner, but the deluded people laughed him to scorn; the consequence was they were destroyed; all the Prophets were Reformers, and also the Apostles; so was the great Founder of Christianity, he was the greatest reformer of all; and if Jesus Christ himself were to come upon the earth again, and to preach against the Church and the State in the same manner he did against the Jewish and heathen nations, his life would assuredly be sacrificed by the relentless hand of the Borough-Judases; for corruption, tyranny, and injustice, have reached their summit; and the bitter cup of oppression is now full to the brim.

By Order of the Committee,

Susanna Saxton, Secretary.

Union Rooms, Manchester, July 20, 1819.

N.B. The Committee will sit every Tuesday Evening, from six to nine o'clock, for the purpose of enrolling the Names of such Members, and transacting other Business relative to the Establishment.

Manchester Observer, 31 July 1819.

Barbarous Treatment of Mrs Scott

The partizans of the Government are ever holding up to public view the horrors of the French Revolution, and cautioning the People of England to beware of plunging the Country into such sanguinary scenes, and yet while with one hand they are penning these precepts of prudence and morality, with the other they are acting over again the Robespierrean part of universal massacre. Can Englishmen remain blind to this duplicity? Let them compare the Regent's Proclamation,[20] or Lord Sidmouth's Circular,[21] or his Letter of Thanks[22] to the Magistrates and Yeomanry murderers of Manchester, with the unparalleled suffering of Ann Scott, in the lock-up, gaol, and hospital of Manchester, and then say whether justice or humanity characterizes the proceedings of the present Ministry and their minions. We here see a Jailer refuse to send medical assistance to a female dangerously ill; we also see him refuse to admit her husband to see her, until he had first been bribed with a sum of money; and finally we see the wretch commit an act of felony, by detaining the money and food (or rather, embezzling it) which her husband committed to his care for her use. Gracious God! When will these proceedings be put a stop to? Will it be believed that for the purpose of perpetrating them, Government are at this moment filling another *Green Bag*?[23] Yet such is the fact, if our information be correct, and correct we entertain but little doubt that it is. Once more we ask, will Englishmen submit *peaceably* to all this? We hope not – for the sake of England we hope not – for the sake of freedom – for the sake of every thing that is valuable to man, we hope that they will shed their hearts' blood, if necessary, to vindicate their rights as freemen and as Britons. We copy the case of Ann Scott from the *Morning Chronicle*,[24] as likewise the letter of Mr Doveton, which exhibits in its true colours the callousness of Aristocratic Ministerial hearts to the sufferings of the Poor, and also their ingratitude to those who have conferred upon them unrequited favours. The Government are making every preparation to crush you to the dust; the Veteran Batallions are once more called out on duty, as we see by an advertisement from the War Office, signed by Lord Palmerston.[25] Will you look tamely on and see all your liberties wrested from you by military force? Never, never. Let *Liberty or Death!* be the motto on your blades, till washed from them by the blood of the tyrants, who shall attempt to overturn the remnant of the Constitution of England, for the purpose of establishing on its ruins a *military despotism*.

Manchester, Oct. 1819.

I, Ann Scott, wife of William Scott, boat-builder, of Liverpool-road, Manchester, declare, that on the 16th of August last, about seven o'clock in the evening, I was violently laid hold of in Deansgate, by Mr Charles Ashworth, said to be a Special Constable, who dragged me to the Police-office, where I remained for about twenty minutes, with several other persons, with whom I was conveyed, under a guard of soldiers, to the New Bailey; here I was committed to what is called 'the Lock-ups,' which is the room that forms a receptacle for all prisoners taken up during the night, for paupers, and for common thieves. In this room, and in such company, I was detained from Monday evening until the following Friday, without being permitted to go into the open air; during which time I had no bed to lie upon, nor any thing on which to repose, except a common form, although the floor was floating with water and filth, produced by the paupers, etc. and their children; nor were either they nor I, nor any other prisoner in the room, permitted to leave it for the performance of the common offices of nature. The smell was consequently so very offensive as to materially affect my health. On the Friday after my arrest, I was taken into the New Bailey Courtroom, where Ashworth the constable charged me before the Rev. Mr Ethelstone[26] with endeavouring to excite the People to commit an assault – a crime of which I solemnly declare I am perfectly innocent. The Magistrate ordered that I should procure bail; which, at that time, I was unable to obtain. I was therefore recommitted to prison, where I was confined with other women, and allowed occasionally to take the air in a small yard; but, in consequence of my sufferings in the Lock-up Room, for the want of air and repose, together with the excessive moisture and bad smell, which I was doomed to endure, I became so very unwell, that I was unable to leave my bed, and where I became so ill, that I informed the Turnkey (Jackson) of my situation, and requested him to let me see the Doctor; but he took no notice of my application, and, locking the cell-door upon me every day, prevented me from communicating with my fellow prisoners. I think I should have died from extreme thirst, had it not been for the humanity of the 'Constable Woman' (as she is called), who attends the female prisoners, by whom I was occasionally supplied with tea, and toast and water, I repeated my complaints daily but in vain, to Jackson; and at length, about six days after, I was confined to my bed. The Doctor then visited me, who immediately ordered my removal to the hospital, where I was carried by the woman constable and another female. In the Hospital, the disease with which I was afflicted, according to the statement of the Doctor, was an inflammation of the liver, accompanied by a high fever. Afterwards, when I had been a fortnight in the Hospital, and suffering under a relapse of the fever, I was permitted to see my husband, for the first time since my arrest, although I had repeatedly entreated that he might be let in to speak to me; and when I saw him I was scarcely able to speak to him. He remained with me about ten minutes, when Jackson ordered him away. I requested the turnkey to let him stay a little; but he answered, 'No!' and compelled my husband to go away. About a fortnight afterwards, I was again allowed to see my husband; but he was not permitted to remain with me above ten minutes, the turnkey standing beside us during our conversation. During the nine weeks that I have been in prison, I was never permitted to see my husband, but the twice that I have stated, although I frequently solicited the Turnkey to let him in. Throughout my confinement, I had only the common gaol allowance, excepting a little tea and sugar, which the keeper said my husband sent me. To this statement I am ready to depose upon oath.

(Signed)

Ann Scott.

Witnesses – P.J. Candelet, Thomas Chapman.

Manchester, Oct. 18, 1819. I, William Scott, of Liverpool-road, Manchester, boat builder, declare, that after I heard of the arrest of my wife, Ann Scott, on the 16th of August last, I went to the New Bailey Prison, in order to see her, but the turnkey refused my admission. I repeated my request for admission several times afterwards, but in vain. I was not permitted, indeed, to see my wife until about a month after her arrest; when, upon giving the turnkey (Jackson) some money, I was admitted, and found her lying a-bed in the hospital of the prison, so very ill, that she was scarcely able to speak. I now staid with her about ten minutes, when I was compelled to go out by Jackson, the turnkey. From that time until her liberation this day, I was never allowed to see her even but once, although I frequently applied for admission at the door of the prison. During her imprisonment I several times sent her food and money, which she declares she never received. To this statement I am ready to depose upon oath.

(Signed)

William Scott

Witnesses – Thomas Chapman, P.J. Candelet.

To these statements, upon which we feel it unnecessary to make any remarks, we cannot help adding the following letter, just put into our hands, from the ministerial member for Lancaster, for whose return poor Scott voted at the last election.

5, Henrietta-street,
Cavendish-square, Sept. 25

My Friend Scott,

I received the petition which you sent to me. I am very sorry to hear the unhappy condition of your wife, in being confined in the New Bailey Prison, on account of some expressions she had used on the 16th August last. As I am totally unacquainted, however, with the nature and extent of her fault, you must be aware how very improper it would be in me to attempt to intercede for her release at your request. I have only to lament, therefore, that I cannot be of service to you on the present occasion.

I remain your friend

G. Doveton.

Cap of Liberty, 20 October 1819.

Letter from the Female Reformers of Manchester

To Wm. Cobbett, Esq.

Sir, The Female Reformers of Manchester, actuated by a lively sense of the manifold services which you have rendered to mankind, and to the sacred cause of freedom, by the gigantic powers of a mind, unsubdued by inveterate and undeserved persecution, beg leave to hail your return to your native land with exultation and joy. They behold in this return a pledge of your undiminished devotion to those principles for which you became self-expatriated, leaving behind you, however, a spark of that celestial liberty which your presence alone, will now fan into a pure and lambent flame, harmless to all but the oppressors and plunderers of the people.

Accept of our grateful homage to your splendid talents and love of virtue, exerted with a vigour neither appalled nor seduced by corruption. Persevere, beloved Sir, with undiminished ardour in the great design of effecting a reform in every branch of a government ...

We presume at the same time to beg your acceptance of a small tribute to your transcendent worth; it is a present somewhat assimilated to your pursuits in life; when you hereafter look upon the writing apparatus thus offered to you, you will not fail to recollect that the Female Reformers throughout the Kingdom are, notwithstanding their sex, equally interested in your past and future labours.

It cannot be unknown to you, Sir, that our intentions have been vilified, and our characters traduced by the unprincipled scribes, of a venal and corrupt press. To you, in your excellent letter to the Female Reformers of Blackburn, we are indebted for a complete vindication of our motives, our conduct and our characters; you have refuted the calumnies of our enemies and proved our innocence and integrity. The days of chivalry are passed; but in you the Female Reformers feel they shall never want a sufficient advocate, and are thankful for the aid you have afforded.

May these trifling tokens of our regard, wielded and directed by your matchless and expanded mind, accelerate the glorious day which we perceive fast approaching our political horizon; may they prove more powerful than the sabres of the cowardly enemy, which we the Female Reformers of Manchester most of us narrowly escaped, and drive corruption to her pristine darkness: then shall the voice of war be heard no more, and our children reap the full fruit of their parents' labour.

With the most sincere and affectionate wishes for the health, happiness and prosperity of yourself and family, we have the honour to subscribe ourselves, for the Female Reformers of Manchester,

Your very obedient and devoted servants,

M. Fildes, Chairwoman,
S. Saxton, Secretary.

Manchester, Nov. 29, 1819.

Cobbett's Weekly Political Register, 29 December 1819.

Notes

1. John Knight (1763–1838) presided at the meeting in Manchester in October 1816 which established a Hampden Club. By 1819 he was regarded as an elder statesman of the movement in Lancashire. He was arrested at Peterloo, but continued activity whilst on bail. He suffered two years' imprisonment.

2. William Fitton was a surgeon in Royton near Manchester, and the leading figure in the Hampden Club there. He was a devotee of Tom Paine and an ardent believer in the rights of man.

3. Samuel Bamford (1788–1872) was the leading radical in Middleton, near Manchester. He wrote an account of Peterloo in his *Passages in the Life of a Radical* (1839–41). At Peterloo he led the Middleton contingent and was arrested and imprisoned.

4. *Black Dwarf,* 14 July 1819, p. 455.

5. Mrs G. Linnaeus Banks, *The Manchester Man*, Manchester 1896, p. 462.

6. Henry Hunt, *Memoirs of Henry Hunt Esq*, 1822, p. 612.

7. Banks, *The Manchester Man*, p. 178.

8. The Hampden Clubs were called after John Hampden (1594–1643). He resisted payment of a tax called 'Ship Money'.

9. Joseph Nadin (1765–1848) was the permanent Deputy Constable of Manchester. He was a notorious figure hated by working-class radicals. As the principal executive agent of the local authorities, it was he who carried out the orders to arrest Henry Hunt and the others with him at Peterloo.

10. William Hulton (1787–1864) was the heir to the Hulton estate, of which he took over the management in 1808. He found coal on his land and increased his wealth. As a Justice of the Peace, he was the senior magistrate on duty on 16 August 1819 and it was he who gave the orders to arrest Hunt and to call in the military to disperse the crowd.

11. The Manchester and Salford Yeomanry Cavalry were set up in 1817 especially to deal with radical activities. Its members were cotton merchants, publicans and shopkeepers.

12. Joyce Marlow, *Peterloo Massacre*, 1969, p. 150.

13. *Peterloo Massacre*, no. 3, p. 42.

14. See biography in Chapter 3.

15. Jane Carlile together with her baby Thomas Paine was imprisoned in Dorchester Gaol in the same room as her husband Richard and his sister, Mary-Anne. Richard and Jane were held from February 1821 to February 1823 and Mary-Anne Carlile from July 1821 to November 1823. Jane and Richard's daughter, Hypatia, was born in prison in June 1822.

16. *Republican*, no. 19, vol. V, 10 May 1822, p. 602.

17. John Belchem, *'Orator Hunt'*, 1985, p. 266.

18. Ibid., p. 272.

19. A term of derision used by William Cobbett in which he included all who served the state as well as the 'system' he hated.

20. The Regent's Proclamation against seditious assemblies, election of 'representatives' and drilling was issued on 30 July 1819 and posted up by the magistrates in Manchester on 3 August.

21. Sidmouth, the Home Secretary, issued a circular encouraging magistrates to arrest persons suspected of disseminating seditious libel.

22. From Sidmouth to the Earl of Derby asking him to thank the magistrates who officiated at Peterloo. He also commended the action of the military especially the Yeomanry under Major Trafford. It was written on 21 August 1819.

23. Green Bag was an allusion to the sealed bags of official documents. The radicals guyed Lord Eldon because he was fond of parading a green bag of incriminatory documents in the House of Lords. They called him 'Old Bags'.

24. The *Morning Chronicle and London Advertiser* started in 1769 as a Whig paper. It later changed sides and became Tory. It ceased publication in 1857.

25. Henry John Temple Palmerston (1784–1865), Tory statesman and Prime Minister 1855–8 and 1859–65.

26. Rev. Charles Wicksted Ethelstone (1767–1830) was Rector of Worthenbury in Flintshire and a Fellow of the Collegiate Church in Manchester. He was easily alarmed and tended to believe all he was told by his spies, who were numerous. He thoroughly disliked radical reformers.

3

The Struggle for the Freedom
of the Press

> To check the circulation
> Of Little Books,
>   Whose very looks –
> Vile *'two-p'nny trash,'*
>   bespeak abomination.
> Oh! They are full of blasphemies
>   and libels,
> And people read them
>   oftener than their bibles
>
> William Hone, *The Man in the Moon*, 1821.

Introduction

The story of the reforming movements that proliferated during the first half of the nineteenth century was based firmly on the need of workers to communicate their ideas. It is no accident that the attempts of successive governments to suppress and curtail the sale of radical journals and newspapers by placing a prohibitive tax on them were referred to as the 'Taxes on Knowledge'.[1]

With growing class consciousness and their identification as the oppressed, working people looked to enlightenment in all its aspects as a weapon with which to secure their emancipation. On the other side of the fence, the ruling class sought to keep people ignorant and isolated from each other. They clearly saw the threat to their entrenched position of a knowledgeable working class able to discuss and plan campaigns against the abuses of the growing capitalist system.

The 20 years following Peterloo were momentous in many ways. The 1832 Reform Act[2] of Parliament indicated to the workers that their political aspirations were not to be won without further struggle. The alliance between the middle class and the workers was ended and campaigning then took place within the established class structure of society. There were some issues of particular interest to middle-class radicals which also sparked interest and action by the workers. But there was one subject on which all radicals agreed during the 20 years, and that was the freedom to publish and to read matter germane to their interests.

34

Women were very active in these campaigns and because this involved publication we probably know more about them than some activists in other fields. The movement's central figure was Richard Carlile. He suffered persecution from the government throughout the period and much of his work had, therefore, to be carried on by his shopmen. (It should be noted that the term 'shopmen' included a number of shopwomen as well.)

In the 1820s Carlile's main campaigning issue was the publication of books and pamphlets considered by the government to be blasphemous. Chief among them were the works of Thomas Paine.[3] Carlile republished Paine's *Rights of Man*[4] which had been proscribed since 1792 as a seditious libel and his *Age of Reason*[5] in which he attacked the notion of the Bible as an inspired book. Publishers had reissued it over the years and had suffered prosecution for so doing. Carlile knew that he was certain to be arrested and tried when he published these works both in expensive editions and in parts at a low price which working people could afford. In spite of all that the government could do, he continued to publish and sell them, and when he was imprisoned he called on his family and those who supported him to carry on the work.

Eventually the government relented and Paine's works were freely published. Carlile claimed that he and his shopmen had achieved the freedom of the press (the press meaning 'printing press', not the newspaper press in the modern sense). But the government had not given up. It had only changed course.

Taxes had been imposed on journals and newspapers for a century at least, but after 1830 the imposition of the tax and the prosecution for selling papers without it intensified. The Newspaper Act of 1798 had required all newspapers to be registered and had placed such a high duty on them that their prices had to be raised to prohibitive heights. Working people got around this in many ways, and possibly the need to club together to obtain a copy of a paper which was then read and discussed collectively was an important step in the formation of working-class consciousness.

Action to prevent workers from gaining political knowledge increased their determination to obtain the freedom to decide for themselves what they should read and discuss. Several Acts were passed up to 1817 which were nicknamed the 'Gagging Acts'.[6] Carlile started his campaigns against these Acts in 1817.

Women involved in Carlile's campaign for the right to publish were his wife, Jane, and his sister Mary-Anne as well as shopwomen such as Susannah Wright. When Eliza Sharples joined him the character of the campaign was changing into the fight against the Taxes on Knowledge and Carlile became a firm advocate of women's emancipation. In a letter written in Dorchester Gaol and published in the *Republican*, he said, 'I call upon every woman, whether old or young, to shake off those prejudices, those trammels in which they have been educated; I call upon them to assert the right of free discussion, and to partake of it ... It is honourable to see a woman distinguishing any kind of corruption and vice and denouncing it, whether it be politics or religion.' He ended by calling on women to join their voices with their husbands in demanding a reformation in the system of government. 'Let them be politicians – let them be philosophers – let them acquire every species of useful knowledge that can be acquired ...'[7]

It is apparent that Carlile's confidence in women and his advice to them to play a part in the affairs of their time struck a responsive chord. In 1833, 150 women in Birmingham signed a letter published in a radical paper called the *Gauntlet* in which they told Carlile that they would 'now place our feet respectively upon the rock of unalterable justice, upon the spire of which we inscribe "Equal Rights and Equal Laws" ...'[8] Participation in the struggle for the freedom of the press had developed women's confidence and understanding so that they were beginning to demand their own emancipation as well as supporting the men in their efforts.

Jane Carlile

Jane Carlile (whose maiden name is unknown) was the daughter of a poor Hampshire cottager. She and Richard Carlile married in Gosport in 1813. For nearly 20 years they were to endure a relationship which was apparently based on incompatibility and in which they both suffered, and they separated in 1832.

Richard's trade of tin plate working was in economic difficulties and he was having to move around in search of work. In order to try to get work Jane and Richard moved to London where they lived in Bloomsbury. They were to have five children: four boys and a girl who was born in prison. Only three of the boys survived and their daughter died from whooping cough in 1825 when she was two years old.

When Carlile started the publication and sale of radical literature, he was harassed by the government. Jane was immediately involved in the situation although, as she confessed in a letter sent from prison, she was not politically aware but acted out of loyalty to her husband.

With her husband in prison, the shop closed down, and some of the furniture removed on the orders of the Sheriff, Jane Carlile endured extreme hardship. She visited her husband in Dorchester Gaol in December and could hardly speak for exhaustion. But within a few weeks she had found the strength to reopen the shop and continue with the sale of radical literature. This continued for 18 months, during which time Jane was hounded by the Vice Society.[9]

She was charged with publishing part of Paine's *Age of Reason* which was said to contribute to 'the high displeasure of Almighty God, to the great scandal of the Christian Religion, to the evil example of all others [and conspiring] against the peace of our said Lord the King, his crown and dignity'.[10] A year later she was prosecuted on two counts for selling Sherwin's *Life of Paine* and for publishing an essay in the *Republican* journal in which the Prince Regent and clergymen were blamed for the state of the country that had given rise to the Peterloo Massacre. Both convictions were overturned on technical grounds.

She was not so fortunate in the next trial. The Attorney General accused her of seditious libel for publishing an essay by her husband in which he characterised King George IV's treatment of his wife, Queen Caroline, as 'malignant, treacherous and abominable'.[11] Caroline's efforts to take her rightful place on the throne were strongly supported by radical opinion.

In deference to Richard Carlile's wishes, Jane appeared without counsel and conducted her own defence. She was convicted but earned the appreciation of her husband. Her fine of £200 was covered by the fact that as a married woman she had no legal standing and could not have a fine assessed against her. But the sentence of two years in Dorchester prison had to be carried out.

The terrible conditions which the Carliles endured in prison caused constraints which led eventually to the breakdown of the marriage. Carlile was an irascible and demanding husband, and after a further ten years of incompatibility, a 'moral divorce' was agreed. By that time Carlile had become attached to Eliza Sharples, whom he later married.

One of the interesting by-products of the estrangement between Richard and Jane was Carlile's interest in birth control, which by implication released him from his family ties. When in 1830 they agreed to separate, Jane was given a £50 annuity and the furniture, in return for moving out of the house with her children. She also took some of the printing stock with her so she could open a shop. When the business failed Jane removed herself from the public scene. She died in 1843. Her three surviving sons became publishers and newsagents. Neither Alfred nor Thomas Paine was successful; Richard went to America and was elected to the House of Assembly for the State of Wisconsin.

Jane Carlile's life was blighted by poverty and degradation. She was loyal to her husband and advocated his unpopular ideas even to her own disadvantage and discomfort. Certainly she played a significant part in the campaign for the right to publish and for the freedom of the press.

Mary-Anne Carlile

After both Richard Carlile and his wife Jane had been sent to prison for selling the works of Thomas Paine, Mary-Anne, Carlile's sister, was persuaded to take over the shop. She was an uneducated woman with few political ideas, but she had strong family loyalty.

She started working in the shop in Fleet Street during her sister-in-law's trial in October 1820. But the Vice Society were soon after her and by the spring of 1821 charges of blasphemy were brought against her for publishing *An Appendix to the Theological Works of Thomas Paine*, a short tract based on an American publication. The Constitutional Society[12] reinforced the situation by charging her with seditious libel for selling an essay by Carlile in which he pointed out that the lessons to be learned from the revolution in Spain could be usefully applied in Britain.

Mary-Anne was tried on both charges at the Guildhall in July 1821 before two Special Juries. On the sedition charge, she was acquitted because the jury failed to reach agreement. But the blasphemy trial took a different course. Mary-Anne conducted her own defence. She read a speech prepared by her brother. This so angered the judge, Sir William Draper Best, that he ordered parts of it to be suppressed because he said that in defending herself from one blasphemy, she uttered a hundred more.

Having been taken from court while the judge expunged her speech from the record, she said on her return, 'If the Court means to decide that an Englishwoman is not to state that which she thinks necessary for her defence, she must abide by the consequences of such a decision.'[13] This obvious lack of justice, together with a sentence of 12 months in prison and a fine of £500, which she had no chance of being able to pay, earned her considerable public sympathy. As she had no money, she had to remain in prison until the government decided that she had served long enough to cover the amount of fine that she was unable to pay. In fact she served 28 months and was not released until November 1823.

Mary-Anne and her brother and sister-in-law and their two small children had to share a prison room. Richard Carlile imposed silence on the two women which they reported 'was not most agreeable'[14] to them. In spite of the constraints of the life in gaol, Richard Carlile and Mary-Anne remained on friendly terms. On her release, she returned to her native Devon where she continued to be a strong partisan of his work.

Eliza Sharples

Eliza Sharples was born and brought up in a middle-class family in Bolton, Lancashire. It was a fervently evangelical family of which Eliza was the most pious member. As a young girl she indulged in prayers, hymn singing and soul-searching to an extent that nearly turned her mind. Her sudden change of direction in the early 1830s after being inspired by the work of Carlile was as complete as her devotion to religion had been. She broke with her family and in 1832 went to London, penniless and homeless, to participate in the radical and freethought campaigns. Richard Carlile was in prison at the time and she began to pay him daily visits in the winter of 1831/2.

Under his direction she started lecturing at the Rotunda[15] in South London where, as 'Isis', she built up a reputation as a speaker of some interest, despite her poor delivery. After six months she was saying that she who had been absolutely without prospect was 'successfully introducing new love, new light, new life into this people'.[16] Her affection for Carlile increased until by 1832 she was spending part of every day with him in prison preparing her Rotunda lectures and planning a 'new life'. In March 1832 she took over management of both the Rotunda and of Carlile's publishing business.

In the spring of 1832 Eliza became pregnant. Carlile wanted her to keep their relationship secret because he feared the backlash in political terms of his making her pregnant and deserting his wife and family. She, however, wanted to be acknowledged publicly as his wife. As soon as it was known that she was pregnant, her visits to the prison were stopped. Eliza found herself alone and poverty stricken again and after the birth of her son, Richard, she suffered a period of acute depression. After his release from prison in September 1833, Carlile published a statement in the *Gauntlet* in which he referred to his 'moral' marriage in glowing terms. He said that he was a radical reformer who had begun to reform at home. 'I have been unhappy and without a home, under one marriage. I am now happy, and with a home, under another marriage.' Eliza also referred to their 'marriage of the soul' and affirmed that it was 'not only a marriage of two bodies but a marriage of two congenial principles, each seeking an object on which virtuous affection might rest, and grow, and strengthen'.[17] However, the world was not yet ready for such advanced views and they were subjected to ribald comments and innuendos all their lives.

While Eliza accepted Carlile's political guidance she developed her own political brand of feminism, especially in relation to the unsatisfactory position in which she found herself as the 'other woman'. Eliza Sharples published the first feminist freethought journal, the *Isis*, in which she advocated the emancipation of women and made confident predictions that it 'must come'. She made a name for herself as a speaker both at the Rotunda and around the country.

Eliza's three children – those who survived childhood – emigrated to the United States. Eliza herself lived for nine years after Richard's death in 1843, for much of the time in extreme poverty. During the last three years of her life, she lived at a former temperance hall at Warner Place, Hackney Road, where she established a coffee house and newsroom. Charles Bradlaugh,[18] the future MP, lodged with the Sharples family at that address while still in his teens.

Susannah Wright

Mrs Wright was a lace-mender living in Nottingham. She was married with a family. When Richard Carlile appealed for volunteers to take over his shop in London and sell radical literature, Mr and Mrs Wright left Nottingham and went to help, becoming the first volunteers to take over the shop.

Susannah Wright is one of the few women whose attitude and activity have been demonstrably supported by their husbands, and indeed Mr Wright continued his support throughout the period of her arrest and eventual imprisonment.

Once the whole Carlile family had been incarcerated, Mrs Wright was the next obvious victim. She was arrested and confined for several weeks in Newgate Prison awaiting trial. Besides the support of her husband, she had loyal friends, for example a Mr and Mrs Jones, themselves activists in the cause of the freedom of the press. The Jones's looked after Mr Wright and the children while Mrs Wright was in prison, and Mr Jones was allowed to be with her in the dock when she eventually came to trial.

During the course of presenting her defence the judge, as so often was the case in radical trials, constantly interrupted her and finally, when she called the Vice Society 'modern Herods, and Pilates, and High Priests',[19] she was prevented from continuing.

During the trial in which she was indicted for selling *Addresses to Reformers*,[20] Mrs Wright succeeded in reading not only the whole text of the Addresses but also W.J. Fox's sermon *On The Duties of Christians Towards Deists*.[21] Lord Chief Justice Abbott[22] found her guilty and committed her to Newgate with her six-month-old baby. Ten weeks later she was sentenced to 18 months in prison and fined £100.

The imprisonment gave rise to a campaign of protest around the country. A group of female friends in Manchester sent collections that they had made, while the people of Sheffield sent a parcel of presents. Her sacrifice was acknowledged in other ways. For example, Allen Davenport wrote a verse in her honour:

For not a name in history's pages
Shall be found more fair and bright,
Which may descend to future ages,
Than the name of – Susan Wright.[23]

Though Susannah Wright was not a robust woman she was strong in her convictions. She described herself as 'truly all spirit and no matter'.[24] She was regarded with admiration and as a role model by her hundreds of followers. In 1822, when she was taken before a magistrate charged with blasphemy, she said, 'I have no fear about me for anything that concerns myself. I should enjoy even a dungeon in advocating such a cause as that in which I am now engaged.'[25]

Among the many women who played a part in the campaigns for the right to publish and sell radical literature, Susannah Wright was outstanding. Richard Carlile said of her, 'Throughout the struggle in which Mrs Wright has engaged, and she was engaged in the hottest part of all, her enthusiasms, her perseverence, her undauntedness, her coolness, were alike conspicuous and excellent.'[26]

Radical Publishers and Printers

Women were often involved in business with their husbands but seldom appeared in reports of their joint activity, because the public aspect of their work was conducted in the man's name. In the radical movement the most active propagandists were frequently the printers and publishers, and often when the man was imprisoned or travelling, the woman kept the business running.

One such woman was Anne Cobbett, who carried on her father's bookselling business after his death. For many years she published her father's work in fresh editions as well as compiling a manual of domestic management.

Alice Mann continued in the publishing business after the death of her husband, James. She was one of the largest provincial radical publishers and booksellers. The provinces played a significant part in the struggle against the unstamped press. Manchester, for example, regularly purchased about 10 per cent of the total number of illegal journals and Abel Heywood was instrumental in coordinating their sale and distribution. In Leeds, Alice Mann played a similar role; in Birmingham, James Guest ran a 'Cheap Book Repository' as a sales centre.

The distribution network of the unstamped involved the participation of many people. Manchester acted as the source from which supplies were distributed to the South Lancashire textile towns and Leeds supplied the manufacturing districts of South Yorkshire.

Books and pamphlets were sometimes published in London and printed and distributed in the provinces. Alice Mann, Abel Heywood and James Guest were all involved in this way.

Alice Mann
There are a few known instances of women taking charge of businesses after the death of their husbands, and some actually carried on businesses as single women. Alice Mann is a typical case.

James and Alice Mann were active in the movement for the reform of parliament from the early 1800s. He suffered during the period of the suspension of Habeas Corpus[27] and served a term in prison for publicising his ideas of annual parliaments, universal suffrage and vote by ballot. The Manns ran a radical bookshop and printing business in Leeds. As well as having a family of nine children, James Mann, together with John Foster, was the leading Leeds radical. It has to be assumed that Alice kept the business and activity going while her husband was in prison.

When James died in 1832, Alice took charge of the business and soon entered into partnership with Joshua Hobson, who moved from Huddersfield in the autumn of 1834. He printed Robert Owen's *New Moral World* from July 1838 to October 1841 and also the *Northern Star*, the Chartist paper which was issued from 12/13 Market Street, Briggate, Leeds, in November 1837. Alice Mann retained the use of the smaller press and published in her own name. She printed such pamphlets as *The Black Book of the British Aristocracy* in which were exposed the vast amounts of money paid by the government to placemen and pensioners. She also printed a *Memoir of William Cobbett*.

Alice Mann must also have retained the bookshop because she was named as the agent for the paper *The Ten Hour Advocate*.

In 1836 Mrs Mann was charged with the sale of unstamped newspapers containing articles 'of a nature calculated to excite hatred and contempt of the government' or 'vilify our holy religion'.[28] Although she was offered punishment on only one count instead of the five on which she was found guilty if she would undertake to discontinue the sale of unstamped newspapers, she refused and served six calendar months in York Castle as well as paying a £100 fine.

During her imprisonment her family kept the business and the shop open. Alice Mann features in history because of the particular circumstances in which she was placed. How many more such active women were lost from the records because they were not accounted for as individuals?

Matilda Roalfe (1813–80)
Born in 1813, Matilda Roalfe lived a normal life as a middle-class young lady conducting a Sunday School class in Edinburgh. But the questions which her pupils put to her made her think seriously about the religion she was attempting to teach. As a result, she became converted to freethought and offered herself as a volunteer to sell the offending literature for which the government was putting so many people in prison. In 1843 she left Edinburgh and went to London to uphold the right of free publication.

In London, she had been associated with George Jacob Holyoake in the Anti-Persecution Union and when she heard that an Edinburgh bookseller was being prosecuted for selling radical and freethought publications she went to help. While Thomas Paterson prepared for his trial, Matilda Roalfe opened the Edinburgh bookshop and announced her determination in a manifesto distributed around the City to sell 'books calculated to bring the Christian religion into contempt'[29] at an Atheistical Depot at 105 Nicolas Street.

She was arrested after police officers visited the shop and purchased *The Oracle of Reason*. She conducted her own defence because she felt that a defence counsel was not to be trusted to maintain the principles on which the defence rested. Despite a packed courtroom obviously in sympathy with her and her cross examination of the police officers (in which they did not distinguish themselves), she was found guilty and sentenced to 60 days' detention.

The police ransacked her shop and house while she was awaiting trial and she returned to find everything in chaos. In prison she was held in vile conditions in a stone cell with a bed that was verminous. Her release was greeted by a huge demonstration of support and a successful social occasion.

As soon as she came out of prison she resumed the sale of the forbidden publications. Shortly afterwards, she married Walter Sanderson and they settled at Galashiels where she stayed until she died in November 1880.

* * *

Petition of Mary-Anne Carlile to the House of Commons, and Correspondence with Mr Hobhouse[30] on the Subject

To the Honourable the Commons of Great Britain and Ireland in Parliament Assembled

The Petition of Mary-Anne Carlile, late of London, Bookseller, now a Prisoner in his Majesty's Gaol of Dorchester.[31]

Humbly Sheweth,

That your Petitioner comes before your Honourable House with a complaint of an undue administration of the laws towards her, on the part of the Judges of his Majesty's Court of King's Bench, and on the part of Sir William Draper Best, Knt[32] one of the Judges of that Court, in particular.

That on the 24th day of July, 1821, your Petitioner appeared in the Court of King's Bench to defend herself against an indictment instituted by a secret association of prosecutors, calling themselves a Society for the Suppression of Vice, but who, in fact, are a set of intolerant, bigoted persecutors, aiming chiefly at the suppression of virtue, or the truths that would inevitably arise from a free discussion of matters of theology and philosophy; in which indictment a selection from a pamphlet, entitled 'An Appendix to the Theological Works of Thomas Paine', was charged as a blasphemous libel; and that in the course of her defence she had occasion to state that the Common Law, on which it was pretended that her indictment was founded, was a common abuse, and although the written defence with which she was prepared to defend herself fully bore out the assertion, and gave a complete explanation of the term used, the Judge (Sir William Draper Best) stopped her defence altogether, and would not allow her to offer another sentence, nor even the completion of that in the midst of which she was stopped, unless she would retract the assertion that the Common Law was a common abuse, and promise not to repeat it. Your Petitioner not feeling disposed to acquiesce in this arbitrary, unjust, illegal, and despotic command, was altogether prevented from making her defence, and the aforesaid Judge called upon the Jury for their verdict, stating positively that the charge of the indictment was proper, and that the selection from the pamphlet in question was a blasphemous libel; upon which unfair assertion a verdict of Guilty was returned without any trial taking place, or without any defence being heard: whilst your Petitioner verily believes, that if she had received a fair hearing, she would have been acquitted of the charge on that indictment, as she was on a subsequent one on the same day, where she trusted her defence to a Counsel, whom the Judge repeatedly tried, in vain, to silence.

That, in the Michaelmas Term last, she employed Counsel to move for a new trial before a full Court, when Mr Justice Best swayed the Court by a statement utterly false, that in the course of reading he had repeatedly complained of your Petitioner's defence before he stopped it altogether, when, in fact, not the least interruption occurred, nor was any objection made to a sentence, or even a word, until the afore-mentioned phrase was uttered, when it was stopped for once and alto-gether, without referring to the copy of the defence for an examination of the bearing of the phrase by the context, or even to see how it was modified by the conclusion of the sentence. In conse-quence of this false statement, Petitioner's Counsel was disconcerted in his argument, having no allusion to any such circumstance on his brief, because no such circumstance had occurred at the time of trial, in support of which assertion your Petitioner can bring forward the most respectable and most efficient evidence, and in contradiction of the statement of the Judge, which she should have done by affidavit before receiving the judgment of the Court, if she had been allowed time, and if she had not been hurried to Prison within two days of her Counsel's motion for a new trial.

That the sentence of the Court upon her after this unjust proceeding was a year's imprisonment in Dorchester Gaol, a fine of five hundred pounds, and securities for seven years to the amount of twelve hundred pounds: whereas, your Petitioner was merely a servant to her brother, and at no period of her life was she ever worth ten pounds; by reason of which fine she has no prospect whatever of being able to comply with the sentence from her own means, and without a remission of the fine, or public charity, she must be imprisoned for life. Such a sentence she submits to your Honourable House is a violation of the law as laid down in the Declaration of Rights, which says, that excessive fines shall not be imposed.[33]

She further submits to your Honourable House, that the denial to her of the right to make a defence, a right never before disputed out of the Star Chamber,[34] is a gross violation of the law and custom of this country committed by the said Sir William Draper Best, and countenanced by the other Judges of that Court; for which she prays the interference of your Honourable House, as the highest tribunal, to a full examination of the matter, alleged in this Petition.

And sheweth, as a matter of elucidation of the severity and injustice of Petitioner's case, that the phrase of the Common Law being in many instances an abuse, is fully borne out by a reference to the Journals of your Honourable House, in which it will be found, that your Honourable House has lately interposed statute laws to repeal the laws relating to what has been called Witchcraft, and the Wager of Battle, as the last relic of the mode of trial by ordeal, such laws having been founded upon erroneous opinions, superstitions, and prejudices, which, from an improved state of knowledge, have fallen into desuetude, or have been considered particularly obnoxious and requiring abolition or correction. Your Petitioner therefore submits to your Honourable House, that it was not sufficient ground for the Judge to have stopped her defence from the use of such a phrase, particularly when it was held forth that the continuation of the defence would have explained and have convinced the Jury of the correctness of the assertion. She submits also, that the Jury ought to have been the Judges of her defence, and they were not allowed to hear it by the undue interference of the Judge.

Your Petitioner further submits, that there is another part of her case worthy of the most serious consideration of your Honourable House. Upon what is called the Common Law your Petitioner was indicted for an alleged blasphemous libel, the selection from the pamphlet setting forth that there was no connection between the books of the Old and the New Testaments; for which assertion, in the very selection alleged to be a libel, the authority of the late Archbishop Tillotson[35] is brought forward, and an inference is drawn that the passages called prophecies in the books comprising the Old Testament are not in reality prophecies of the person of Jesus Christ, as mentioned in the books of the New Testament, by which the divinity of the Great Reformer of the Jews is disputed. Now, an act of your Honourable House, passed in the 53d of George the Third, entitled 'An Act to relieve those Persons who impugn the Doctrine of the Holy Trinity', which enactment implies the encouragement and legality of disputing the divinity of Jesus in the legality of impugning the doctrine of the Holy Trinity; nay, so wide a range does this legality to impugn the doctrine of the Holy Trinity take, that the persons who come under the denomination of Atheists may claim a legal right to impugn every principle of Theism[36] under its sanction, by saying, that the doctrine of the Holy Trinity is the doctrine of the Christian Deity, and an Act of the British Legislature, passed so late as the year 1813, has expressly and literally made it lawful to impugn that Deity, in direct contradiction of the principle, that Christianity is part and parcel of the law of the land and of the pretended Common Law which is still kept in practice; and in consequence of the provisions of this Act of your Honourable House, the sect denominated Unitarians,[37] for whose relief it was avowedly passed, professing to worship one God only, in unity and not in trinity, who have now chapels or places for worship and lecturing erected in almost every town in the country, are continually describing the sacred person of Jesus Christ, whom Christians worship as a branch of their Deity, as the Peasant of Judea and the Carpenter's Wife's Son, thereby stating that they believe him to have been a mere man; in which they are not only tolerated, but feel themselves secured by an express law, as above-mentioned.

Your Petitioner therefore humbly prays, that your Honourable House will obtain for her that justice which has been denied her in the Court of King's Bench, rescue her from the unjust judgment under which she is now suffering and the penalties imposed on her; and further, that your Honourable House will in its wisdom think fit to render the laws more decisive and intelligible on this head, as the late pretended proceeding by Common Law against your Petitioner has been in evident contradiction to the statute law above-mentioned.

And, as in duty bound,

Your Petitioner will ever pray,

Mary-Anne Carlile.

Dorchester Gaol, Feb. 28, 1822.

Republican, 3 March 1822.

Letter from Jane Carlile[38] To Mrs Elizabeth Gaunt, Manchester

Dorchester Gaol, May 4, 1822.

Dear Madam,

My warmest thanks accept for the very handsome little Pair of Shoes you have been so kind to send me, of your own manufacture, and be assured they shall be the first on the feet of my daily-expected infant, whose birth shall be announced to the Female Republicans of Manchester as early as possible, if every thing passes off as well as I hope.

My spirits and constitutional strength are good, or I should have every thing to dread in child-birth in such a place as this, where humanity is a marketable commodity, and where, what is still worse, I am one of those excluded from the market, at any price.

My very close confinement has greatly augmented the sufferings of pregnancy, but my humane and very Reverend Keepers have nothing but inveterate prejudices for my accommodation. Up to this moment we are locked into one room, and such seems likely to be the case at the moment of my labour.

For the small presents of Cotton and Needles, which accompanied the Shoes, my thanks are offered wherever they are due.

The pleasure which is derived from such acts of kindness and affection from Females to whom I can be only known by name, is a complete balance to the mind for the pain of imprisonment. I cannot treat imprisonment with so light a heart as my husband does, as it has tended to disperse my children; to bring whom together makes me wish for liberty more than any thing else. However, the time will now soon arrive, and neither my children or myself will ever have occasion to blush at the cause of my incarceration.

I was neither a politician nor theologian before my imprisonment, but a sentence for Two Years has roused feelings in me that I might never have otherwise possessed. I have been made to feel the necessity of reforming the abuses of the Government; as I am sure, that under a Representative System of Government no Woman would have been sent to Prison for Two Years, for publishing an assertion that tyrants ought to be treated as dangerous and destructive beasts of prey. I have been made to think it, as well as to publish it.

I am, Madam, respectfully yours,

Jane Carlile
Republican, 10 May 1822.

Letter from Joseph Lawton to Mrs Carlile

Salford, Manchester, Sept. 30, 1823.

Madam,

I hope you will excuse me troubling you with the following list for insertion in 'The Republican' the sum of which, One Sovereign, was paid to you by me during your stay here, from a few of your friends of the Salford Reading Society,[39] as a small tribute of esteem for your having been as Mr Carlile observed a greater sufferer in your mind than himself for the cause of liberty and free discussion, and who still bears with great fortitude the *heart rending* idea of being so far separated from your husband, his whole frame debilitated by so long an imprisonment, and that imprisonment undefined!

We hope you will still prefer the honest and wise councils of your husband to the artful and hypocritical suggestions of the corrupt and venal.

To you, Mr Carlile, his sister, and all the persecuted friends of liberty I shall ever feel indebted.

Joseph Lawton

	s.	*d.*		*s.*	*d.*
Joseph Blondell	2	0	Joseph Lawton	3	0
T. Barton	1	6	John Lawton	2	0
An Enemy to Persecution	1	6	T.T. Monthly, up to June		
William Drinkwater, an			22	2	0
admirer of Paine	2	0	George Longbottom	2	0
Thomas Benbow	1	0	John Foulkes	2	0
J.P.	1	0			

Republican, 24 October 1823.

Letter from Nottingham Supporters to Mrs Wright[40] and her Reply

To Mrs Wright, Cold Bath Fields Prison, London

Nottingham, March 10, 1824.

Dear Madam,

The Committee of the subscribers to the fund for the relief of persecuted friends of reform, and free discussion, beg your acceptance of three sovereigns, as they think it will be a small acknowledgement, for your undaunted spirit in withstanding the base and vile gang of persons who support the dogmas of the Christian Religion by persecution, by terror, by fine (which is robbery) and imprisonment (which is murder.) Instead of proving by fair argument, the mysteries of their doctrine; they fly to the strong arm of power; knowing, that there they will be supported by corrupt Judges and a packed Jury, as in your case and many others. But we trust their race is run, and that mankind will in spite of kingcraft and priestcraft, seek that information which will prove to them, that truth will prevail and triumph, in spite of all the gangs of persecutors in the universe: and by free and fair discussion, no longer be deluded by the dogmas of idol worshippers, whose God is money, and whose religion is to fleece the people. Hoping these lines may find you and yours well, and in good spirits to support you through the time of your imprisonment, and that you may live to see yours, and all mankind's enemies meet the punishment due to their crimes, is the ardent hope of,

Dear Madam, your friends and well wishers,
(Signed in behalf of the Committee.)

Moses Colclough and John Doubleday

To the Committee of the Subscribers to the Fund for the Relief of the Persecuted Friends of Reform Established in Nottingham

Citizens and Townsmen,

I thank you for the remittance of three sovereigns, and for the gratification which every notice of this kind imparts to a prisoner in a good cause. My sentence of imprisonment would soon expire, were it not that I am one of the victims of that modern practice of the Judges, which imposes such a fine, as puts an objectionable reformer of their ways and means under the footing of a felon or a person insane, and subjects one to imprisonment during his Majesty's pleasure or until the Lord Chancellor's doubts are settled upon the matter! His conscience stirring! And Mr Peel[41] in a satisfied and forgiving humour! Which form the most tedious prospects that any one can have to look forward to.

As to my health, it was too much impaired by the treatment I received in Newgate[42] to be recovered whilst I am a prisoner. I suffer much from fits and a variety of other complaints. My spirits are as good as ever: in truth, *I am all spirits and no matter;* for I am a mere shadow, a real disembodied spirit. If I take a flight into another world, I shall leave nothing but my mantle behind, as Elijah did, or as the Jew Book says: the whole of which I do not, and hope you do not believe.

With a duplicate of thanks,

I remain your spiritual friend,

Susannah Wright
Republican, 9 April 1824.

Eliza Sharples' Editorial to the Readers of *Isis*

It is announced as of authority in the newspapers, that Lord Althorp[43] does not intend to make the repeal of taxes on knowledge a cabinet measure; which means, that he does not intend to repeal them at all, if he can help it; and I dare say the 'noble lords,' particularly the 'noble Lord' Eldon,[44] will not find it to be prudent so to do. The answer to this proclamation is, that like Irishmen with their tithes, we will repeal them ourselves, as far as possible. This publication is a partial repeal of them. Whig tyranny is more atrocious than Tory tyranny, more to be resisted, more to be denounced, more to be hated. For Tory tyranny, there is an apology in education, though not in morals and in politics. Whig tyranny has no apology but its hypocrisy. We have proof enough that the Whigs wish to keep every thing as near as possible to its present state: that is, they wish if possible, to collect the present revenue of fifty millions for the state and ten for the church. There is a very agreeable feeling associated with the fingering of large sums of money; as agreeable to dishonesty as to honesty. Whigs have this feeling as well as the Tories. They are not light-fingered gentry; but heavy-fingered gentry. The siftings of fifty millions through the various public offices is an onerous task and justifies *liberal* takings.

However, we shall see that many things will be done, which will not be cabinet measures, and many things contrary to the wishes of the administration. Little is dreamt in the king's cabinet, of what is passing in the cabinet of the public mind. We shall see more about it after two or three more genuine public agitations, which when made will never be reduced to a former stagnancy. The promise of the future justifies a little patience; but let us be so far impatient as to leave nothing undone, that may be now done. Let us be so far impatient as to be active and zealous in doing present good, and in preparing the dull public mind for a better state of things. Let us be so far impatient, as to be spreading all possible knowledge, and making all possible resistance to that which is wrong.

Isis, 27 October 1832.

Declaration of 150 Female Volunteers in Birmingham and its Vicinity

Be just, and fear not.

TO MR RICHARD CARLILE

Respected Sir,

We take the present opportunity of expressing to you our deep sympathy for your past sufferings, and at the same time our admiration of your unflinching conduct in the sacred cause of freedom. Some men may ask, why do women make it their business? Our reasons are two: first, because Englishmen have neglected theirs; and, secondly, because our interests are inseparably connected with the welfare of men: and, being so, we are bound to co-operate with them for the general good. Others may ask, what can women do? To such we would reply by asking, what have not women effected? None but a novice can doubt our ingenuity, and none but a fool would set our power at nought. The clergy will tell you that one of us, singly, conquered Sampson, the strongest, and that women were the instruments whereby Solomon, the wisest of men, was subdued. But some may want more modern proofs of our superiority. Let such consult literature, and, when they have done so, we have no doubt they will begin to beg our pardon. Others may say we are wanting in courage. They who may think so, we would point to the city of Paris, where our predecessors nobly fought, and bled, and conquered too. But it may be asked, what do you mean to do? Our reply is, we purpose to do what in us lies to reduce the taxes of our country to the most moderate amount, and to make an end of all wicked and wasteful expenditure. For this purpose, Sir, we tender to you the ingenuity of our heads, the devotion of our hearts, and the assistance of our hands. We would caution our countrymen not to be deceived. Our deliberate conviction is, that it is not in paper nor in promise to impart permanent prosperity to our unhappy country. We have often trusted, and we have been betrayed – we have repeatedly believed, and we have been deceived. Let the working men of England be united in the bonds of a holy brotherhood. This will make even tyrants respect them; and why – because they will be as Gods, knowing good and evil. At the present time the men of England are the veriest asses on the face of God's earth. But we would hold, or we shall wrong the brute creation. The clergy tell us that Balaam's ass[45] reproved his tyrannical and unruly rider. If so, Balaam's ass was a better reformer than most men in our day. We conceive that one of the principal causes of our national calamity consists in working men trusting to the honour of idle men for assistance. Hence, we hear so much about this good man, and that liberal-minded man, and so on. Allow us to observe, that we disclaim all personalities. By this means, ambitious and designing men seek to rise upon the ruins of the reputation of others; and, after reaching their purposed aim, with a scowl of contempt they look down upon their numerous followers, and leave them the wretched and disappointed victims of their own vanity. Do mice go to the cat for security? Or does the hare run to the hounds for protection? They know better. Would to God that men possessed as much intelligence. Till they do, we hope we shall hear no more about their being superior to the rest of God's creation. A short time ago we were taught to believe that a reformed House of Commons would consult our interests: but whas [sic] been its conduct? Why, the professed stoutest opponents of corruption have had the unblushing impudence to stand up and declare that the middle classes were in a worse condition than the working classes were. If this doctrine is not confusion worse confounded, we should like, in the name of common sense, to know what is. After this, we shall not be surprised to hear of the bishops telling us that they are worse off than any body. What are the men of England about? Are they dead, or are they dreaming? The name of the evils under which we groan is *legion*, for there are many. Owing to the facilities which machinery affords, our families are either but partially employed, or totally without labour. Of course we believe that machinery was designed to be a blessing, but, by being changed from its original purpose, it has become a curse to the community. But why stand we here all the day idle? The clergy will tell us that these sufferings are for our sins. To this charge we plead guilty; for our sins are great in permitting the clergy so long to impose burdens upon us which are past endurance. For this sin we humbly seek God's pardon; but, as we hope to obtain it, we stedfastly purpose to lead new lives, being determined to keep the church from in future forcing her hands into our pockets. We have been guilty of another sin; namely, in our permitting our children to be tutored in meanness and slavery, inasmuch as the little learning which they acquire is prostituted for the vilest purposes. Thus they are taught, almost before they can speak, to 'order themselves lowly and reverently towards their betters' – towards a number of persons, forsooth, who have the honour of doing nothing – who neither toil nor spin, but who, while we do both, are idly reaping the fruits of our painful industry. Let no man misunderstand us. Our children shall order themselves respectfully both before and behind their betters; but we will teach them to look elsewhere to find them. Whenever an honest individual displays more virtue and courage than ordinarily manifests itself, the scoundrels of our country begin with all the fire of furies as one man to denounce him. We hear then exclaiming, shocking! What insubordination! But, Sir, the long night of ignorance and superstition is fast waning away, and it will soon be morning. The enemies of our country are by signs silently intimating to each other that *all is lost*. The lion at last has awakened – his hoarse voice is heard through the British empire, while every meaner beast in the forest begins to start back, conscious of his unparalleled prowess. The press is working, knowledge is spreading, error is vanishing. As yet our condition is deplorable; for what can be more painful to hear than what we have been compelled to endure – even our children crying for bread, when we had not any to give them? And this, too, in a land of plenty! This, too, in a land of industry? But, say the clergy, God has declared that man shall live by the sweat of his brow. What sapient gentlemen they are, cunningly to escape the curse themselves by not labouring; and while we are labouring and sweating, they craftily carry off the means of our subsistence. Thus, virtually, after telling us that God has cursed us, they kick us into the bargain. Perhaps they are trying to kill two birds with one stone; but we mean to stop this game. These, Sir, are the blasphemers of our God! These are the 'baptised infidels'! We will repel the vile calumnies thus brought against our Maker. We will assert eternal providence, and justify the ways of God to man, by declaring, that there is enough for each, enough for all, enough for evenmore. But again, when the clergy wish to impress upon our minds all the solemnities of an eternal state, they remind us of the latter day, on which it is said an angel shall descend from heaven, and taking a mill-stone in his hand, and placing one foot upon the sea, and the other foot upon the land, dashing the stone into the sea, he shall swear by him that liveth and reigneth for ever and ever that time shall be no longer. We do now place our feet respectively upon the rock of unalterable justice, upon the spire of which we inscribe, 'Equal Rights and Equal Laws,' and with the 'Rights of Man' enclosed in our hands, and with more than twenty millions of British subjects at our back, we swear, by the power of Providence, and the omnipotence of the people, that boroughmongery, compulsive taxation, corn-laws, monopolies, national church, gentlemen paupers, with all the vile vermin which eat up and destroy the inheritance of our God, shall exist no longer.

Sarah Potter, Holt-street, Aston, Birmingham.
August 8, 1833.

Esther Heath, 297, Summer-lane. Mary Spink, Lancaster-street. Ellen Hollist, Loveday-street. Catherine Bloor, 41, ditto. Sarah Cox, 44, Summer-lane. Ann Cox, New Summer-street. Catherine Burdett, Tavern-street. Elizabeth Coton, Grosvenor-row. Sarah James, Henige-street. Hannah Beech, ditto. Sarah James, junior, ditto. Elizabeth Amos, 86, Lawley-street. Rebecca Eve, 10, Halford-street. Rebecca Eve, junior, ditto. Jane Butler, ditto. Harriet Thorn, ditto. Ann Key, 120, Pritchet-street. Mary Boulton, Holt-street. Sarah Prince, Brierly-street. Ann Jones, ditto. Mary Davis, 64, Summer-lane. Sarah Cox, ditto. Sarah Slater, 28, Fleet-lane. Mary Povey, Tower-street. Mary Grice, Brierly-street. Mary Allen, Great Dartmouth-street. Susannah Allen, ditto. Sarah Wilkins, Crisp's-buildings. Ann Shotton, Brewery-street.

Ann Cope, Dartmouth-street. Sarah Cope, ditto. Eliza Rogers, Great Brook-street. Hannah Newnham, 86, Coleshill-street. Sophia Allen, Great Barr-street. Harriet Wordsworth, ditto. Elizabeth Eginton, ditto. Ann Thirsfield, Gosta-green. Maria Thirsfield, ditto. Harriet Chiles, Holt-street. Jane Norris, Well-lane. Mary Jenkins, ditto. Ann Penn, 2, Court, Summer-lane. Hannah Penn, George-street. Lavinia Corns, Holt-street. Jane Ofeney, Pritchet-street. Hannah Edwards, Union-street. Eliza Edwards, ditto. Mary Ann Thorn, 17, Hospital-street. Lucy Wilkes, 7, Court 1, Weimon-street. Jemima Colledge, 1, Weimon-row. Elizabeth Legg, 112, Tower-street. Margaret Pease, Henrietta-street. Jane Welding, Little Hampton-street. Ann Welding, ditto. Martha Parsons, Windsor-street. Rebecca Harris, ditto. Mary Thomas, Pritchet-street. Sarah Jones, Aston-road. Jane Chilton, ditto. Mary Wright, Hockley-street. Sarah Wright, ditto. Caroline Hollist, 126, Pritchet-street. Hannah Davis, Aston-road. Ann Pemberton, ditto. Elizabeth Jones, ditto. Ellen Murchen, Pritchet-street. Fanny Smith, Aston-road. Sarah Smith, ditto. Ann Smith, ditto. Sarah Smith, junior, ditto. Jane Smith, ditto. Caroline Smith, ditto. Ann Hollis, Pritchet-street. Elizabeth Chilton, Aston-road. Diana Murchett, Pritchet-street. Maria Portlock, ditto. Jane Bloor, ditto. Ann Tundy, ditto. Ann Gee, ditto. Elizabeth Gee, ditto. Phœby Griffiths, ditto. Mary Lavender, ditto. Ann Goddard, ditto. Emily Wilson, 12, Tower-court. Phœby Hunt, ditto. Ann Bennett, ditto. Ellen Bennett, ditto. Elizabeth Bennett, ditto. Catherine Newey, ditto. Ann Holding, ditto. Susannah March, ditto. Mary Towers, ditto. Hannah Parsons, ditto. Helena Phillips, 63, Tower-street. Martha Eccles, Bradford-court, Tower-street. Maria Sisen, ditto. Mary Bodell, 29, Breckland-street. Hannah Hunt, 9, Court, Summer-lane. Susannah Taylor, ditto. Sibyll Patrick, 9, Court, Briarly-street. Mary Gordon, Stoneyard, Tower-street. Mary Allen, Tower-street. Sarah Goderich, 11, Court, Briarly-street. Elizabeth Pagnell, 6, ditto. Ann Hadcock, 1, Court, Ward-street. Mary Johnson, 52, Briarly-street. Catherine Bullow, Great Leicester-street. Lucy Reddin, Church-street. Sarah Rook, Slaney-street. Mary Kesterton, Fleet-street. Ann Squelch, Summer-lane. Ann Swadkin, Hospital. Mary Kesterton, ditto. Ann Vaux, Church-street. Jane Knight, 15, Court, Briarly-street. Ann Pearson, 28, Brickell-street. Sarah Pearson, 28, ditto. Mary Edwards, 30, Pritchet-street. Mary Heath, Union-court, Snowhill. Sarah Smith, 11, Court, Little Charles Street. Susannah Day, Bradford-court, Tower-street. Jane Kesterton, ditto. Sarah Banks, ditto. Susannah Banks, ditto. Mary Banks, ditto. Maria Yardly, 13, Court, Tower-street. Jane Crane, 13, ditto. Charlotte Mellows, ditto. Ellen Crow, ditto. Mary Saucer, ditto. Maria Mellows, ditto. Jane Banks, Pritchet-street. Ann Clemmons, 14, Court, Tower-street. Eliza Barlow, ditto. Charlotte Fletcher, ditto. Mary Roberts, ditto. Sarah Richardson, Tower-street. Eliza Hill, ditto. Mary Ann Smith, Slaney-street. Ann Chambers, ditto. Susannah Sly, ditto. Jane Turner, Park-street. Catherine Hughes, ditto. Eliza Walton, Allison-street. Julia Sutton, ditto. Esther Cope, Coventry-street. Mary Ann Mericks, Lanch-street. Ann Maria Sansum, Loveday-street. Mary Ann Brown, ditto.

Gauntlet, 25 August 1833.

Matilda Roalfe's Activity in Edinburgh

Before this number is in the hands of our readers, Miss Roalfe will be an inmate of a dungeon, classed with thieves and treated as one, for the *crime* of having published infidel books. She received notice to prepare for trial in the Sheriffs Court on Tuesday last. That we can foretell the result with infallible prescience is a proof of the undying virulence which is mixed up with that precious compound – true christianity. If our law officers should charge a person with blasphemy for having boiled a tea kettle on a Sunday, there is not a sound christian jury in the three kingdoms that would not find a verdict of guilty. We hate the Hindoo religion for its burning of widows; we hate mythologic, savage and catholic rites for their bloody and cruel orgies, and shall we not hate christianity for its immolation of men and women in gaols for the conservation of its absurd and dangerous tenets. Victim after victim is immured, and now Miss Roalfe is added to the number. Will it only be registered as an ordinary transaction? Will it pass by as a tale told? No; it will remain for ever in the memories of those who love integrity of expression; and while the regard for freedom and truth exists, christianity will be detested.

Glasgow – A public meeting has been held in this town on behalf of Dr Kalley. It was called on a requisition to the Lord Provost and held in the Gælic church. Baillie Anderson was in the chair. Dr Heugh, Mr A. Mitchell, Dr Bates, Mr Jno. Wright, Dr Wills, Dr Watson, and Mr Thompson, of Nile Street, were the speakers on the foreign sympathy side. Mr Southwell, Mr Adams, a chartist preacher, and an Irishman, whose name we cannot learn, spoke in favour of a home sympathy for those suffering for conscience sake in Scotland. Mr Adams declared his intention was to move a resolution that should bring out the 'insincerity' of the gentlemen on the platform; and two policemen stepped up to him, seemingly for the purpose of removing him; but they did not do it. Mr Southwell drew a parallel between Dr Kalley and the Edinburgh victims; he was often interrupted by the disapprobation of the meeting; but by the intervention of the chairman – who behaved with more justice than the Lord Provost of Edinburgh – Mr Southwell was heard to the end.

Movement, 27 January 1844.

The Apprehension and Treatment of Miss Roalfe

The following from Miss Roalfe to the Secretary of the London Anti-Persecution Union will be read with interest and concern by the friends of liberty.

Edinbro', Dec. 14, 1843.

My dear sir,

A combination of circumstances prevented me from fulfilling my promise of writing to you yesterday. In the first place I found my home, as you may well suppose, in a wretched state of disorder on my return from prison. It took the greater part of yesterday to restore it to anything like a degree of comfort. Next I had the shop filled with persons who called to see me, some prompted by regard, and others by curiosity, and last though not least, the house was surrounded by a riotous mob, whose hissings and hootings at times almost stunned me. Never did I witness such a scene as took place the night of my liberation; the moment it was ascertained that I was at home, a crowd began to assemble, and in about half an hour some hundreds of persons had collected, and before ten o-clock they baffled all description. If you can imagine an *Indian war-whoop* then you may form some idea of the yells of these disciples of the meek and lowly Jesus. Several of the committee of the Anti-P.U. were at my house, some of whom attempted to put up the shutters; but part were seized by the mob, and others were struck; one young man in particular was struck by a medical student on the head with his stick, which cut it open. At last with the assistance of a number of the police, we succeeded in dispersing the mob. I fear, however, that I shall experience considerable annoyance for some time to come, as I am blessed with a neighbour who is a Methodist local preacher, and who is the principal actor in the scene.

I am not aware at what Court I shall be tried, but I *fear* at the Sheriff's; I say I *fear*, because although I should, no doubt, have a shorter term of *imprisonment* if tried at that court, yet, as I intend to defend *myself*, it would more benefit the cause to which I am devoted, to be tried at the High Court of Justiciary.

At my seizure I did not lose a great deal of stock. I had taken the precaution to remove the principal part, having received intimation that the 'Fiscal' intended to honor me with a visit. I sold last week two books to a person who I was informed was a sheriff's officer; another was waiting outside the shop. The books I sold him were the 'Trinity of Trinities' and the 'Bible an improper book'. As the man went out of the shop I heard some of the persons outside the shop say – *'She's nick'd'*, which seems to be the Lord's way of settling business in these parts.

The examination was a private one, and the books with which I am charged to have vended, are those before-named, and copies of the *Oracle of Reason*, 91, 94, and 100; also 'God *versus* Paterson', 'God-ology', and one 'Home thrust'.

When committed to prison I was put into a wretched stone cell, and after waiting in vain for my dismissal I was told by the turnkey that the lights were about to be extinguished and that I had better go to bed, as there was very little chance that I should leave that night. But on preparing for rest guess my surprise and disgust, on discovering my bed covered with *vermin*! I instantly made an alarm and insisted on being removed into another cell, which was accordingly done. I stated that I should make a complaint, but as the turnkey was particularly civil I said no more about it. Since my return home however I have had considerable difficulty in freeing myself from the impurities of that place.

Mr Finlay, jun., has just brought me a letter from his father who has written for his tools; he is therefore allowed to work at his own trade. He is quite well in health, and desires to be remembered to all friends.

M. Roalfe.

Movement, 30 January 1844.

Miss Roalfe and her Persecutors, or error, versus truth

Mr Editor,

From the *facts* I have to state, it will be evident to all parties that Miss Roalfe really acted the part of a heroine on her trial, that she took her stand in the strictest sense of the word upon principle, and upon principle alone. She never attempted to meddle with the case legally, but boldly and unhesitatingly denied the justice of such prosecutions whether legal or not. She did this in the very teeth of the Procurator Fiscal himself; knowing full well that it would subject her to all the horrors of prison discipline, with communications from friends cut off on every side, and to the most rigid solitary confinement. Can we say too much, or too highly estimate her conduct, when, had she been disposed, to take advantage of legal quibbles, she might have escaped the law most effectually; for the sheriff told her that if she said that she was ignorant of the contents of the books when she sold them, why then it would be a very different thing, in fact the case would fall to the ground. Besides, in the quotations made from those books prosecuted, there are some of the most palpable blunders possible to be made, not simply one or two, for in no less than a dozen different places the books are falsely quoted by the over-zealous supporters of God's Holy Word; and had Miss Roalfe thought proper to avail herself of these things, she might have escaped their clutches. She knew of all those legal flaws before the day of trial. I subjoin a few of the misquotations:

1st. Page 73, 'God v. Paterson'. In quoting Mr Southwell's[46] article, the 'Jew Book', it stands in page 7 of the indictment as follows: 'It is a book which contains passages so outrageously disgusting and scandalously indecent, that were it called the word of God, no modest woman would suffer it to be read in her house.' While it stands in God v. Paterson, 'that were it not called etc'. so that the entire sense is altered, and persons prosecuted for selling a book which never contained the words indicted.

2nd. In page 14, the Indictment in quoting page 76 of 'God v. Paterson', instead of leaving out a word, they have thought proper to put one in, which is not to be found in the book, last line but one the words holy, holy, are quoted, while only one 'holy' is there.

3rd. The article 'God checkmated by the Devil', must certainly have had a very extraordinary effect upon the copyer, more than the reading of it did upon Mr Levie the witness; for there are seven misquotations altogether.

Page 15 Indictment, 78 'God v. Paterson', in line 7, the word 'that' is in the Indictment and not in the copy.

Page 17 Indictment, the word 'not' is inserted instead of the word 'did'.

Same page, the word 'shortly' is made to precede the words 'he promised', instead of 'in better plight'.

Page 18 Indictment, 78 'God v. Paterson', line 7, second paragraph of 'God checkmated by the devil', the word 'all' is left out.

Page 19 Indictment, line 10, second paragraph, the word 'them' is left out. Three lines lower down the word 'will' is put instead of the word 'shall'.

Page 24 Indictment, 79 'God v. Paterson', last line but one of the second paragraph, the word 'and' is left out.

In 91, *Oracle*, the word 'up' is left out, page 29 Indictment. Same page, *Oracle*, page 30 Indictment, when speaking of the Jews, Egyptians, and their jewels, the word 'of' is inserted when it has no business there; and in 'Godology', third paragraph, the word 'before' is left out in the Indictment.

I make no further remarks, but that we cannot fail to think that Miss Roalfe knowing all this, and not taking the advantage of it, set a worthy example, for when contending against a bad law, should we take advantage of it, it would seem that we thought it of some value.

I will send you a copy of 'God *v.* Paterson', and 'Godology', marked, so that you can see the difference.

W. Baker.

P.S. I have sent a parcel to you containing a sample of bread, cheese, pea-soup, Scotch kale or porridge, and treacle water, with an account of how much of each is given to the prisoners at a meal in Calton Gaol, the bread and cheese is that which Mr Finlay had for his dinner on Sunday, the day before he was liberated. I propose that they should be taken care of, to form, with a copy of all the prosecuted books, papers, and indictments, summons, and other relics of Infidel martyrdom, an *Infidel Museum*. A copy of all Infidel works might be deposited with you, so as to form a library for reference, such as is not to be found in any place in the United Kingdom. – W.B.

[Note – M. Ryall,[47] W. J. Baker, and several of us have long had in contemplation the establishment of an extensive and unique *Museum*, in which not only infidel relics, but the gods of all nations, as far as practicable, shall be assembled and arranged in mythological order. More of this anon. – Ed. M.]

Movement, 24 February 1844.

Miss Roalfe

We give the following important and interesting news on the authority of a correspondent. The Glasgow Branch of the Rational Society intends presenting Miss Roalfe with the sum of ten pounds, being the amount of the fine the authorities required her to pay as an alternative to imprisonment. The presentation is to take place at a soirée to be held in the Hall on the occasion of her liberation.

Movement, 9 March 1844.

Miss Roalfe's Soirée

The Soirée and ball in honour of Miss Roalfe, was held on Monday, March 25, in the Calton Convening Room, Mr Charles Southwell, M.C. Mr Robert Affleck, chairman. On Miss Roalfe entering the room, three rounds of enthusiastic cheering greeted her. There was a good band, good accommodation, good attendance, and good everything, not excepting good profits. The greatest satisfaction was felt, and the affair was considered to exceed anything of the kind that had taken place among our Edinburgh friends.

Movement, 6 April 1844.

Notes

1. See Chapter 4, n. 17.
2. The Reform Bill of 1832 was passed by a Liberal government in the teeth of strong opposition from the Tories. It enfranchised people with property qualifications and gave representatives to a number of large towns or cities such as Manchester.
3. Thomas Paine (1737–1809). Writer whose work had very considerable influence in the US during the War of Independence, in France during the Revolution and in England. The radicals used his works as their guidelines and many were imprisoned for selling them when the government decreed that they were seditious and blasphemous libels.
4. Thomas Paine, *Rights of Man*, 1791 and 1792 was a reply to Edmund Burke's *Reflections on the French Revolution*. Paine was outlawed in England when it was published.
5. Thomas Paine, *Age of Reason*, 1793–4. An outspoken deistical commentary on the Bible which brought much criticism on Paine.
6. The Gagging Acts in 1817 and the Six Acts in 1819 suspended Habeas Corpus which enabled the government to imprison radicals without trial.
7. *Republican*, 8 February 1822.
8. *Gauntlet*, 25 August 1833.
9. Society for the Suppression of Vice and the Encouragement of Religion and Virtue established 1802. It concentrated on opposing radical publishers.
10. *Mock Trials of Richard Carlile*, 1822, p. 16.
11. *Republican*, 1 December 1820.
12. Constitutional Society for Opposing the Progress of Disloyal and Seditious Principles, founded May 1821 for the purpose of curbing the radical press.
13. *The Defence of Mary-Anne Carlile*, 1821, p. 10.
14. *Republican*, 10 May 1822.
15. The Rotunda building stood at the corner of Blackfriars Road and Stamford Street. It dated from the late eighteenth century and in 1790 was used as a Natural History Museum. During 1818 and 1819, William Hazlitt lectured there on English poets and comic writers. There was a library and reading room attached to the Hall. Richard Carlile took it over in 1830. William Cobbett, Daniel O'Connell, Feargus O'Connor, Rev. Robert Taylor and Robert Owen as well as Richard Carlile and his wife, Eliza Sharples (*Isis*) lectured there.

16. *Isis*, 10 March 1832.
17. *Isis*, Preface 1832, pp. v–vi.
18. Charles Bradlaugh (1833–1914), secularist leader and propagandist of birth control, women's suffrage and trade unionism. Insisted on affirming instead of taking an oath on entering parliament.
19. Joel H. Wiener, *Radicalism and Freethought in Nineteenth Century Britain*, 1983, p. 90.
20. *Addresses to Reformers*, 1821.
21. W.J. Fox, *The Duties of Christians Towards Deists*, 1819.
22. Charles Abbott 1st Baron Tenterdon (1762–1832), Lord Chief Justice 1818–32.
23. 'The Captive' by Allen Davenport in *Republican*, 9 January 1824.
24. *Republican*, 16 July 1824.
25. *Black Dwarf*, 2 April 1823.
26. *Republican*, 16 July 1824.
27. See note 6.
28. Stanley Chadwick, *A Bold and Faithful Journalist, Joshua Hobson 1810–1876*. Kirklees Libraries and Museum Service, 1976, p. 23.
29. Matilda Roalfe, *Law Breaking Justified*, 1844, p. 12.
30. John Cam Hobhouse (1776-1854), Under Secretary of State for Home Affairs. Refused to present Mary-Anne Carlile's petition to the House of Commons.
31. See Chapter 2, n. 15.
32. Sir William Draper Best, 1st Baron Wynford (1767–1845), suppressed part of Mary-Anne Carlile's defence and treated his court to frequent sermons addressed to the accused.
33. Act declaring the Rights and Liberties of England and the Succession to the Crown 1689.
34. The Star Chamber was a court held in Westminster which was abolished in 1641. It has become proverbial as a type of arbitrary and oppressive tribunal.
35. John Tillotson (1630–94), Protestant preacher who tried to wean hearers away from Puritanism. Also preached against atheism and Roman Catholicism. Archbishop of Canterbury 1691.
36. A religion which acknowledges the existence of a personal God as a supernatural being endowed with reason and will and able to influence people's lives.
37. People who believe in one God but reject the doctrine of the Trinity.
38. See her biography on p. 36.
39. Salford Reading or Zetetic Society. A discussion group seeking truth by free enquiry and exchange of opinions. The word Zetetic was first used by a group in Edinburgh (Richard Carlile's letter to James Affleck, Edinburgh, 5 January 1822. In *Republican*, 18 January 1822 p. 83). Zetetic means 'proceeding by enquiry – a seeking after truth'.

40. See biography on p. 40.

41. Sir Robert Peel (1788–1850), Tory MP 1809, Home Secretary 1828-30, Prime Minister 1834–5 and again in 1841.

42. Name of a celebrated London prison.

43. Lord Althorpe (1782–1845), Chancellor of the Exchequer and Leader of the House of Commons. Later became 3rd Earl Spencer. The Factory Act of 1833 is frequently called Lord Althorpe's Act.

44. See Chapter 2, n. 23.

45. Numbers, XXII, verses 27–33.

46. Charles Southwell (1814–60), freethought lecturer and social missionary. Publisher of the *Oracle of Reason*, 1841, for which he was imprisoned and fined.

47. Maltus Questell Ryall (1809–46), member of the Lambeth branch of the Rational Society and Secretary of the Anti-Persecution Union, 1842.

4
Friends of the Oppressed

Defiance is our only remedy; we cannot be a slave in all: we submit to much – for it is impossible to be wholly consistent – but we will try the power of *right* against *might*; we will begin by protecting and upholding this grand bulwark and defence of our rights – this key to all our liberties – *the freedom of the press* – the press, too, of the *ignorant and poor*! We have taken upon ourselves its protection, and we will never abandon our post; we will die rather.

Henry Hetherington, *Poor Man's Guardian*, 9 July 1831.

Introduction

From 1830 the struggle for the freedom of the press took on a new aspect. The government changed tack and stopped prosecution for the publication of blasphemous libels to concentrate instead on banning the sale of the unstamped newspapers.[1] The great 'Battle for the Unstamped' began in earnest and many women were involved in it as sellers, publishers and printers.

In London in 1832, a number of the unstamped sellers formed a group called the 'Friends of the Oppressed'. Their progress and activities were reported in the *Poor Man's Guardian* in 1832 and 1833.

The aim of the society was to assist the wives of those who suffered in the fight for the cause of the people. Their hope was that the formation of a female society would 'excite the male population to still more strenuous efforts in support of a really free and untaxed press.'[2] At the inaugural meeting they decided to record the members in a book and keep strict account of all money. They elected officers and applied the principle that proceedings would be conducted only by women.

The cases applying for financial relief were interviewed at the Institute[3] in Theobalds Road on Monday evenings. The wives and families of the men who were in Lancaster Castle[4] for selling the unstamped papers were among the early recipients.

One of the speakers at the meetings was the *Isis* editor, Eliza Sharples.[5] Possibly it was she who was behind the decision taken at a public meeting in December 1832 to abolish the 'absurd and superstitious practice of Churching women'.[6]

In October 1832 they went to Marlborough Street House of Correction to welcome Mary Willis who had been held for 14 days for selling the *Poor Man's Guardian*. She had been released earlier; but finding her in the neighbourhood, they placed 'the honest and intrepid old lady'[7] at the head of the procession and then marched to the Institute in Theobalds Road where they gave three cheers for the *Poor Man's Guardian* and then dispersed.

A number of women are mentioned as being officers of the society: Jane Hutson, Sarah Odom, Mrs Orey, Mrs Boume, Mrs Olding, H. Ayliffe. They played an important role as sellers of the unstamped papers, and found strength in joining together in the society. They disappeared from the stage of history after a year's activity; it is possible, however, that some of the same women were involved in the London Female Chartists group in the 1830s.

* * *

Formation of a Female Society

On Monday afternoon, at 3 o'clock, a meeting will be held at the Institution, Theobald's Road, for the purpose of forming a Society to aid and assist the wives and families of those who suffer in the cause of the people. Tea will [be] provided at 8*d* each.

Poor Man's Guardian, 14 July 1832.

Female Society, entitled 'The Friend of the Oppressed'
On Monday last a meeting of females was held at the Institute of the Industrious Classes, Theobald's Road, to take into consideration the propriety of forming a Society to assist and protect the wives and children of those who suffer in the people's cause; and we were highly delighted to perceive so large and respectable an assembly of females in pursuit of this laudable object. Every day brings forth additional evidence of the popularity of our cause, and we anticipate that the formation of this female society will 'renew a right spirit within us,' and excite the male population to still more strenuous efforts in support of a *really free and untaxed press*. What course will the dastardly and contemptible Whigs now adopt? Will they add to the cruelty and injustice inflicted daily upon the destitute cripples and starving old men by entering upon a war against *petticoats*? Let our readers peruse the accounts in the present number of the unjust and illegal convictions against our unhappy fellow-countrymen for selling the *Poor Man's Guardian*, and we are sure they must, like ourselves, loathe,

abhor, and detest, these despicable reptiles, *the Whigs*;[8] who, having the power to prevent, are base enough to permit, the perpetration of the most atrocious cruelties against the poor men, for merely vending cheap knowledge. We thank our fair countrywomen for this public expression of their sympathy and support. It is peculiarly opportune and felicitous. It will call forth the latent courage of their husbands, brothers, and sweethearts. It will stimulate them to fresh exertions in the glorious contest of *right* against *might*, and will induce them to swear, in the emphatic language of 'Lord' Grey,[9] that rather than be conquered in this all-important struggle, *'They will die in the last ditch in defence of their Order!'*

The following resolutions were unanimously adopted –

That a female society be formed, for the purpose of affording aid to the wives and children of those persons who suffer in the people's cause, to be entitled the 'Friend of the Oppressed'.

That a fund be raised by the subscriptions of the members, at not less than one penny per week, by donations, and by voluntary contributions.

That a book be kept for the purpose of enrolling members' names, and entering monies received.

That such relief and assistance shall be rendered to persons suffering from oppression as shall be deemed expedient by a majority of the members present at a meeting called for the purpose of investigating and deciding upon claims for relief.

That a book, containing an account of money expended, specifying the particulars in full for which the money has been voted, shall be open to the inspection of the contributors at all meetings of the society.

That the society meet on Monday next, July 23, at five o'clock.

A committee and treasurer was appointed to carry the above resolutions into effect, when the meeting adjourned till Monday next. Tea will be provided, at sixpence each, for those who think proper to take refreshment.

Poor Man's Guardian, 21 July 1832.

The Female Society, entitled 'The Friend of the Oppressed' Will hold a public meeting on Tuesday, August the 14th, 1832, in aid of the Wives and Children of the Men confined in Lancaster Castle. The proceedings will be conducted by females. Business will commence at 8 o'clock precisely. Admittance 3*d*. each.

Cases considered worthy of Relief are to be delivered to the Female Society at the Institution, Theobald's Road, on Monday evenings, between the hours of five and seven o'clock. They will be investigated and attended to.

(Signed on behalf of the Society)

Jane Hutson, Sarah Odom.
Poor Man's Guardian, 4 August 1832.

The Female Society, entitled 'The Friend of the Oppressed'
We were much gratified at witnessing the spirit displayed by the members of this Society on Monday last. They mustered in great force, and accompanied the National Union of the Working Classes to Copenhagen House, to celebrate the Second Anniversary of the Glorious Three Days. We understand that the number of members is rapidly increasing, and we perceive, by an advertisement in the present number of the *Guardian*, that they purpose holding a public Meeting, in aid of the wives and children of the men confined to Lancaster Castle. It appears the proceedings will be entirely conducted by females, and we have little doubt that the novelty of the thing will insure an overflow. We most cordially wish success to their laudable efforts.

Poor Man's Guardian, 4 August 1832.

Eliza Sharples' Lecture

The Editress of the *Isis* will lecture at the Theobald's Road Institution, on Tuesday evening, August 15th, at eight o'clock, in behalf of the Victim Fund established by the ladies – admission three pence.

Poor Man's Guardian, 11 August 1832.

Meetings of the Female Society

Public Meeting of Females

On Tuesday Evening last, a Meeting of the Ladies' Society, 'The Friends of the Oppressed', was held in the Institution of the Working Classes, Theobald's Road. A very spirited discourse was delivered by the Editress of the Isis. The result of the Meeting is, that, after paying the expences, £1. 11s. remained to be forwarded to the wives and families of the men confined in Lancaster Castle, for whose benefit the meeting was held.

The Society meets every Monday afternoon, from Five till Seven in the Evenings, at the Institution, Theobald's Road. We call upon our intelligent countrywomen to rally round this Society, and assist them in their sacred efforts to protect from starvation the wives and children of those who fall victims to the *cowardly despotism* of the 'Useful Knowledge'[10] Administration!

Poor Man's Guardian, 18 August 1832.

Friends of the Oppressed

The members of the Female Society, entitled 'The Friends of the Oppressed,' met on Wednesday afternoon at the Institution of the Working Classes, Theobald's Road.

The state of the Society was taken into consideration, and found to be in a very flourishing condition, having added many new members, all of whom appeared to be inspired with a zeal quite equal to that displayed of old by the Grecian nations.

The Secretary read a communication from Manchester, from the wives of the four victims, confined in Lancaster Castle by the base Whigs, acknowledging the favour conferred upon them by this Society.

It was resolved to convene a Public Meeting on the 12th of September, to forward the object of this Society – which is to support and comfort the wives and children of all who may be called upon to suffer in the glorious struggle for freedom.

The first fruit of this liberal and high minded Society having been applied to the wives and families of the *Lancashire Patriots*, will doubtless produce beneficial effects all over the country, and we shall be much mistaken if the example thus set by the females of the Metropolis, is not followed by every good hearted female in the kingdom.

The Society meets every Monday from 5 to 7 o'Clock, for the purpose of entering new Members, and receiving subscriptions for the common cause.

Poor Man's Guardian, 1 September 1832.

Mary Willis's Release from Prison

Liberation of the Female Victim

Mary Willis, who was committed from Marlborough Street to the House of Correction for fourteen days, for selling the *Poor Man's Guardian*, was liberated on Wednesday last. Her liberation was not expected to take place till Thursday, and the Female Society, of which she is a member, had determined to bring her from the prison in procession; she was, however, discharged the day before, and a few of the members, amounting to about one hundred, hastily assembled, and proceeded with banners to the prison to demand Mary Willis, but she had previously left. She was taking some refreshment in the neighbourhood. The honest and intrepid old lady was then placed at the head of the procession, and it moved from the prison down Hatton Garden, up Holborn and Red Lion Street, through Red Lion Square, into Kingsgate Street, where they gave three cheers for the *Poor Man's Guardian*, and separated at the Institution, Theobald's Road.

Poor Man's Guardian, 6 October 1832.

Public Ball

The Female Society, entitled 'Friends of the Oppressed', will hold a Public Ball at The Temple of Liberty,[11] Kings Cross, on Monday, October 29. Single tickets 1s; Double Tickets 1/6d each. To be had of H. Hetherington[12] 13 Kingsgate Street; of Mrs Hutson, 58 King Street, Seven Dials; and at The Temple of Liberty, Kings Cross.

On Monday next, October 22nd, at eight o'clock in the evening, the Society will hold a Public Meeting at the same place – admittance 1d. The members of the Society are requested to attend the Committee on Monday next, from five to seven o'clock in the afternoon, at the Institution, Theobald's Road.

Poor Man's Guardian, 20 October 1832.

Jane Hutson's Report

Female Society

A Public Meeting of the Female Society entitled 'Friends of the Oppressed', will be held at the Institution, Theobald's Road on Tuesday, Dec. 11, to aid and assist the victims of the rural tyranny of the farmer-overseers of Chilbolton, near Winchester, and to prevent, as long as possible, the dreadful sentence of those over-paid and over-fed Dogberries, Messrs Pollen, Curtis, and Ironmonger, from being put into execution. When these brave men asked for food or employment, their sentence by the magistrate was *'Go and starve!'* – because you belong to the National Union. We, therefore, call upon every male and female to come forward and assist. Several females will address the meeting. Admittance One Penny.

The Committee of the Society attend every Monday Evening at the Institution, Theobald's Road, from Five till Eight, to enrol Members and receive contributions, and to investigate all applications for relief, and other public business.

There will be a good fire in the room to make the members comfortable.

Jane Hutson, Sec.

Poor Man's Guardian, 8 December 1832.

Meetings at Theobald's Road Institute

Female Society

A Public Meeting of the Female Society entitled 'Friends of the Oppressed' will be held at the Institution, Theobald's Road, on Tuesday, December 4th for the purpose of setting an example to females, by taking the first step towards entirely abolishing the absurd and superstitious practice of Churching women. The proceedings will be conducted by members of the Society, and the proceeds of the meeting will be given to the Victim Fund.[13] Chair to be taken at 8 o'clock. Admittance one penny. The members of the Society will, in future, meet every Monday evening, from 5 to 8, at the Institution, Theobald's Road.

Poor Man's Guardian, 1 December 1832.

Female Society of Friends of the Oppressed

On Tuesday night a public meeting of this society was held at the Institution, Theobald's Road.

Mrs Olding in the Chair.

Mr Mee opened the business of the evening. He observed that a free press was of the utmost consequence in securing justice and the rights of man, and hence the opposition which tyrants always exercised towards it. The ladies were always known to be the friends of the oppressed, and they did themselves honour in the present instance, by coming forward to support Mr Hetherington in his struggle for a free press. Some might object to support any person in an illegal act, but it was always held to be right when the good of the country required it, to act in opposition, and even overturn, existing laws and powers, as in the case of the dethronement of the Stuarts. Men, then, whose conduct, though illegal, was calculated to advance the universal interests of the people, ought to be supported. The stamp duty, however, was an evil and unjust impost, and though some might have no objection to pay it, it ought to be resisted. He then alluded to the £54,000 secret service money, expended by government in paying spies and the present stamped press to misrepresent the people. Had the stamped press done its duty the country would have been relieved long ago, but their's was a mere matter of pounds, shillings, and pence. He called upon the working classes to show some mark of respect to Mr Hetherington, instead of giving their pence to buy pieces of plate for a deceitful ministry (hear.) If the cheap political publications were increased and supported, the result would be an increase of intelligence, freedom, and happiness, indeed if they were not supported, and those who published them more encouraged, the people must expect to fall into greater depths of misery than ever (hear.)

Mrs Hutson alluded to the incarceration of Mr Hetherington, and observed that in such times as the present they ought to be particularly active and unflinchingly staunch against their enemies. The Tories were their enemies, but they were open and undisguised; while the Whigs were treacherous and deceitful, for when out of place the freedom of the press and liberal measures were always on their lips, but as soon as they were in the possession of power they did all they could to crush liberty. The schoolmaster,[14] however, had gone abroad, and she hoped the schoolmistress too (laughter and cheers.) It only required activity and firmness to deliver themselves from tyranny, and if they would do as she wished they would go in a body to the House of Commons and demand the release of all the martyrs to the freedom of the press. Castlereagh,[15] by his Six Acts,[16] intended to keep the people in ignorance, and the Whigs opposed those acts, but now they supported them and carried them into execution; and they had incarcerated men for repeating the very sentiments which had previously fallen from the lips of Lord Brougham himself. She concluded by calling upon them to exert themselves in their own cause, and they would secure the release of their champion as soon as the reformed parliament met. They ought to support Mr Hetherington and family during his imprisonment (applause.) She concluded by proposing the following resolution:

That we view with horror the degradation to which we are brought by the accursed taxes on knowledge,[17] for the removal of which petitions have been so often presented in vain; and that having found Mr Hetherington to be a man determined to brave the storm of oppression, and to give to the world cheap political knowledge, for which he has been condemned to pay a heavy fine and suffer a long term of imprisonment, we are determined to do all in our power to assist him, and we call upon the people, and especially our countrywomen everywhere, to aid him in his struggle to secure a cheap and free press (cheers).

Mrs Orey, in seconding the resolution, recommended a union of interests among the working men, on the principle of exclusive dealing, for by such means only could they take care of their order. The Church and the State were combined against them, the one throwing dust in their eyes while the other picked their pockets (hear and laughter.) Having made some remarks on the past conduct of the Whigs and Tories, she alluded to the exertions of Mr O'Connell[18] in the cause of freedom, and the advance his opinions had made in spite of the powerful opposition raised against him, which proved that the progress of freedom could not be resisted. Mr Baring had said that the working men were too ignorant to manage their own affairs, and he did all he could to keep them in ignorance, but that wiseacre was greatly mistaken, as would be seen in a short time. After pointing their attention to the state of Mr Hetherington now in prison, she concluded by seconding the resolution.

Mrs Boume gave an account of Mr Hetherington's capture.

After a few words in support of the resolution from Mrs Ayliffe, it was unanimously adopted.

J. Sears a boy who had been confined in the New Prison, Clerkenwell, with Mr Hetherington and Mr Pilgrim (the publisher of the *Cosmopolite*)[19] detailed the cruelties to which he had been subjected.

The meeting then adjourned.

Poor Man's Guardian, 12 January 1833.

Female Society
The Friends of the Oppressed are particularly requested to attend on Monday, next, the 28th, at the Institution Theobald's Road, as there is business of great importance and to receive the quarterly cards.

The Working Man's Friend and Political Magazine, 26 January 1833.

The Female Society Entitled the 'Friends of the Oppressed'
This Society meets every Monday evening in the Committee Room at the Institution, Theobald's Road from 5 to 8 to enroll members and receive contributions, and to discuss politics and other public business.

Jane Hutson
Secretary
Poor Man's Guardian, 23 February 1833.

The Female Society, called the 'Friends of the Oppressed'
On Wednesday next, March 6, 1833, a public meeting of this Society will be held at the Institution, Theobald's Road. The Chair to be taken at 8 o'clock in the evening to adopt measures to avert as much as possible the sanguinary measures proposed by Earl Grey to delude the already crimson died [sic] earth of our sister country with the blood of its starving population. All lovers of freedom are particularly requested to attend. Admittance to the Union 1*d*; to the public 2*d* each. The Produce, after expenses paid (if any) to go to the Female Victim Fund.

N.B. This Society meets every Monday evening from 5 to 8, at the Institution, to enrol members and other public business.

Jane Hutson Sec.
Bonnet Rouge, Republican, 2 March 1833.

Meetings at the Chapel, High Street, Borough

A Public Meeting of the Female Society, entitled 'Friends of the Oppressed', will be held at the Chapel, Chapel Court, High Street, Borough, on Monday 10 June in aid of those noble minded men who are persecuted by the odious Whig Government for attending the meeting held on the Calthorpe Estate.[20]

H. Ayliffe, Hon. Sec.
Poor Man's Guardian, 8 June 1833.

Female Society

At a meeting of the Female Society, the 'Friends of the Oppressed,' was held at the Chapel, Chapel Court, High Street, in the Borough, on Monday evening, June 10, 1833, in aid of the victims of Whig brutality, and to express their sentiments upon the late atrocious attack of the police upon a peaceable meeting of the people at Cold Bath Fields, the following resolutions were unanimously agreed to.

1. We, the members of the Female Society of London, 'The Friends of the Oppressed,' view with alarm the late atrocious attack of a brutal, military police upon an unarmed and peaceable assembly of the people at Cold Bath Fields, on the 13th May, 1833; and that, considering such a violation of the rights of the people ought not to be forgotten, are unanimously resolved to aid and assist, by every means in their power, any legal method that may be devised, in order to bring the authors to condign [sic] punishment.

2. That the conduct of the Whigs, since they have been in office, has been such as to forfeit all confidence on the part of the people; and that we, the females of London, cannot therefore consistently regard them as the lawful rulers of this country.

3. That we sympathise with our unfortunate fellow-countrymen, now in the hands of government; and that, considering they have only acted legally and consistently with the just rights of freemen, namely, that of assembling to discuss their grievances, and what was best calculated to ensure their future happiness, are resolved, with heart and hand, by public subscriptions and otherwise, to assist them, their wives, and families.

4. That the verdict returned by the Jury, held on the body of the policeman Culley, was given consistently with the evidence of the witnesses, and the solemn oath by which they were bound; and that their magnanimous resistance to the dictates of the tyrannical coroner, Mr Stirling, demands our united thanks; and that we, the Females of London, Members of the Society, the Friends of the Oppressed, tender them with sincerity and heartfelt gratitude.

5. That we, the Members of the Female Society, view with indignation the conduct of government in quashing the verdict of the seventeen honest and intelligent men, and we fear England will be enslaved, unless the people stand forth and vindicate their rights.

Poor Man's Guardian, 15 June 1833.

Male and Female Reformers of Hyde and Newton

To the Editor of the *Poor Man's Guardian*

To the praiseworthy and noble-minded Jurors of the justly slain Cull[e]y

Gentlemen, – To you, the Defenders of that bulwark of British liberty – the Trial by Jury. Do the Male and Female Reformers of Hyde and Newton, return you their sincere thanks, and that heartfelt gratification, for your talent and composure, your determination and perseverance, your careful discrimination of evidence, the unshaken manner in which you repelled the dictation of your partial Coroner, and your sense of duty to petition the House of Commons against Whig Destruction, have conferred a lasting honour upon you, and set a good example to all other jurors. May you live a long, a prosperous, and a happy life, is the sincere wish of us all.

Samuel Sidebottom

On behalf of the male and female Reformers of Hyde and Newton. Newton, June 30th.

Poor Man's Guardian, 13 July 1833.

Case of Mrs Wastneys

The humble Memorial of the Undersigned Inhabitants of Newcastle-upon-Tyne and its vicinity, to the King's most Ex-Majesty.

Sire, – We, the undersigned Inhabitants of Newcastle-upon-Tyne, and its vicinity, appeal to your Royal Clemency in favour of a female named Wastneys, who was committed on the 5th day of March last, and is now confined in the gaol of this town, under sentence of six months imprisonment for offending against the Act passed in the 60th year of the reign of his late Majesty King George the Third, by having sold Unstamped Newspapers.

The Prisoner states that she is now suffering a severity of punishment, which your Memorialists think could never have been contemplated by the law; being associated with convicts who have broken through the authority not only of Acts of Parliament, but also of the sacred obligations of Moral Principle.

We need not suggest to the humanity of your Majesty all the circumstances which plead in extenuation of the offence of the unfortunate wife and mother now imprisoned, but we venture to allude to the fact that some of those who have the honour to act as your Majesty's Servants, had previously taught the people to expect the repeal of the Act under which the prisoner now suffers.

Encouraged by a confidence in that clemency which consecrates Power, your Memorialists hope that the circumstances of this case may obtain for the prisoner some considerable mitigation of the sentence.

And your Memorialists shall ever pray, etc.

Here follows nearly a thousand signatures.

Poor Man's Guardian, 17 May 1834.

Notes

1. The fourpenny duty on journals and newspapers imposed in 1819 made them too expensive for working-class readers who were forced to club together to buy copies and read them collectively. In the autumn of 1830 an agitation against the 'taxes on knowledge' began and numerous sellers were imprisoned. Hundreds of unstamped journals were published and sold illegally during the following six years before Lord Melbourne reduced the tax to one penny in 1836.

2. *Poor Man's Guardian*, 21 July 1832, p. 470.

3. The Institution in Theobald's Road was used as a base for the National Union of the Working Classes. There were six such meeting-places around London in 1832. Lectures and social events were held there.

4. Lancaster Castle was used as a prison. The radicals arrested at Peterloo were taken to Lancaster Castle in the charge of Joseph Nadin, the Deputy Chief Constable of Manchester. It continued to be used to house radicals arrested during the campaigns of the 1820s and 1830s.

5. See biography in Chapter 3.

6. This refers to the ritual cleansing of women after childbirth by attendance at a church ceremony where thanks was given for the safe arrival and health of the child and mother.

7. *Poor Man's Guardian*, 6 October 1832, p. 559.

8. The Whigs were the political party which after 1688 aimed at subordinating the power of the Crown to that of parliament. It was a Whig

government that passed the Reform Act of 1832. The Whigs became the Liberal Party.

9. Earl Grey (1764–1845), leader of the Whig Party and advocate of a moderate approach to politics.

10. The Society for the Diffusion of Useful Knowledge was founded by Charles Knight and sponsored by prominent Whig politicians to circulate doctrines of a broadly utilitarian character without pandering to the lowest tastes. It tried to avoid political controversy and to divert people from radical ideas.

11. The Temple of Liberty, Cumberland Row, Kings Cross, London, was one of the headquarters of the National Union of the Working Classes.

12. Henry Hetherington (1792–1849), printer and publisher. Active in forming the first Mechanics' Institute in London and the early Trade Unions. Editor of the *Poor Man's Guardian*, which deliberately flouted the law by selling without the government tax stamp. Instead it carried a printing press as a logo, with the motto 'Knowledge is Power'.

13. The Victim Fund was established in July 1831. It was organised to assist all sellers of the Unstamped Press. It flourished during 1832 and up to July in 1833.

14. The schoolmaster referred to Lord Brougham (1778–1868) who sponsored the Society for the Diffusion of Useful Knowledge. He was guyed in the radical press in cartoons portraying him as a schoolmaster.

15. Lord Castlereagh was an Anglo-Irishman who believed that the country was on the verge of a radical revolution. He was hated for his role in the Peterloo Massacre, and in Shelley's *Mask of Anarchy*, he was the first target: 'I met Murder on the way, He had a mask like Castlereagh'.

16. The Six Acts were passed into law by the end of 1819 after the Peterloo Massacre. They were aimed at repression and prevention of radical activity and sought to control the calling of meetings and publication of radical material.

17. The Taxes on Knowledge were, in the public mind, the stamp duty on newspapers although they also covered taxes on paper and such limitations as a levy on advertisements.

18. O'Connell, the 'Liberator', was an active and popular campaigner for Irish Home Rule. He was MP for Clare in 1823 and later for Dublin. He joined other radical members in calling for a campaign to obtain the repeal of the taxes on newspapers.

19. George Pilgrim was editor of the *Cosmopolite*, published March 1832–November 1833. It reached a circulation of 5,000 and advocated radical reform on all fronts.

20. In May 1833 a political meeting in Cold Bath Fields, Calthorpe Street,

off Grays Inn Road, was declared illegal by the government. A clash took place and a constable, Robert Culley, was stabbed. The killer was never found.

5
Female Political Union of Manchester

On the death of Henry Hunt, 20 February 1835

During the thirty and odd years that he has taken a prominent part in the struggles of his country, he was never known to desert a cause he had espoused ... Whatever he undertook he performed ... To him the post of danger was the post of honour; wherever the cause of liberty entailed peril on its defenders ... his spirit was ever the same - the spirit of a brave Englishman who loved justice for its own sake and hated tyranny because tyranny caused the misery of his fellow citizens.

Poor Man's Guardian, 21 February 1835.

Introduction

Manchester people held Henry Hunt in high esteem following the Peterloo meeting in 1819. He could always be certain of support in the north-west and when, in 1830, he was elected as Member of Parliament for Preston, he assumed the mantle of radical representative for the whole country. In particular, he was considered to represent the people of Manchester and Lancashire.

In the increase of activity preceding the 1832 Reform Act, a number of groups were formed. There was general dismay among radical opinion at the terms in which the Reform Bill was published. It became apparent that the years of campaigning by working-class radicals were going to be discounted and that the proposed changes would enfranchise only comparatively well-off householders.

It was also a period of increase in trade union activity under the growing influence of the Owenite socialists. In London, a Metropolitan Trades Union had been formed and this became the National Union of the Working Classes[1] in the summer of 1831. The policy of the union was to 'obtain for every working man, unrestricted by unjust and partial laws, the full value of his labour, and the free disposal of the produce of his labour.'[2] This policy was put to meetings around the country and in Manchester to a meeting of Female Radical Reformers who drew up a eulogistic address to Henry Hunt.

It is interesting that the women set out their policy as 'Universal Suffrage – Annual Parliaments – and Vote by Ballot' and designated themselves a Branch Political Union as an auxiliary of the National Union of the Working Classes.

* * *

Address to Henry Hunt, Esq., M.P.

From the Female Radical Reformers of Manchester
Most excellent and respected Sir,
We, the female Radical reformers assembled at the Forrester's Arms, Sothern Street, Liverpool New Road, Manchester, for the purpose of forming a Branch Political Union, as an auxiliary to the National Union of the Working Classes – upon the just principles of Universal Suffrage – Annual Parliaments – and Vote by Ballot.

Sir, it was agreed that an address and vote of thanks should be forwarded to you for your undeviating exertions in that House, misnamed the Commons of England, on behalf of the poor, the needy, and of those that had none to help them; for which we beg, Sir, you will be pleased to accept our sincere and heartfelt thanks.

When we take a retrospective view of your proceedings for the last 26 years, we are led to admire your patriotic conduct: confident are we that you are the only honest patriot within St Stephen's walls. Your patriotic actions are so numerous that we are at a loss where to commence in order to do you justice. However, we will endeavour to enumerate a few of them, in order that we may be enabled to place them upon record against that day when we expect retributive justice to overtake those bad men who may survive death's final stroke.

Sir, what satisfaction and delight have some of us found in perusing your excellent memoirs; and with disgust do we read the account of those men in power, who had the temerity to thrust you out of office for being kind to those who were so unfortunate as to have recourse to parochial relief at the time you was [sic] churchwarden; here's an instance of your philanthropy, when you raised their scanty pittance something nearer to apparent comfort.

Again, Sir, your conduct at the various contested elections, such as Westminster, Bristol, and other places, calls aloud for our wonder and admiration; because you so manfully stood against the factions of both Whig and Tory. We need not go into any lengthened detail, by referring to anything that has taken place so far back as above alluded to: no, Sir; we have plenty of matter of later date which we hope will never be erased from our minds while life remains.

Worthy Sir, your glorious conduct on that never-to-be-forgotten, that never-to-be-forgiven bloody massacre, the 16th of August, 1819, when 618 were killed and wounded on St Peter's Field – the danger you underwent – and the sufferings you endured in prison are still fresh in our memories: your conduct whilst there, when the authorities were brought to their understanding – the gaoler disgraced and dismissed – the gaol razed to the ground – and the prisoners made more comfortable. We do expect to see that day when satisfaction will be obtained for these deeds. Again, Sir, we, the female reformers, being mothers, daughters, sisters, and relatives to those who have been for a long time struggling for liberty, feel it our duty to render them a helping hand at this momentous crisis; seeing, as we do daily, our children on the brink of starvation, owing to profligate government. Then, respected Sir, allow us to offer a few more reasons why we are led to admire your valuable services. The manner, Sir, in which you acted on various occasions gained you 3730 independent voters at Preston,[3] and when the corrupt press had been heaping every species of abuse in order to lower you in the estimation of the productive classes of the three kingdoms, you never relaxed in your endeavours in the good cause of liberty. Where, we would ask, can that man be found for the last 160 years, that has acted so independent on the behalf of the people, as you have by resisting the enormous grants. The various motions you have made in that House relative to the odious Corn Laws[4] – the yeomanry cavalry, with the length of time they have been quartered upon the public. We admire you, Sir, for the spirited manner you have acted in publishing your excellent letters, and exposing those blood-thirsty Manchester yeomanry: these, Sir, and a many others for which we have not room, we return you thanks. We are determined to support you with our lives, and to instil into the minds of our children what oppression has done for them.

Dear Sir, we would conclude by saying, go on and prosper, and your name will be handed down to posterity, when a monument will be erected to commemorate the noble, manly, and patriotic conduct through life: wishing you may yet live to see your country emancipated from those overbearing two-fold oppressors; namely, a bloated oligarchy and a tyrannical aristocracy, we are, Sir, on the behalf of the female Radical Reformers of Manchester,

Your most obedient and admiring servants,

Hannah Brooks, President,

Ann Foster, Secretary.

Poor Man's Guardian, 21 January 1832.

Letter to the Female Radical Reformers of Preston

London, May 28, 1833.

My Excellent and Patriotic Friends,
Your splendid present, the silver cup, and your still more welcome and heart-inspiring address, were presented to me yesterday, in the presence of many thousands of our fellow-countrymen and country-women, who were assembled in the metropolis to propose an act of justice to the brave Jurymen of Calthorpe-street, who gave a verdict of 'Justifiable Homicide' on the death of Robert Cull[e]y,[5] a policeman, who was slain in attempting to *disperse a peaceable meeting, on Monday the 13th inst.* It is impossible for me to find language adequate to express my feelings of gratitude for this fresh testimony of your kindness, approbation, and confidence, so eloquently and so feelingly detailed in your truly patriotic address. Permit me, however, to say that neither time or circumstances will ever make me alter the high opinion that I have always entertained of the virtue and the patriotism of the Female Reformers of Preston. The only return I can make for such unbounded confidence and esteem is this – if ever I am called into a situation which will give me the power to accomplish those objects for which I have, during a pretty long life, been struggling, and for which you have honoured me with this new mark of your approbation, no consideration upon earth shall deter me from endeavouring to realize them. In the fond hope that I shall ere long have an opportunity, to thank you, my fair and brave friends, in person, I shall only say that I am, and ever shall be, to the latest period of my existence, your grateful, devoted, and affectionate friend,

H. Hunt.
Poor Man's Guardian, 1 June 1833.

Notes

1. The National Union of the Working Classes was a centre of organised working-class radicalism and supporters of the unstamped press. The government was unduly fearful of its influence and it was riddled with spies and plain-clothes men.
2. 'A Penny Paper for the People', *Poor Man's Guardian*, 29 April 1831, p. 6.
3. As an ancient borough, Preston had a population able to claim voting rights. In the election of December 1830, Henry Hunt was elected to Parliament with 3,730 votes.
4. The object of the Corn Laws was to prevent the price of grain from rising too high. Supporters of the Corn Laws claimed that protecting grain brought poor land into use and therefore gave employment; that

it freed the country from foreign dependence and enabled the landed proprietors to patronise manufacturing industry. Opponents such as Cobden and Bright and the Anti-Corn Law League advocated free trade. Because the price of corn governed the price of bread, the laws were unpopular with working people.

5. See Chapter 4, n. 20.

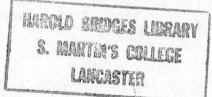

6

The New Moral World

I have proclaimed important truths to the world, and if they were not regarded by the world, it was because the world did not understand them. Why should I blame the world? I am in advance of my time.

Robert Owen in George Jacob Holyoake,
Life and Last Days of Robert Owen of New Lanark, 2nd edn, 1859, p. 21.

All social movements, all real advances made in England in the interests of the working class were associated with Owen's name.

Frederick Engels, *Herr Eugen Dühring's Revolution in Science*,
Karl Marx–Frederick Engels Collected Works, vol. 25, 1987, p. 249.

Introduction

Robert Owen inspired the working class with his vision of a socialist society. He was tireless in advocating his ideas about the structure of society and he stimulated discussion on the evils of the capitalist system and how they could be overcome. He was the founder of the Cooperative Movement; he raised the demand for factory legislation and experimented in primary education. He was instrumental in drawing attention to the terrible exploitation of very young children in factories and he had a fundamental belief in the innate ability of people to raise their standards and live in neighbourly cooperation.

Owen was not a feminist. In general he did not differentiate between men and women, looking on them as people with similar disadvantages and similar potential. It was the Owenites, his followers, who saw the natural development of his ideas applied to women; and it was women who latched on to them and flocked to listen in their thousands to lecturers spelling out the basic concepts of women's emancipation.

Where Owen's social policy pronounced an egalitarian future, the women socialists interpreted this in terms related to their immediate experience. They raised the issues of the inequality of the law, the grossly male-orientated marriage situation, the lack of adequate education for women which led to their exclusion from work or participation in political affairs and the denial of their basic rights as citizens.

The socialist missionaries who went around the country preaching the gospel of emancipation met with extreme antagonism from the entrenched powers. They persisted despite being subjected to both physical and intellectual opposition.

Several attempts were made to coordinate activity in 'women only' organisations though women were also involved in the general groups that flourished during the 1830s and early 1840s. In a few cases, women were officers in mixed groups and attended as delegates in their own right at Congress. This culminated in a Female Socialist writing from Edgbaston in 1839 to ask for a rule that equal numbers of men and women be on branch committees. That, she commented, would give the men an opportunity to educate the women, if they found them wanting.

One feature of women lecturers such as Emma Martin and Margaret Chapellsmith was the breadth of their interests, ranging from the progress of the industrial revolution, the marriage system, the philosophy of religion, and the rights, duties and education of women. Reports of their lectures often included a comment on the clarity of their exposition and the pleasure the audience derived from their delivery and eloquence.

Emma Martin, for instance, was described as 'a small lady of attractive expression with dark luminous eyes, a pleasant far-reaching voice and a womanly woman'.[1] As one of the complaints levelled against them by their opponents was that they were she-devils and unwomanly in their conduct, it is refreshing to find that they were accepted as normal human beings and found to be attractive personalities by the huge audiences that flocked to hear them.

Margaret Chapellsmith (1806–80)
Margaret Chapellsmith was born Miss Reynolds and early in her life became strongly influenced by the works of Cobbett. In 1836, at the age of 30, she began writing articles on politics for the *Dispatch*.[2] Later she became a freethought and Owenite lecturer. In 1839 she met and married John Chapellsmith and in 1842 she set up in business as a bookseller.

John Chapellsmith was a fervent supporter of his wife in all her activities. On occasion it is even recorded that he could be found pouring the tea at a social where she had been the chief speaker. Margaret Chapellsmith, together with Emma Martin, advocated Owen's views on 'Marriage in the New Moral World', and her lectures, like Mrs Martin's, were rapturously received, especially by women. The lectures also became the target of violent demonstrations by people opposing her.

Like Eliza Macauley, Margaret Chapellsmith was particularly interested in economic theory, and in 1841 she condensed and edited a version of Cobbett's *Paper Against Gold*[3] which was printed and published in Manchester by Abel Heywood.[4]

In 1850 the Chapelsmiths emigrated to New Harmony[5] in America. Margaret continued writing and contributed a number of articles to the *Boston Investigator*.

Eliza Macauley (178?–1837)

Left an orphan when she was an infant, Eliza Macauley had to support herself from an early age. She became involved in acting, first locally and then in London, where she arrived in about 1805. By the late 1820s she had abandoned the idea of a career in the theatre and she took up preaching in a small chapel in Grub Street. From there she became involved in the Owenite movement which was beginning to gain momentum.

By the 1830s she was deeply involved in London Owenite activities. She announced herself as part-proprietor of an Equitable Exchange Bank and addressed herself eloquently to the females in her audience. The Equitable Exchange was a short-lived cooperative experiment in which a tradesman took the product of his labour and was given 'Labour Notes' to the value of time spent in production. He was then able to 'spend' the notes within the Exchange. Unfortunately there was a limited variety of products available and people had to do part of their shopping outside. This involved selling their product on the open market in order to obtain money – and so the Exchange collapsed.

By 1835 Eliza was in the debtors' prison at the Marshalsea from where she published her short memoirs. She died in 1837 while on a lecture tour.

Emma Martin (1812–51)

Born in Bristol in 1812 to a prosperous cooper, William Bullock and his wife Hannah, Emma Martin was brought up in a conventional religious home. She took part in a church belonging to the Particular Baptists (a branch of the Baptists who believed in salvation only for the elect) and when she was 18 she became a school teacher with her own Ladies' Seminary.

In 1831, she married a businessman, Isaac Martin, and by him had three daughters. But it was not a happy marriage and after hearing an Owenite missionary, Alexander Campbell,[6] lecture in Bristol in 1839, she moved towards freethought.

She started on a career as a lecturer on educational and feminist issues and as a visitor she attended the Owenite Congress held in Birmingham in 1839. During the year before the following Congress, Mrs Martin moved from Bristol to London and started lecturing as a socialist. Her marriage broke with her move and since her property, by law, remained her husband's she was without means of keeping herself or her daughters.

However, she set out on a highly successful lecturing career in which she concentrated on physiology, the condition of women and socialism. She developed her feminism and argued the case that woman's subordinate position was due to lack of education; she blamed the marriage system which made a woman an object of a commercial transaction. Later, as her interest in and knowledge of Owenism developed, she changed her views and said that women's inferior status was the product of the system of society in which private property and competition were at a premium.

Emma Martin became one of the best known of the 'infidel'[7] lecturers. She debated against a number of clerical opponents and commanded huge audiences of several thousand people, especially women. Her views on marriage, which reflected Owen's, and her advocacy of divorce struck a responsive chord in many women's hearts in an age when women were expected to remain tied to a marriage in which they had every possible obligation no matter how unsatisfactory the relationship might be.

Mrs Martin was paid a small amount by the Owenite Central Board for lecturing and from time to time she earned money as a teacher and later, as a midwife. She and her daughters ran women's clinics, and the girls made elastic bandages.

Not all Emma Martin's lectures were peaceful and successful. She faced strong opposition from the Church and when in 1842 blasphemy prosecutions were brought against the 'infidel' missionaries, Southwell, Holyoake and Thomas Paterson, she became active in the Anti-Persecution Union. In Glasgow she led a crowd of 3,000 to a church to criticise a minister's sermon; in Hull, she lectured in spite of attempts by the magistrates to prevent her, and in Leicester she filled the market square after the Assembly Rooms had been closed to her. A scheme to re-open the Rotunda,[8] scene of Eliza Sharples and Richard's Carlile's successes, unfortunately came to nothing. She would have been a worthy successor to them as resident lecturer.

When she was 33, she began living with Joshua Hopkins, an engineering worker, and she bore him a daughter, Manon, in 1847. This second marriage brought her great happiness and some stability. However, soon afterwards she contracted tuberculosis and in 1851 she died, at the age of 39.

She was a courageous and hard-working speaker who advocated feminist issues at a time when to do so engendered fierce opposition. Her publications were avidly read by women and an assessment of her on the occasion of the publication of one of her penny pamphlets said, 'This lady's activity is incessant. One day she sends all Hull into convulsions by an attack on the missions, next she upsets a missionary society in

Manchester, she hurls a pamphlet missive against the theists one day, incontinently projects another against the mission-money seekers, and ere this be well dry from the press will have a fresh paper pellet in readiness for active service.'[9]

George Jacob Holyoake in his address at her funeral described her as 'Beautiful in expression, quick in wit, strong in will, eloquent in speech, coherent in conviction, and of stainless character, she was incomparable among public women.'[10]

* * *

Public Meeting at the Institution of the Industrial Classes Gray's Inn Road[11] Equitable Labour Exchange

Miss Macauley was then introduced to the meeting amidst very great applause and said that she was part proprietor of an Equitable Exchange Bank. She felt it her duty to address and excite her own sex. She said that moral courage was now wanted; and that female exertion was now wanted. She enlarged very eloquently on this subject, and her remarks met with great approbation. She said that tradesmen now took the Labour Notes and that they had offers of provisions.

Crisis, 25 August 1832.

The Independent Exchange Bazaar

Independent Exchange Bazaar[12]
For rapidly improving the condition of the Productive Classes, and of Society at large, is now open in the Gothic Hall, New Road, Marylebone; and affords an opportunity for all Persons who either possess, or can fabricate, or produce Goods, Merchandize, or Provisions, of any kind, to dispose of the same immediately on a system of Equitable Exchange.

The Council appointed to conduct the operations of this most important Establishment, have now the satisfaction of stating, after an experience of eight weeks, that the beneficial progress of the concern has far exceeded their expectations, as also those of the parties who have disposed of their goods by placing them in the Exchange Bazaar; and of others who have remained deeply interested spectators of the course of an experiment, which has determined, that it is in the power of all industrious human beings of both sexes, immediately and advantageously to dispose of the produce of their skill and labour.

The principle on which the Exchange Bazaar is conducted, is as simple as it is efficacious.

Each Depositor of Goods or Provisions puts a value on the articles deposited by him, or her; and if the valuation be approved by the Council or Committee, appointed to revise the same, the amount is immediately paid to the Depositor in the Exchange Notes of the Institution, with which Notes, the Depositor purchases any suitable article that may be contained in the Bazaar – and which, indeed, are already received by several shopkeepers and others, not connected with the Establishment, in payment of purchases made from them.

The result of this operation is equivalent to the introduction of a vast amount of additional money into the country – with peculiar advantages which no other money possesses; for, first – the Notes of the Exchange Bazaar[13] represent always the exact quantity and value of the goods which are actually within the Bazaar; always increasing as the quantity and value of the goods increase, and decreasing, on the other hand, as the quantity and value of the goods are diminished: second – the new, truly valuable, easily attainable, and most useful money thus created, is incapable of being usuriously employed, since it cannot bear interest, but can only be expended in purchase of the goods, the actual value of which it truly represents.

The advantages to be derived from this Institution will be in proportion to the variety of goods fabricated and deposited in the Bazaar. Hence it becomes the duty of all parties to exert themselves, to bring in, or induce others to bring in, such goods as they themselves want, and which for some time they may not find there. Let this suggestion be *practically* attended to, and we shall soon experience its beneficial result.

The Government consists of a President and Council; the Officers are Secretary and Resident Agent.

1. The Council appoint the Valuing Committees, who are selected from among the Members. It is the duty of the Valuing Committee, to estimate the cost price of materials, and, in all practical cases, to add sixpence per hour for the average time necessary to manufacture or work up the same; and thus to lay the foundation of an equal reward for labour.

2. If a value so placed on the Goods, be approved of by the person to whom they belong, the President and Council authorize the issue of an exchange order, enabling the depositor to obtain whatever goods he may select from the Bazaar.

3. All goods left with the Agent before four o'clock, p.m. are valued the same day, when an exchange order immediately issues.

4. To cover the expense of the Establishment, one penny on a shilling is added to the cost price of labour and materials.*

---

* Materials mostly consist of labour, and will gradually find their way into the Bazaar, and become articles of exchange.

5. The principal object of the Association is the giving facilities to the creation and distribution of *New Wealth*, so as to enable all wealth producers and consumers, mutually to benefit each other, without *injury to any*; and the benefits being also immediate, and not *remote* – for their extent and value are in *proportion to the numbers and variety of occupations of the parties acting in union with each other*.

Isis, 8 September 1832.

National Equitable Labour Exchange[14]
Charlotte Street, Rathbone Place
Female Employment Association

A number of ladies, who have witnessed the benefits which have been derived by many industrious females, from the Equitable Labour Exchange, have resolved to form an Association of Ladies, for the purpose of extending the advantages of the system to all who may be disposed to partake of them. The only difficulty in the way of which, appears to be the obtaining for those whose only capital is their industry, the materials necessary for their useful employment; to do which, it is proposed that each Associate shall advance weekly, such sum as her convenience will admit, but not less than sixpence, for which advance, in the following week, Labour Notes to the same amount shall be received by the subscriber, which Notes will entitle the holders of them to select any goods they may require from the stores of the Exchange; and it is presumed, that there is no one who will not be able to select useful articles from these stores, to the amount of some few shillings per week.

With the funds thus raised, it is intended to purchase the most necessary and useful materials for wearing apparel, and to distribute them to such of the Associates as are in want of employment under the superintendence of the committee, and in conformity with the rules of the Association; which has the fullest concurrence of, and will receive every possible encouragement from the managers of the Exchange, in which the productions of the Associates will be deposited, where a market will be always open for them, without fear of its being overstocked, or the value of the articles being depreciated. The management of the Association to be vested in a President, Vice President, Treasurer, Secretary, and Committee.

The Associates who are employed to be divided into classes, of not less than seven each, including a leader, who shall be a member of the committee.

Each class header will collect the subscriptions from her own class and pay them to the Treasurer, give out the materials to be made up, receive the articles when finished, and deposit them with the committee; who, in conjunction with the Valuators of the Exchange, will fix the price at which the goods are to be taken into the Exchange.

The committee to purchase the materials at the best markets at ready money price, to fix the amount to be paid for making the various articles, and to make a report of their proceedings at the meeting of the Association, to be held one evening in each week.

The Secretary to keep the accounts, examine the invoices of the materials, and give an order on the Treasurer for their payment, take minutes of the business at the weekly meetings, and carry on the necessary correspondence. The whole of the business of the Association will be conducted by ladies, but they will be most happy to receive the donations or subscriptions of such gentlemen as well as ladies, who are favourably disposed to the objects contemplated by the Association.

Ladies desirous of joining this Association, are requested to apply at the Institution in Charlotte-street, or at 9, Tavistock Place, Tavistock Square, where all particulars may be obtained, and where donations will be received.

Crisis, 20 April 1833.

Public Meeting of the Delegates of the United Trades Thursday May 16th

A delegate from one of the Ladies' Societies said the number of their members amounted to about 60, and that they employed seven or eight of their members. She said much good had been done by the assistance given them last week in exchanging their notes for money.

Crisis, 25 May 1833.

Moral Union of the Women of Great Britain and Ireland

Plan of a Practical Moral Union of the Women of Great Britain and Ireland, for the purpose of enabling them to attain a superior physical, moral, and intellectual character.

The general arrangements of society, hitherto formed in ignorance, having impeded the course of that universal sympathy so necessary to happiness, it is anticipated that an association combining all classes of women, who shall have one great and interesting object in view, will naturally give a beneficial impulse to those moral and intellectual qualities which all possess.

That self-interest being the universal motive to action, it is intended to show that the measure proposed will be one step towards attaining that happiness which all desire.

That the character of woman having been formed by circumstances, all in opposition to her nature, which has never yet been properly understood or attended to, it is peculiarly her interest to assist in removing these opposing circumstances. That, therefore, it is necessary for the benefit of this, and of all future ages, that women should endeavour, by a system of mutual aid and kindness, to surround each other with such circumstances as shall truly and fully develop the entire character, and secure to them those privileges for which they are by nature intended.

That the acquisition of the knowledge that we are the creatures of circumstances, will of itself enable us to form new circumstances that will be most beneficial for the whole of society.

That the laws which regard women, having been formed upon a false estimate of their nature, are, consequently, all unjust and unnatural.

That, therefore, they are called upon to cultivate their whole being physically, morally, and intellectually; thus *compelling* society to reverse its unjust and unnatural decrees; but that this can be done only by an extensive union of the women themselves.

To effect these very desirable results, it is proposed that a society be formed of women only, each to be considered a member by contributing the weekly sum of one penny. That the amount of subscriptions be made public at each quarterly meeting, and that, at the end of one year, the whole be appropriated to such a purpose as shall appear most advantageous.

That a committee be formed, consisting of thirteen, who shall elect from among themselves a provident treasurer and secretary, and that a quarterly election or re-election take place of the whole committee.

That collectors be appointed, who shall pay in the amount of collections weekly, to one of the committee, who shall pay the amount over to the treasurer at each meeting of the committee.

That a meeting of the committee take place every fortnight, a meeting of the committee and collectors every quarter, and a general meeting of the committee, collectors, and members half-yearly. It is confidently expected that much that is of the greatest importance to the happiness of society, will be effected by this association – the broad line of demarcation which has been drawn between the different classes of women will be effaced – they will be in the frequent interchanges of the best feelings of human nature – they will become conscious of the power they possess to free themselves from existing errors – and they will be taught by one another, how they can best exert that power for the benefit of the whole human race.

Crisis, 17 August 1833.

Society of Industrious Females

Public Meeting of the Trade Delegates August 15, 1833
The Society of Industrious Females Miss Green gave a most cheering account of the progress of this most interesting Society. She stated they were now ready to undertake any orders that may be brought them. We earnestly recommend this Society to the support of every friend of the system. Their weekly report from August 2nd to August 9th is as follows:

Receipts in cash	£0.16.6	} Total £1.19.3
Receipts in notes	45h:3s	
Expenditure in cash	£0.13.5	} Total £1.1.2
Expenditure in notes	15h:3s	
Commission	1s.11¼d	

Crisis, 24 August 1833.

A Male Criticism of Women-only Unions

Fatal to the advancement of women would be an exclusive union; the line of separation would be extended between the sexes, and destructive to the happiness of the human species. Are the interests of man and woman separate, or is their interest one and the same? Ought an *equal means* of education to be extended to man and woman without any regard to sex? Ought equality of *right* and of *condition* so prevail without any privilege to either sex? If these questions are answered in the affirmative, then the projected state of society of women would be inconsistent with the above admissions. If woman denounce the right usurped by man of legislating exclusively for the whole, how can she expect but every rational man will not protest against woman being the legislator, excluding man from any participation in that right? On this ground, we contend, woman is equal with man by the laws of our physical condition, which is far from being of such an intricate and mysterious nature as some have supposed, there being general laws applicable to the species. Each has the same wants – food, clothing and shelter; each acquires knowledge through the medium of the senses; each is susceptible of happiness and misery, of pain and pleasure. Do the laws of our nature show we are destined to live together in a social state? If monasteries for men and nunneries for women be not a violation of the laws of nature then we should return to that state; but if they are a violation of our social condition, then the projected society of women would be pernicious. Let man see his own interest in restoring woman to freedom, then will he himself be free. An ignorant woman will not find admirers for symmetry alone and man for his physical ability or riches.

B. Warden[15]
Marylebone
Crisis, 24 August 1833.

Moral Union Formation

To the Women Friendly to the 'Rational System'
The plan for forming a practical moral union among the women which appeared in the *Crisis* of last week, seemed likely to prove so beneficial to all concerned in furthering the object, that several ladies have already formed themselves into a committee, and will be happy to answer any further enquiries addressed to 14, Charlotte Street, Rathbone Place.

Crisis, 24 August 1833.

Eliza Macauley's Lectures

St Simonian Lectures,[16] On the Rights of Industry and on Female Emancipation, every Friday, at 8 o'clock in the evening, at the Burton Rooms, Burton Crescent.

Miss Macauley is engaged by the St Simonians and will lecture at the above rooms on Monday 20th January, at the same hour.

Poor Man's Guardian, 11 January 1834.

Anna Wheeler's Letter to the French Socialists and their Reply

We publish the following extract from the *Tribune des Femmes*, a French periodical, as it refers to the letters of Concordia[17] published in the *Crisis*. The French women evidently regard themselves as far in advance of our fair helpmates on this side of the water – and are rather a little surprised that English women should talk of emancipation: they have been accustomed to regard them, no doubt, as a sort of voluntary slaves. The women in France are certainly far in advance of English women, and we have no doubt but the emancipation of woman will be first consummated over the water. But England is the land where the emancipation of man must take place – it is evident that nature has destined the two countries for these two departments; hence political liberty, which is the male department, is more abundant here – and moral or social liberty is more abundant in France. The political will come first, but the social is the grand consummation. We can see no country in the world so far advanced as England in the career of male emancipation; an event which is most likely to be accomplished by the Unions – as an example to all the world: but if the English outstrip the French in moral socialism, they must get wings to their heels *instanter*. But can moral socialism be accomplished before political emancipation? Impossible. These are the two pillars of the new world, the Jachin and the Boaz, the right leg and the left. If the right leg moves on, the left is sure to follow; but it requires you to move both legs before you can move one step.

From the *Tribune des Femmes*
We receive from England occasionally letters published in the *Crisis* by women, and feel anxious to communicate to our readers the pleasure we experience in finding the subject of female emancipation so forward in the British empire. One of those letters, signed 'Concordia', is directed to Mr *Robert Owen*, as we might in France address Mr *Charles Fourier*,[18] who is here what Mr *Owen* is in England, a man of sincerity, who wishes with all his heart and all the faculties of his genius to ameliorate the human species; but we could likewise tell him, You did not know, nor do you comprehend *woman*. How could your male heart correctly appreciate our sentiments, since the slavish state in which your sex keeps us, has never allowed our faculties to be freely developed? And still you dare call upon the world to put in practice a new Social System!

Legislators, and all you system-makers, what is the use henceforth to build for us splendid *'Boudoirs'*? For if fatally we are precluded from making the least change in them, we shall soon feel dull and heavy; if we are not to participate in the divisions, appropriations, and decorations of our dwellings, in a word, in every thing connected with *taste* and *sentiment*, we renounce acknowledging you as the arbiters of our happiness, and we refuse you the right of directing our destinies.

The complete emancipation of woman, therefore, must be the fundamental principle on which should rest, to be successful, the new Social System we are labouring to establish.
Paris, February, 1834.

'Suzanne'
Crisis, 8 March 1834.

Frances Morrison in Manchester

Manchester (Branch 34), New George-Street, Shudewell [Shudehill]

It is but a short time since this branch was established, and owing to various difficulties which attended the opening of it, its success has been materially retarded. But the principles of truth require no extrinsic aid to ensure their ultimate prosperity, and our recent progress gives cheering assurance that she *will* triumph in despite of the attacks of her enemies, or the snares of her pretended friends. The lecture in the morning was better attended than usual, and in the afternoon the audience was still more numerous, but in the evening we had a lecture from a lady of the name of Morrison,[19] widow, I believe, of the late editor of the *Pioneer*, and then the place was crowded to suffocation. She commenced her lecture with astonishing firmness and composure, and seemed throughout to evince a spirit of devotedness to the cause she advocated which rose superior to the strange position which she, for the first time, occupied. The subject of her lecture was confined principally to the feeling or principle which should guide or actuate those call-themselves Socialist. Her manner was peculiarly energetic, her arguments well-arranged, and her remarks judiciously adapted to the occasion, and characterised by remarkable simplicity and delicacy. She was listened to with respectful attention and seemed to give general satisfaction. She is the first female in Manchester who has had the nerve to come forward in practical advocacy of our views, and it is hoped that her example will operate as a stimulus to others to lend their exertions in promoting the great cause of Socialism, whose interests are so completely identified with their own. An animated discussion followed, which was opened by Mr Johnson, lately a Baptist minister, who was replied to by Mr Southall; we had then a female opponent who occupied the next ten minutes, and was answered, apparently to the satisfaction of all, by Mr Shephard. Mr Johnson then resumed, and Mr Clarke, one of our lecturers, closed the discussion; after which I had the pleasure to announce that the lady (Mrs Morrison) would lecture again next Sunday evening. I remain, sir, yours respectfully,

H. H. Horton, Chairman.

Star in the East
July 14 1838.[20]

New Moral World, 21 July 1838.

The Funeral of a Socialist

Sir,

I was highly gratified, on Wednesday last, by a most interesting, and, in London, uncommon procession, namely, the funeral of a child, which was borne by six little girls, dressed in white, each carrying bouquets, composed of heart's-ease, forget-me-not, and roses, apt emblems of the young and fading flowers of mortality, followed by numerous friends. I was pleased to find that this was a Social funeral, and, upon inquiry, learnt that it was the infant son of Mr Alger, the late secretary to the London Institution. I followed it to the burial ground; the body was lowered into the grave, and the children threw their flowers into it, and then sang a delightful hymn, connected with their principles. The whole scene was, to my mind, as well as many other spectators, delightful; and seemed, indeed, to remove the useless gloom generally connected with the transmission of mortal mould to its fellow-earth. I think, if all your funerals were conducted on a similar plan, it would produce a most pleasing effect. It was wished that the usual service could be dispensed with, but the custom of the place will not yet comply; part only was read, but I could not help observing the cold and unconcerned manner in which this duty was performed. No heartfelt sympathy was there; *money* was in every word and look. I do not blame the man; *circumstances* were the cause. Late events have made me acquainted with Socialists, and feeling interested for the principles, I take the liberty of forwarding the above; if you think it worthy of insertion in *The New Moral World*, it is at your service.

I remain, yours, respectfully,

A Female Observer
New Moral World, 4 August 1838.

Female Improvement in Birmingham

Sir,

Having, for some time, attended the lectures and discussions of the socialists, and heard much talk about the emancipation, education, etc., of females, and their right to equality with the other sex, I wonder our social friends should so far follow the priesthood as to preach one thing and practice another. If they really and truly desire to see the females intelligent and useful members of community, why not establish a rule throughout the branches to have an equal number of females with the males on their councils, and introduce them into their private meetings, and, if they find them ignorant, endeavour to imbue their minds with useful knowledge. This being done, I think many of them would soon acquire sufficient strength of mind to speak their sentiments in public – and not allow parson Foye, with 'his some how or other', when speaking of the trinity, to refer to 'the poor silly women', as he was pleased to do, at a late discussion in this town; for, if some of them could have summoned courage to reply to him, and spoken what they then thought, he would not have found them quite so silly as he wished to make them appear. It being so novel a thing for females to speak in public assemblies, and the idea of all eyes being, at once, directed towards them, is it at all marvellous that, however they may feel excited, or disposed from what they hear, that a sufficiency of courage is wanting to speak their sentiments? And here I would just remind Mr Foye that, whatever opinion he may entertain of us, there are many females far enough advanced to know better than go to his church, and pay him a shilling for offering up thanks, in their name, for certain mercies received, when, at the same time, should a poor unfortunate being step in, whom circumstances have not favoured with the means to pay, they must return home short of the blessing, if so it may be called.

I hope, however, the time is not far distant, when both men and women will learn to think and act for themselves; for, as far as I can judge, if prayers and thanksgiving are pleasing to the great Creator, the response of a grateful heart in secret must be more acceptable than paying a priest to offer what can only be termed a second-hand thanksgiving, at an uncalled for expense. I hope my fellow females will rouse all their energies, and let the priesthood see that we have moral courage to depend upon our own exertions, with the confidence that the God who made us, is both able and willing to make us happy, without their canting, hypocritical nonsense; and as woman is said to have been first in the transgression, let it not be said that she is last in promoting the regeneration of mankind.

A Female Socialist, M.B.

Edgbaston, April 16th 1839.

New Moral World, 27 April 1839.

Woman and the Laws

Reverence for woman is the test of civilisation. Man rises in proportion as woman is less depressed.

It is, I confess, an ungracious task to review the laws, or to cast censure upon the conduct man has pursued, in reference to woman. For, as we take pleasure in dwelling on the virtues and the beauties that will mark the actions of individuals, in those happy days, when moral cultivation shall be the grand desideratum in youthful education; so, of course, are we averse to speak upon the defects and the depravities an unwise development of character gives rise to; thus must there be but little of congeniality or attraction for ourselves in the subject under consideration.

But, though our experience may be brief, and though we may be disposed to look with feelings of a charitable, and, therefore, favourable kind, on human motives and intentions, yet our scrutiny has not been so confined as to prevent our gaining an insight into some of the causes that produce the complication of female wrongs, of which our present system furnishes such ample proofs; nor is our sense of justice so weak, our love of humanity so feeble and uninspiring, as to lead us to be guilty of treason against this knowledge, by an attempt to disguise or conceal our real sentiments.

The opinion of the humblest, as of the most exalted, is, as I view it, to that individual, his or her property to be respected, whether deemed right or wrong, nor to be slighted without consideration. It, alone, is as the drop in the ocean, signifying little; yet we know that of the minute atom, the single drop, is the earth composed, the sea made up. Wave could not follow wave; the tide of human progression could not flow along as we have evidenced it has, were there no power of union in the fluid, of harmony and coalition in the separate individual opinions.

It is this feeling which should prompt every woman to ask herself whether her position is such as to enable her to promote, as largely as she thinks herself capable of, the happiness of those around her, more especially of her own sex? No one, I am sure, whatever her station, but must discover how small the treasure of happiness she is capable of imparting, compared with her wishes, and the power she feels herself to possess for the performance of that highest earthly good – the power of rendering others more virtuous, more happy! We may err in our conclusions, and in our mode of expressing them; but let us not, through fear of so doing, remain silent, and expose ourselves to the chance of hearing from the thoughtless and inconsiderate of the other sex the following, which appear to me, pet phrases, reserved for occasions when allusions are being made to the unhappy condition of woman, such as 'they really are quite contented as they are, and are unconscious of their thraldom; therefore, it is quite nonsense for us to make a stir about them, when, perhaps, they wouldn't thank us for it'; 'they, who desire it, will be free; and if women, along with the desire, had any strength of capacity, they would not have been enslaved in the nineteenth century; but they are, evidently, very much our inferiors'; then, if these fail, we have a long tirade about the 'charms of domestic life and the home fire-side'; the necessity of woman's being constantly at home to cheer and soothe man's rough and wayward temper, 'the beauty of female gentleness, modesty, etc. etc'; which, if women be permitted more freedom, will all be lost to them? In such and similar wild jargon, do men, old and young, indulge, when the dread of woman's enlightenment takes possession of their minds.

Let us not withhold from civilisation the credit that is its due, in relation to science, and the increase of the comforts and luxuries of life. But, at the same time, we cannot deny, if we apply the text mentioned at the head of this paper, that in reference to woman and to our state of morals, slight indeed has been the advantage. Yet, who that have thoughts beyond those of their childhood, will dispute the importance of an advance in the latter, being equally as essential as in the former; or refuse to admit that the morals of a people are intimately connected with the degree of intelligence that belongs to its females? Moral improvement is the point to which our aims should be directed – in which our hopes of happiness should be centered. Without it we can enjoy no real social pleasures; for the root of them all is in morality; in its expulsion do we chase from our hearts sentiments the most delightful to cherish! We bear about with us the cheerless gloom of winter, for there can bloom no spring, there can reign no summer to vivify and enlighten – to charm and gladden the homes and family of man – while the searing, destroying thoughts and purposes that now deprive the earth of its freshness and purity, shall be allowed to corrupt and degrade it.

And while woman is oppressed as she has been, and now is, by the laws of her country – while her education is conducted in blind obedience to custom – immorality must flourish. Legislate happily for the interests of woman; educate her wisely for taking her part in society; and a beneficent state of morals will necessarily follow.

Shame on the world! In madness or in pride,
Has woman's mental birthright been denied?
Be she the weaker, kindly give her might;
Be she man's equal, then it is her right:
Whether or not, 'tis *policy* to dower
Woman with wisdom, since she *must* have power –
The power to sear or soothe; to blight or bless,
To mar or make, *all* moral happiness.
Mrs Grimstone.[21]

Who will presume to say, that the laws of this, or of any country, calling itself civilised, are just in their treatment of woman? The pretext assigned by man, for keeping absolute dominion himself, and allowing woman to have no share in framing the laws, is, I believe, the physical and mental superiority of himself to the other sex. But, if this were admitted, is it right that punishments for infraction of those laws should be as severe in the one case as in the other? Woman, 'the gentle race and dear,' is recognised equally as strong in mind and body when the hour of trial and infliction arrives. The tender limbs, the weak muscle, or the feebler mind of woman have had no influence with man, when he has had to pronounce her condemnation! The torture, the stake, the axe, or the gibbet, have not spared *her*; until a very few years the lash numbered *her* as its victim. In fact, no species of punishment has been introduced, at all supporting the proposition of woman's inferiority in strength of body or of mind; each have ascribed to her an equal power of judging correctly; an equal strength in the endurance of physical suffering. Is it wrong to wish woman to have a share in framing the laws? Looking around, and seeing the vast amount of evils that poison each wholesome current, which should supply purity and peace throughout the whole frame-work of society, traceable, as we consider they are, to the defective state of our laws and institutions, are we deficient in thought, or in correct feeling, when we desire to have those laws new modelled, those institutions otherwise arranged? And that woman, whose part, hitherto, has been only that of suffering from them, may lend her assistance in rendering them more consistent with truth and justice? We have yet to learn that it is an error so to do; or that, in so doing, we shall be led to think less warmly of those beautiful and finer traits that should, and one day will, adorn the character of woman.

There is much talk about family interests and family affection; but how are these dealt with in our code of laws? The law of inheritance, of marriage settlements, and of dower; the law of divorce, and that which relates to the custody of infants, etc. etc., do they evidence a regard towards the promotion of family affection? Does it not frequently oppose the son to the mother, the brother to the sister, the husband to the wife, and the father against the mother of their children! The laws here alluded to, have reference only to parties endowed with some portion of the great desideratum – wealth; they, therefore, are taken especial care of, for so the law directs. But there are in society some who have no wealth; they have families, however, and how are the interests of these families secured? What does the law for them? I know not what it may promise to do, but we behold it doing absolutely nothing; family interests in these cases are not understood. If there is any doubt, look at the families of the poor, industrious, and suffering millions! But to maternal affection, what want of respect, what gross violation is shown? The mother, in the highest circles of life, when separated from her husband, in accordance with the law of divorce, may have all intercourse with her children denied to her, however free from suspicion her conduct may have been; while, in consonance with the New Poor Law, the wretched creature, deficient, perhaps, in her morals, destitute of food and shelter, and, with these, of every thing that can render the society of her child aught but a torture, *is commanded to fulfil her maternal duties.* Threats of the tread-mill, of transportation, of the exquisite refinement upon cruelty, which has succeeded to the application of the lash, in respect to woman – namely, solitary confinement in dark and dismal cells, with diet of bread and water, are continually being acted upon! What mockery, then, for man to talk of consideration for woman's delicacy of nerves and feelings, while he calmly assents to the continuation of horrors such as these!

Unkind world! It is not the mother alone, but it is the whole of society that is interested in the welfare of the young life, that, in the future, will either ornament or be the disgrace of his country. The mother – how affecting to think of her in the house of greatness, weeping because her child is not near her, to lisp the accents of its love, or to gather fresh instruction from her lips; then to see the poor mourner, to whose sorrows, sufficient to bow down the strongest spirit, is added that of finding herself, alone, bereft of the support of *one* human being out of the great family of man, all that the law has left of friend or parent to smile upon, to succour, or to protect her hapless, injured child. We will no longer dwell upon the effects of laws that we hold in so much abhorrence, as that we have described. It is enough that we find the same spirit of oppression in which the laws first took their rise manifestly in operation now; centuries have passed away, each one marked with the strongest proofs of woman's suffer-ings, from man's injustice; yet, no strenuous efforts have been made to crush the domination of this spirit, or to abate its virulence. And shall not the present generation commence, if they cannot succeed in accomplishing the whole of this great purpose? To continue in the path of error, when we know it to be such, is an evident departure from our duty, which cannot be too strongly impressed on the mind. To exert ourselves, in order that we may quit that path, and enter upon another, where the several relations of life shall be maintained with propriety of word and action, and woman be considered as worthy the esteem, the confidence, the full respect, of the race of man, in return for her care, tenderness, and affectionate sympathy – to exert ourselves, I repeat, in endeavours to attain this state of felicity is no idle pursuit, nor is it calculated to lessen the desire we all have to become wiser and better.

Kate.[22]

New Moral World, 29 June 1839.

Margaret Chapellsmith's Lectures

Manchester District – On Wednesday, the 4th ultimo, Mrs Chapell-smith, of London, commenced a course of four lectures, in the lower room of the Hall of Science, Campfield.[23] The first lecture was on 'The Progress of Machinery, and the Remedy'. The matter was exceedingly good and well arranged; numerous facts were adduced to exhibit the consequences which had proceeded, and were likely to proceed, from the application of mechanical power, with a system of individual competition; and the remedy, co-operation, was pointed out with great force and eloquence. Mrs C.'s delivery is very good, and from the very favourable impression made upon an excellent audience, we doubt not but that her other lectures will be bumpers. She has also commenced similar courses of lectures in Stockport, Oldham, and Bolton.

New Moral World, 21 March 1840.

Progress

Barnsley – Mrs Chapellsmith delivered a lecture in the Odd Fellow's Hall, on Monday evening, the 11th inst., on the Marriage system proposed by the Socialists. The lecture was well attended, and was most favourably received. The demeanour of the Lecturer was of such a character, as entirely to preclude any thing disrespectful being said either of her or the cause she so ably advocates. No opposition was offered, and it is hoped that Mrs C. will shortly again favour the friends here with another lecture. Individuals not at all connected with Socialism were so pleased that they offered subscriptions to assist in defraying the expences of the lecturer.

New Moral World, 23 May 1840.

Mrs Chapellsmith in Scotland – The following is a brief statement of Mrs Chapellsmith's labours in the cause of Social Reform, in Glasgow and the surrounding towns, during the past month. At the above place, on Sunday, May 21st, she gave her 'Experience or her Reasons for becoming a Rational Religionist'. This lecture was received with evident signs of great satisfaction by an audience which was too large for the room. On Monday she lectured at Paisley on 'Marriage', to the largest audience they ever had there. On Wednesday, Thursday, and Sunday she lectured at Glasgow, on the 'Formation of Character'; 'Practicability of Communities'; and 'Marriage'. On Monday, June 8th, she lectured at Kilmarnock on 'Marriage'. There were about 300 persons present. Many disgusting remarks were made upon Mrs C., and upon the subject of her lecture, previous to her entering the room. Many of the audience laughed, and looked deridingly, at the commencement of the lecture; but, as she proceeded, they became surprised; from surprise their looks changed to those of attention; and at length they became deeply interested. On Tuesday she lectured on the 'Progress of Machinery'; and though the audience was not so large, the results were equally satisfactory. On Thursday and Friday she lectured at Glasgow. On the latter evening the audience was not so large (about 300). Opposition was courted, but none could be obtained. On Sunday, June 14th, she lectured in the morning and evening at Paisley, to audiences of betwixt two and three hundred each time. On Monday the room was crowded to hear her 'Experience'. On Tuesday and Wednesday she lectured at Kilbarchan, in a room capable of holding about 240 comfortably, but into which 300 were crammed. No opposition could be obtained here. In Glasgow, on Sunday morning, June 21st, Mrs C. delivered a lecture on the 'Protestant Reformation'; and in the evening she lectured again. On this occasion the room was crammed to suffocation, and many were refused admittance. This lecture was re-delivered on Tuesday night at a Methodist Infant School, which is situated in another part of the town. When she left the place a number of children and young people who had evidently been set on, commenced hallooing and throwing stones, and shouting 'Owenite', 'Socialist', 'Mrs Chapellsmith'. Some of the stones hit the persons who were escorting her home; and one woman darted forward and snatched her veil, with the intention of doing mischief, which was prevented by a companion of the woman drawing her back. The mob followed for seven or eight minutes, until Mrs C. and her party reached the police office, when they withdrew. On Thursday, Mrs C. lectured at Johnstone, on 'Marriage'. There were about 350 persons present. The lecture was received in the same manner, and attended with the same satisfactory results as at Kilmarnock. On Friday, she lectured on the 'present condition of Society', which though as well received, was not quite as well attended. On Sunday, June 28th, she lectured at Glasgow, 'on the rights, duties, and education of Woman', and on Monday, at Rutherglen, a small town near here. There were about 120 present. The only objection made, was to having called working-men *creators*, instead of *producers* of wealth. On Friday, she lectured at Irvine; on Wednesday, at Ayr; on Tuesday, at Irvine again; and on Friday, at Stewarton. There have been no lectures on Socialism previous to these, at the last three places. They were attended by a genteel class of persons, and are likely to be productive of benefit to the cause. With respect to the press, the *Glasgow Constitutionalist*, and the *Paisley Advertiser*, have been bestowing the most virulent abuse upon her. They term her a disseminator of disgusting blasphemies and immoralities – a she-devil – and other characteristic terms. However, as a set-off to this, we insert the opinions of another opponent. It is from the 'Pepper Box'.

We don't understand Socialism. We have a mortal hatred of all *isms* whatever, because we consider that in *ism* there must of necessity be sectarian-*ism*. We are no way acquainted with the views of the Socialists, but we like the name, for profoundly social are we ourselves, and disposed at all times to hob-nob it with any good fellow who possesses a good upper story. A good fellow did we say – yes, a good fellow, whether of the masculine or feminine gender; and that in the shape of a travelling fellow – a comical fellow – a bed fellow – or, if you will have it, a lecturing fellow. Now, though we profess not to understand the mysteries of Socialism, or how all mankind would be happy if placed within the walls of a parallelogram, yet we have a deep respect and a sincere love for all who from the fount of true benevolence seek to wash away the stains that have hitherto disfigured and blackened the countenances and hearts of the human family; and of this description do we regard the highly intellectual and accomplished lady who is now seeking to promulgate her views of human improvement, in the Hall of Science. There is a depth of feeling, a correctness of taste, an elegance of manner, and an easiness in Mrs Chapellsmith's orations, that at once, despite our hatred of *ism*, places her in our estimation as worthy to be listened to; and if in error, worthy to be refuted; which, with the help of common sense, we will endeavour to do in our next.

The following is our opponent's 'common-sense' refutation of Socialism:

We have really no time this week to fulfil our promise of refuting the new schism, call *Socialism*, but we are, nevertheless, resolved to fulfil our pledge, when once we have had time to comprehend what the Socialists would be at. We merely understand – and they must excuse our extreme ignorance – that they want to make men and women live in respectable parallelograms, with schools and colleges in the corner, and cookshops in the centre, and that they are to live and be merry for to-morrow they die. Now, we have no objection to the good living – turkies [sic], and capons, and roasted and boiled, and plenty of every thing, vegetable and animal, which the stomach can desire and digest, are all capital things; and could we be assured of an eternal feast of this sort, we would be a Socialist to-morrow: but imaginary feasts and real feasts – utopian schemes and cold reality, have ever proved to be two different things; and till we have a truly *practical* lesson of the working of the system, we must consent to jog on in the old beaten track of the competitory system. Our opinion really is, that the Socialists are a set of men and women, whose philanthropy, or cynicism, have disqualified them for holding a place in society as it is at present constituted, and that they should employ the *rent* to the hiring of vessels, and transport themselves to some uninhabited island as fast as they can. We went and heard Mrs Chapellsmith on Sunday evening, and were quite charmed with her manner of lecturing, we have so seldom an opportunity of witnessing anything so splendid in the female form and character; but as for her opinions of the monetary system, we can only believe them when we are convinced that British society has been only retrograding since the days when the peasant feasted luxuriantly on threepence-halfpenny a-day. We think that in our own time mankind in general are not worse off than they were. They are not so well as they should, or deserve to be; but still, truth is truth, and our artizans, in general, are better clad, housed, and fed than in any former period of British history.

We admit the injustice of the aristocracy – the avarice and hypocrisy of the priesthood – the insolence of the Tories – the truckling of the Whigs – the morality of the Chartists – the piety of the Socialists; but withal, we are chary about embracing any scheme for the regeneration of the human family, till we are persuaded of its not being liable to those objections which experience has ever demonstrated attendant on plans, by which want, and the fear of want, has been held up as things that can be dispensed with, in urging on the great march of intellectual and moral improvement.

New Moral World, 1 August 1840.

Emma Martin's Lecture Tour

Northampton – Mrs Martin lectured at our Institution yesterday afternoon, on the errors of our present Social System, particularly as respects the condition of women; after displaying the great and appalling evil of society as at present constituted, and the opposition generally made to all improvements, she dwelt upon the inefficient education of her own sex, especially in those arts and sciences which would assist them in the discharge of their duties as wives and mothers, and commented upon the apathy existing among women upon this important subject. The audience was numerous and respectable; and I think I may say the only feeling of the company were those of admiration of the lecture itself, and of the very pleasing and impressive manner in which it was delivered. In the evening Mrs M. again lectured on the religion of the New Moral World; the foundation of which was stated to be universal benevolence. Mrs M. instituted a comparison between the various religions of the world, and proved that that advocated by Robert Owen contained all the best parts of each, and was calculated in a superior degree to satisfy, direct, and elevate the human mind. It was true it had no creed – no ceremony – except the charity she recommended could be termed so. She concluded one of the most powerful, pleasing, and instructive addresses I have ever heard, by inviting any lady or gentleman to come forward and object to any thing she had advanced, if they dissented from her views, saying that by these means she might be led to refute any objections which the arguments contained in her lectures had not fairly met. No one, however, came forward for that purpose; but three persons came forward as candidates of the branch.

J. Gurney, Secretary.
New Moral World, 30 May 1840.

Macclesfield, Jan. 27 – On Sunday, Monday, and Tuesday evenings, the 17th, 18th, and 19th instant, we had a course of lectures from the talented Mrs Martin, whose powers of oratory and logical skill must convince the most scrupulous, that *woman* is capable of being trained and educated equal with man. The order of her lectures ran thus: 1, 'Religion of the New Moral World'; 2, 'The Doctrine of Responsibility'; 3, 'The Marriage System'. It is unnecessary to say more upon these lectures, here, as the audiences were so well satisfied with the arguments adduced by the lecturess, that, at the concluding lecture, they passed the following resolution:

Resolved – 'That it is the opinion of this meeting, that Mrs E. Martin will render the cause of human improvement a great and lasting benefit, if she will kindly condescend to have her three lectures published.'

This resolution was passed unanimously.

New Moral World, 6 February 1841.

Darlington, March 6 – A course of four lectures has been delivered in this town, by Mrs Martin, of London, to highly respectable and attentive audiences. On Sunday evening last, the lecture was on the 'Philosophy of Religion', when Mrs Martin clearly proved, that the only true religion was the religion of nature, and that all religions founded on particular creeds, were false. On Tuesday evening, on 'False Religions of Ancient and Modern Times', when the lecturess clearly demonstrated to the audience, that the whole of the rites, ceremonies, etc., of the pseudo Christian religion, were founded on, and derived from, the heathen mythology of times long prior to the period ascribed to the birth of Christ. On Wednesday evening, on 'Responsibility to Man and God'. Mrs Martin commenced by giving a brief explanation of human nature; shewing the ignorance of legislators and priests, of all ages, on the subject; next shewing the relation men (living in a state of society) bear to each other; and, lastly, the relation subsisting between man and God, proving that man could be no more responsible to God for his actions, the necessary result of his organisation, and the circumstances in which he was placed, than a machine could be to its maker for any defect in its construction. The last lecture was on 'Marriage and Divorce'. The lecturess, after animadverting on the unequal education of the two sexes, and the ridiculous distinctions created in society, through excess of wealth and abject poverty, laid down the only system by which the union of the sexes ought to be regulated, viz., the mental, moral, and physical fitness of the parties forming such union. The great and important truths contained in these lectures, were delivered in such a clear and energetic manner, as could not fail to bring conviction to the minds of all present, and a more interesting course of lectures has not been delivered in this town. The priests were boldly challenged (not only in the placards announcing the lectures, but also during each lecture), to come forward and defend their system, but not one of them dared to come forward. They know they cannot much longer support their system against the power of truth, and are therefore obliged to allow it to die its own natural death. That we may soon have the pleasure of preaching its funeral sermon, is the wish of

Robert Pincher, Sec.

New Moral World, 20 March 1841.

Reports from Mary Wiley[24]

Institution, 6, Frederick-Place, Goswell-Road, March 18 – I have great pleasure in informing you that to the parental government established in our branch may be mainly attributed the improvements which have taken place, and which are now in progress in the affairs of the branch, and in the institution generally. For the due execution of the business of the council, heads of departments have been appointed; to each has been appropriated the management of one of the five departments into which our business is divided – namely, finance and correspondence, lectures and discussions, library, notices and orders, and music and singing; the whole being under the direction of the president. A class for mutual instruction in the Social principles is also formed, consisting of the female members of our branch. Their first meeting was held on Sunday, March 13, when the following rules were unanimously adopted –

1st – To meet on Tuesday evening in each week at half-past eight, for mutual instruction, and to cultivate a knowledge of the Social principles.

2nd – That a moderator be appointed at each meeting.

3rd – That the meeting commence their business by reading a portion of some of the works of Mr Owen, as the foundation or text for the conversation of the class.

4th – That a tea party take place the first Sunday in each month.

5th – That the meetings of the class be open to all ladies who are desirous of Social improvement, and are willing to adopt the religion of charity.

6th – That gentlemen shall be admitted by card of introduction, obtained of the secretary.

In the evening we had a lecture on 'Phrenology', by Mr Jenneson, which created considerable interest; so much so that there was an unanimous request that the subject should be resumed on the following Sunday. The lecturer expressed his dissatisfaction with the principles laid down in the various treatises on 'Phrenology' – namely, that the size of the brain is the index of the mental power, and that the form indicates the moral feelings and physical propensities; and argued that the whole character of man is mainly formed by the influences of the circumstances by which he is surrounded; that the quality of the organization, rather than size or form, determine the general character of the mind; that the quality must uniformly be a consequence of the training and education imparted to the individual. The varied influences of education, trade, profession, civil institution, religion, and country, were illustrated by a diagram demonstrating in the clearest manner the true formation of character.

Mary Wiley, Sec.
New Moral World, 26 March 1842.

Institution, 6, Frederick Place, Goswell Road, Dec. 4 – Messrs Ainslie and Hughes, the Secretary, and one of the preachers of the London City Mission, having commenced a counter-agitation in this quarter of London, and our friends being prevented from replying in their chapel, they have resorted to the only other method left, and distributed tracts liberally at the door; and two of the friends are delivering lectures in reply on Sunday afternoon, on the origin of all religions.

Our efforts are still directed to various improvements which are in progress in the Institution, in order that it may become as one of the strongholds of Rationalism. We wish to make it attractive and respectable; and have therefore introduced vocal and instrumental music.

We have had Dr Bird to lecture; it was a model of eloquence and sound argument combined.

Mrs Chapellsmith followed, on Nov. 20, her subject was, on the Rights, Duties, and Education of Women; and the subject was resumed on the following Sunday. Mrs Chapellsmith attracts more than any lecturer in our institution; on this occasion she surpassed her former efforts: this was evinced by the strong feeling shown by the delighted audience, the expression of which was not to be restrained.

In answer to a question, whether the degradation of women was to be attributed to phrenological inferiority, of the circumstances of their domestic slavery and want of proper education – she answered, if inferiority was to be admitted, it must be attributed to both causes; the mental culture of the female is neglected; and the efforts she makes to emancipate herself from domestic thraldom, and the slavery of superstition, are frequently chilled and depressed by priestly power and the tyranny of custom: thus is her phrenological development first rendered weak, and that weakness is attempted to be perpetuated by injustice in the arrangements of the circumstances permitted to surround her. Much interest was created at the conclusion by Mrs C. publicly naming a child; this gave her an opportunity of contrasting the Rational arrangements in religion, political economy, and education, with the competitive mal-arrangements of society. Our institution is now open during the week as a lady's school; Miss Thetford, one of our members, having consented to conduct it; with a view to introduce as much of the Rational principles as present circumstances will permit.

Mary Ann Wiley, Sec.
New Moral World, 10 December 1842.

Betsy Willis

Wallingford, March 14 – Since my last report I have had the opportunity of visiting several of the dissenting ministers of different denominations of this town, whom I had supplied with Mr Owen's works, and who are now reading the *New Moral World* regularly. I was received by all of them in a very friendly manner. They all thanked me very kindly for what I had sent them, and express a wish, if it was possible, to see the system in practice. At one of these gentlemen's residence I have been met by several violent opponents; and after they had spent their furious and abusive language against Mr Owen, I asked them if they had ever read any of Mr Owen's works. They said they had not. I then said I did not wonder they saw it in the light they did, from the false reports that had been circulated, and in a short time I was able to cool them down to a reasonable argument, and have not only parted from them in good friendship, but have prevailed on most of them to read for themselves. Not one of them has ever showed any dislike to me for my principles; all expressing their belief that I was perfectly sincere. One thing has been in my favour, as it appears to me, that I have their good opinion. My conduct through life must be well known, as I have been in business in this town now just forty years. I have more readers than I can supply. Many good mechanics and trades' people, who are afraid to acknowledge their principles openly. I enclose you a note I received from a schoolmaster. I do think if I can find a leader we should soon form a good class here. I hope I shall soon be able to pay them all a visit, and see what I can do. Having received the power to shield myself with the impregnable armour of truth, I have been able to weather the storms most gloriously, and have nothing to fear, even should the tempest be more violent. All is calm and sunshine both within and without.

Betsy Willis
New Moral World, 9 April 1842.

Emma Martin's Funeral Oration for Richard Carlile

*A Funeral Sermon, occasioned by the death of Richard Carlile, preached at
the Hall of Science, City Road, London, by Emma Martin.*
London: Watson, Paul's Alley, Paternoster Row.

The authoress of this discourse is one of those admirable women who
prove that the appellation of 'better half' of mankind, is no fictional
compliment, but a sober and cheering verity. No woman ever before
said the bold and excellent things which continually fall from the lips
of this lady. Not less quick in perceiving just principles than energetic
in advocating just action – she stands forward in denouncing conventional wrong, when men are found cold, calculating, and prudent.
When public meetings have been held to solicit protection for parties
imprisoned for opinions' sake – no matter what their opinions were –
no matter whether they were atheists or not – no matter that men had
certain squeamish fears about taking an unqualified part in their
defence – no matter who approved or who disapproved – without
caring for certain respectable cant, relative to feelings, propriety, and
decency outraged – she stood the eloquent and uncompromising
defender of every man and woman's right to speak their own sentiments in their own words. In this generous spirit she has, in her
discourses, paid a noble compliment to Carlile. The remarks on the
injurious direction given by rulers to public opinion is excellent – the
estimation of the value of Mr Carlile's recent policy is accurate – and
the promise that religion shall yet pay dearly for the shortened days of
our champion of the press's liberty, is bravely given, and it is the duty
of every infidel to see that it is religiously fulfilled.

G.J.H.
Oracle of Reason, 22 April 1843.

The Ladies' Class of the Rational Society

The Objects and Laws of the Ladies' Class,
Branch A 1 of the Rational Society[25]
Established February 4th, 1844.
OBJECTS

To promote the individual and collective happiness of every man,
woman, and child, without regard to sect, country, colour or class.
1st. By the circulation of useful, practical information.
2nd. By the cultivation of social and industrial habits, and the taste
for literary and scientific pursuits – including the song and the practice
of the pianoforte.

3rd. By acquiring a practical knowledge of the science of human nature, the science of the formation of character, and the science of society, as developed in the outline of the Rational System of society; and by giving all possible assistance to the establishment of Communites of united interest.

4th. By taking an active part in the business of the Branch, and assisting each other in times of affliction.

RULES

1. That all members of this class, whose husbands are paying to the General Fund, shall pay one penny per week; and all females, whether wives of non-members or otherwise, shall pay twopence per week, and sixpence entrance. This shall constitute them members of the Rational Society.

2. That this class meet every Sunday afternoon at three o'clock for the transaction of general business, the reception of members, and the free expression of opinion on all subjects; and on Tuesday evenings at seven o'clock, for mutual instruction, etc., and at such other times as they may determine.

3. That a Health Insurance Fund for themselves and families be connected with the class, subject to the following regulations:

Name: Health Insurance Fund for Females and their Families.

Objects: To provide medicine and medical attendance for themselves, their husbands, and children.

Subscriptions: For each member of the class one penny per week, and the same for each member of her family, to be paid in advance.

All surplus funds to be at the disposal of the class.

New members can only join this fund on the first Sunday in each month, and must declare themselves in good health at the time.

All members are free to the benefits of the fund immediately.

All parties not paying up their subscriptions at the end of each quarter will not be entitled to further benefits until arrears are paid.

The medical attendant shall wait upon each applicant on the receipt of a note or message, and shall send the medicines to the patient if required. All glass to be either returned or paid for; and all applications, when practicable, to be sent to his residence before eleven o'clock in the morning.

Government: The fund shall be managed by a Committee, consisting of President, Treasurer, Secretary, and three members of the class.

The whole class will be under the general superintendence of the President and Council of Branch A 1.

Officers of the Class

President .... Mrs Eliza Skelton
Treasurer .... Mrs Mary Ann Abbey
Secretary .... Miss Charlotte Hudson
Medical Officer .... Mr George Bird

7, Union Place, New Road,
(Opposite the Marylebone Infirmary.)

In the evening, Mr Ellis[26] lectured to a crowded audience, 'On the inutility and injustice of Prosecutions for Blasphemy'. It was a powerful and eloquent exposure of the injustice, irrationality, and evils of persecution for opinion's sake; but space will not permit us to give an outline. Mr Ellis concluded his lecture by a most powerful appeal to his audience, in behalf of the 'Anti-Persecution Union'.[27] At the end of the lecture, a collection was made in aid of the funds of the committee of this Branch, when the sum of nearly four pounds was realized, making in all, between six and seven pounds collected by the committee in aid of the 'Anti-Persecution Union'. We understand that our friends of the Glasgow Branch intend presenting Miss Roalfe with the sum of ten pounds, at the expiration of her imprisonment; these are examples worthy of imitation, by all friends to freedom; and which, if responded to by our friends of the other Branches throughout the country, will give a deadly blow to all persecutions for opinion's sake.

New Moral World, 16 March 1844.

Emma Martin's Second Tour

Mrs Martin's Tour – Mrs Martin has delivered a course of three lectures in Leicester which were well attended. In Nottingham she announced a sermon on the execution of Saville, from the text, 'Their feet are swift to shed blood, destruction and misery are in their path, and the way of peace they have not known'. She engaged the 'Assembly Rooms' for its delivery, but that being held by parsons and magistrates, its use was refused. Not to be prevented fulfilling her object, she delivered her sermon in the market place, where she had the satisfaction of addressing 5000 people, and the mayor, who was present, and who we believe is a liberal man, had the gratification of seeing that although the brutal exhibition of a *public murder*, attended by priestly teachers, may bring together a multitude, that there are other and better who for wiser purposes can gather the people together, and turn their thoughts into nobler channels. Mrs M. lectured in the evening in the same place. A tea party was held in honour of Mrs Martin, at which the affair of the market place was described as 'the best thing which had happened for socialism there'. Two pounds were presented to her by way of compensation for losses through being deprived of the Assembly Rooms. Mrs M. next lectured in Derby, and on Sunday last in Manchester. On Sunday, Sept. 1, she lectures in Preston, and on Monday and Tuesday, Sept. 2, 3. On Wednesday, Sept.4, she lectures in Bolton. Mrs Martin's address is Hall of Science, Manchester, to which place applications can be made by Branches desiring her services.

Movement, 31 August 1844.

Mrs Martin's Tour
(From a Correspondent)

Considering that the *Movement* should be made more the recorder of the doings of infidels all over the country than it has been, I will trouble you with a remark or two relative to Mrs Martin's doings in these parts.

Being at Nottingham when Mrs Martin was there, I was cognizant of the proceedings relative to her sermon on 'Capital Punishments' noticed in a recent number of your journal. The room was taken and paid for – no questions being asked as to the class of persons intended to be admitted, but on placing a board, on which was a placard stating the admission to be *one-penny*, at the door, the shareholders, in the person of a priest, who is one of them, declared the sermon should not be delivered, as such a price would admit all the 'scum of the town', 'the sweepings of the streets' – such was the classic language with which one of *god's own* chosed to honour those whom kingly tyranny and priestly delusion had made poor. Well might Mr Owen say 'the mere theological made mind is not only the most useless and irrational, but it is also the most injurious upon earth'. At the time of meeting the people collected in hundreds, and loud murmurs of disappointment were heard in all directions, until some one in the crowd proposed that Mrs Martin be requested to write an address on the subject. The subscription was immediately made. She agreed. The address was written and issued immediately, calling upon the people to attend in the Marketplace, on Sunday, at three o'clock, at which time Mrs Martin made her appearance in an open carriage, and delivered her sermon to an audience of at least five times the number that could have obtained admission to the room that had been taken for the purpose. I hardly need say the sermon was of the right sort, and went to the very root of the evil, whence has originated the crimes that have rendered capital punishments apparently necessary. Kingcraft and priestcraft, and the Bible as the text book of both, were denounced as the great obstacles to the improvement of the people.

Christianity was shewn to be the best apology for crime, while it was the most decided opponent of every thing that could elevate, enlighten, and improve mankind. These sentiments were received with the most evident satisfaction – a proof that the people are prepared to hear the whole truth on such subjects. Anti-Theological sentiments are not so frightful to the great mass of the people, as some of our *half* 'theologically made minds' (which half Mr Owen tells us is so much insanity) would have us believe. Finding her sentiments so favourably received, Mrs Martin announced her intention of delivering another address in the evening. The people assembled in the evening in numbers at least equal to – some say greater than – in the afternoon. The subject was 'The Bible and Missionary Societies' – exposing their follies and crimes; a fruitful theme, which I assure you had justice done it, with perfect satisfaction to the audience, who were heard inquiring in all directions at the close, 'when will she come again?'

Afterwards we had four lectures in Derby, at the Old Assembly Room, at which nothing unusual occurred. With the exception of an attempt, by a well-dressed drunken christian, to create a disturbance on the fourth night, the lectures have passed off well.

H. Roche.
Movement, 14 September 1844.

Persecution in Hull

Persecution of the meanest and most despicable kind has been commenced in Hull. Mrs Martin lately delivered a lecture in that town, on the Crimes and Follies of Christian Missions; Mr Watson, who let his room for the purpose, has been fined by the Magistrates (on summons) £1 and 9s. costs for doing so; and Mr Johnson, Bookseller, who it appears took twopence of one James Freeman, has been fined in the same way, £20 and costs, for the same offence. There is something manly in prosecutions for blasphemy, compared with this petty malignity. A man indicted is heard in his own defence, but in this case, with scarcely a hearing, a man is ruined for doing only that which other public parties, Dissenters and Churchmen, are doing daily with impunity. The Police were immediately in possession of Mr Johnson's house and property, and on Monday the sale of his property was to take place. One result of this persecution is, the determination of the people of Hull, to have a Hall of their own. Now that religion has peeped out on the good people of Hull in its native form, they will deserve to live for ever under its curse, if they do not bestir themselves to strike it down. Mrs Martin is agitating the town, and we call on the friends of the Anti-Persecution Union, to immediately send in subscriptions, to enable the Union to act as may seem most fitting.

Mrs Martin

This lady who has been lecturing on the 'Missionary Imposture', has created marvellous excitement in this town of piety and spinning jennies; one of the great missionary meetings was announced to be held in Mosely Street Chapel, Sept. 30, and Mrs M. placarded her intention of being present, which seems to have brought thousands there. Just as the first resolution was about being put to the meeting Mrs Martin rose, in one of the pews, and desired permission to speak; upon this she was assailed with yells from all parts of the Chapel, which were answered by vehement cheering from more than half the persons present, who seemed friendly to Mrs M. being heard. One female saint, near Mrs Martin, threatened 'to poke her umbrella through Mrs M.'s bonnet'. The whole Police Corps appear to have been sent for by the Chairman, and entered the meeting; but a number of sturdy mechanics belonging to one of the principal firms in the town, surrounded Mrs M. and protected her from arrest. Placards we are told have since been put out headed something to this effect, 'send for the Police – the Missionaries are in want of the Police!' And Mrs Martin has delivered a lecture on her 'Adventures at the Missionary Meeting'. Mr Geo. Smith,[28] of Salford, has been threatened with prosecution for selling blasphemy, and the religious world of Manchester seems turning up side down, poor thing!

Since writing the preceding, we have had a very warm letter from Mr Smith of Salford, fully corroborating the preceding statements. From his letter it appears that the meeting was opened with prayer, but when Mrs M. appeared, instead of calling upon God the preacher called upon the Police, they knew who was most likely to help them. Mrs M. was struck at with sticks, and it was an elegantly dressed lady who actually poked her precious parasol at Mrs M.'s head.

We understand that the Inhabitants of Colne, where Mrs Martin has visited, have erected a tent for her accommodation.

At Hull, Mrs Martin has held a discussion within these few days, with a Rev. Pulsford, at which high prices were offered for Tickets of Admission. The subject of discussion was 'the Evidences of Christianity'.

Movement, 16 October 1844.

Mary Jenneson's Report from the Finsbury Institution

Finsbury Institution, Branch 16 – We are endeavouring at this Institution to become conservatives of the Social principles. In prosecution of this object, we have continued from the commencement of the present quarter a consecutive course of lectures on Rational principles and practice. Mr Shorter followed up the lectures on the Formation of Character by one on the Principles, Laws, and Objects of the Rational Society. The next was Answers to the Objections to Socialism, which consisted of a review of the attacks on the philosophy of Socialism contained in the lectures published by the Rev. J. Cubitt on the Doctrine of Circumstances. In the third lecture, Mr Shorter replied to the objections alleged to exist in the way of Socialism by the defenders of the Malthusian[29] theory. The efficacy of our friend's arguments was manifest by the profound attention and marked approbation, which was not to be suppressed, particularly on the occasion of the reply to Mr Fox,[30] which, as an example of general eloquence and sound reasoning, has not been surpassed at this Institution. After these excellent discourses, our friend, Mr Cooper,[31] favoured us with two lectures, one on Marriage and Divorce, the second on Rational Religion as a Means of securing Happiness to Mankind, and to extinguish Misery among the Human Race. We have been compelled to depend on our own local resources for lectures for a considerable length of time, but this has occasioned us no cause for regret at present. Mr C. is a decided favourite here, and always attracts crowded and respectable audiences. Indeed, we found this to be decidedly the best policy to bring before the public boldly and unequivocally the leading principles of the Social System: our friends always exerting a careful discretion, I am happy to say, in excluding mere controversial and sectarian disputations, which have hitherto had so injurious a tendency, creating feuds and party spirit, where only charity, union, and national conciliation should exist. One proof of the efficacy of our course of proceeding we can give. We have in course of delivery a series of lectures, on Wednesday evenings, on philosophical and scientific subjects, Dr Bowkett, of Poplar, having been requested to deliver one on his plan to abolish poverty, by enabling the industrious classes to obtain freehold property by forming themselves into associations for that purpose. The propositions of Dr B. being generally approved of, it was thought advisable to call a public meeting to consider the same, which accordingly took place, (Nov. 5) Dr Bowkett in the chair. The meeting was well attended. Resolutions were passed unanimously approving of the plan. The requisite number of names are enrolled, viz., 100, and we are now enrolling subscribers to another association of 100 more. Many of these persons are most respectable inhabitants of the district, who have agreed to associate with our members and friends, without making distinction of class, sect, or party, for the attainment of what they conceive to be a practical individual improvement, and ultimately a national benefit – thus proving how much our progress and permanent standing in any locality depends on a conciliatory bearing towards our opponents. Upon the whole, our progress is satisfactory. We called a meeting of our members to consider the communication from the Central Board relative to the day's wages subscription, and several of our members responded to the call.

Mary Jenneson, Sec.
New Moral World, 6 December 1844.

Notes

1. George Jacob Holyoake, *The History of Co-operation*, 1906, p. 241.
2. See Chapter 7, n. 4.
3. William Cobbett, *Paper Against Gold*, 1815, 2 vols. A collection of 32 articles or letters first published in the *Political Register*.
4. Abel Heywood (1810–93) Chartist, radical and bookseller. Possibly the best-known victim of the agitation for the freedom of the press. He was the leading distributor of cheap periodicals in south Lancashire. He was twice imprisoned for selling the unstamped papers and twice became Mayor of Manchester.
5. An Owenite community in Pennsylvania, America. Robert Owen and over 900 people attempted to live there and when Owen returned to England, his son, Robert Dale Owen, remained in the community.
6. Alexander Campbell (1796–1870), prominent Scots Cooperator, imprisoned for selling the unstamped press. A social missionary, he was Secretary of the Glasgow Carpenters' Union.
7. When a series of legal actions was instituted by the Church of England clergy to prevent lectures being given in the Halls of Science on Sundays, the Rational Religionists replied by establishing the hall as a place of worship belonging to a body of Protestant Dissenters and registered at the Bishop's Court. This brought it under the Act of Parliament which licensed it to be open for divine service. Some lecturers then took the oath of allegiance to the Church and were able to conduct services in the Hall. But those Owenite missionaries who refused to participate in such a subterfuge continued to defy the law and were frequently imprisoned for it. They were called the 'infidel' missionaries.
8. See Chapter 3, n. 15.
9. *Movement*, 27 November 1844, p. 437.
10. George Jacob Holyoake, *The Last Days of Emma Martin*, p. 4.
11. The National Equitable Labour Exchange was opened on Monday 17 September 1832 in premises in Gray's Inn Road near King's Cross. The logo of the *Crisis* is a representation of the building.
12. There were a number of attempts to open exchange bazaars at which goods produced by producer cooperatives or individuals could be exchanged for notes denoting the labour time involved in the production. William King, who had been editor of the *Brighton Co-operator* was

instrumental in establishing the Exchange at the Gothic Hall, New Road, in April 1832.

13. Labour notes were an attempt to obtain for the producer the full value of his work by cutting out the middleman. Notes were given on the basis of a ten-hour day at six pence an hour. All rates of labour together with the value of the raw materials used were expressed in terms of the hourly unit. A commission of one penny in the shilling was charged to cover the costs of the exchange.

14. 14 Charlotte Street was opened on 1 May 1833 as a social institution where lectures could be given and trade union branches meet. It was also the venue of the Equitable Labour Exchange.

15. B. Warden was a saddler and harness-maker, co-founder of the Metropolitan Trades Union and active in the British Association for the Promotion of Cooperative Knowledge.

16. See Chapter 8, n. 12.

17. See biography of Anna Wheeler in Chapter 10, p. 205.

18. A French Utopian-Socialist (1772–1837).

19. See Introduction to Chapter 8.

20. *Star in the East* was published in Wisbech 1836–40.

21. Mary Leman Grimstone was a feminist of a radical liberal hue whose writing was published in the Owenite press.

22. Catherine Isabella Barmby (1817–53), a feminist and Socialist who often wrote in the *New Moral World*. She used the pseudonym 'Kate'. There is a full biography in Bellamy and Saville, *Dictionary of Labour Biography*, 1982, vol VI, p. 10.

23. The Hall of Science at Campfield was opened by Robert Owen in January 1840. This was the largest of such halls and could seat almost 3,000 people. A full programme of lectures, discussions and social events was held there.

24. Mary Wiley was Secretary of the Finsbury Branch of the Association of All Classes of All Nations. She was the only female to give continuous leadership over a number of years. She attended the Congress in 1843, the only female delegate, although several other women went in an unofficial capacity. The lack of women in leading positions in the formal Owenite organisation was a constant subject of controversy.

25. In 1842 the Owenite organisation known as 'The Universal Community Society of Rational Religionists' was renamed simply 'The Rational Society' with the aim to make man a rational being and society united, wealthy, intelligent and happy.

26. John Ellis was an Owenite missionary with extreme views on marriage, on which he wrote a pamphlet.

27. The 'infidel' missionaries formed the Anti-Persecution Union to campaign against the persecution and imprisonment of its adherents. Its main journal was the *Oracle of Reason*.

28. George Smith was a prominent member of the Association of All Classes of All Nations – not to be confused with Joseph Smith, also of Salford, who financed the building of the Salford Social Institution in Great George Street in 1835.

29. Thomas Robert Malthus (1766–1834), clergyman and economist. Author of *An Essay on the Principles of Population* which was used by reactionaries to justify a number of attacks on working people's standards of living. His adherents followed his ideas and called themselves Malthusians and his doctrine Malthusianism.

30. William Johnson Fox (1786–1864), unitarian minister, publicist and political organiser. Editor of *True Sun* and *Monthly Repository*.

31. Robert Cooper (1819–68), a Manchester radical who became a prominent Owenite lecturer.

7

Marriage and the New Moral World

That the mutual affection of the people concerned should be the one paramount reason for marriage, outweighing everything else, was and always had been absolutely unheard of in the practice of the ruling classes; that sort of thing only happened in romance – or among the oppressed classes, who did not count.

Frederick Engels, *The Origin of the Family, Private Property and the State*, London 1940, p. 85.

Even love is sold; the solace of all woe
Is turned to deadliest agony.

Percy Bysshe Shelley, 'Queen Mab', v. 189.

Introduction

Frederick Engels asserted that Robert Owen's main contributions to progressive thought were his attempt to outline the future communist community and his views on marriage.

Women were not only treated as non-entities legally, they also suffered all the worst consequences of the rapidly developing competitive system. From the time of the slave state, women had been regarded as commodities to be used in commercial transactions between men. But the feudal state, whilst it failed to recognise or alleviate the worst abuses so far as women were concerned, did make family life more tolerable. While industry was based in the home and the members of the family were involved in production, women played a dignified role in the process. But the advent of technological change which took manufacture away from the home and lured women and children into the factories as cheap labour, while the traditional male head of the family unit became unemployed, made significant alterations to women's position both in society and in the family.

It was considered normal to apply different moral standards for men and women. Chastity was expected of women and execration followed any lapse; but for men, normality was the full exercise of sexual freedom.

Women who chafed under the obvious injustices heaped on them or who had personal experience of an unhappy and unsatisfactory marriage seized on the possibility of change held out in Owen's views on 'Marriage in the New Moral World'. The notion that children should be considered a social responsibility attracted women who felt the need to develop their talents and interests without being tied to perpetual childbearing and raising.

Women welcomed discussions on the marriage state, contraception and divorce and turned out in huge numbers to listen to lectures on these subjects and to participate in the ensuing debate.

Before legal changes made civil marriage a possibility, the Owenites instituted marriage ceremonies in which the partners made a public declaration of their intent to live together. At first these declarations were considered to be somewhat clinical as George Jacob Holyoake noted: 'No bright chamber, hall or temple to give distinction to the ceremony; only the business office of the Registrar of deaths infusing funeral associations into a wedding.'[1] But the socialists responded to such complaints by providing their own wedding ceremonies. Even before the new Marriage Act permitted civil ceremonies, the Owenites had performed simple secular services at New Harmony in the US where Owen's son, Robert Dale Owen, and Mary Robinson had signed a document waiving his 'unjust rights' over the person and property of his wife.

As well as secular marriage, the Owenite socialists performed 'Naming Ceremonies' and secular funerals so that the influence of the 'priesthood in the old immoral world' was reduced so far as possible.

Not all socialists went as far as Owen himself wanted. In a letter to Owen published in the *Crisis* as early as 1833, Concordia (Anna Wheeler) cautioned him to proceed at a pace at which society was able to follow. Otherwise, she forecast, 'the individuals who attempt to brave the public scorn, or to force it to reverse its decrees, only engage in a struggle which will finally end in the destruction of their happiness, and the injury of their cause'.[2]

* * *

The Marriage Ceremony Superseded

At Lawrence Street Chapel, Birmingham, May the 4th, after the morning service was over, Four Christian Dissenters, desiring the congregation to stop, 'took the marriage affair into their own hands', in the following manner:

(Copy)

Before this congregation, I, Charles Bradley, jun., give you, Emma

Harris, this ring to wear as a memorial of our marriage, and this written pledge, *stamped* with the impressions of the 'United Rights of Man and Woman', declaring I will be your faithful husband from this time henceforward.

(Signed)

Charles Bradley Jun.

(Copy)

Before this congregation, I, Emma Harris, receive this ring to wear as a memorial of our marriage, and give you, Charles Bradley, jun., this written pledge, *stamped* with the impressions of the 'United Rights of Man and Woman', declaring I will be your faithful wife from this time henceforward.

(Signed)

Emma Harris.

(Copy)

Before this congregation, I, Roger Holinsworth, give you, Mary Louisa Bradley, this ring to wear as a memorial of our marriage, and this written pledge, *stamped* with the impressions of the 'United Rights of Man and Woman', declaring I will be your faithful husband from this time henceforward.

(Signed)

Roger Holinsworth.

(Copy)

Before this congregation, I, Mary Louisa Bradley, receive this ring to wear as a memorial of our marriage, and give you, Roger Holinsworth, this written pledge, *stamped* with the impressions of the 'United Rights of Man and Woman', declaring I will be your faithful wife from this time henceforward.

(Signed)

Mary Louisa Bradley.

(Witnesses) Charles Bradley, Sen.
Hannah Bradley.
William Harris, Sen.
Elizabeth Harris.
Thomas Tennant.
Frances Bradley Tennant.
Edwin Bradley.
Charles Squire,
And forty-two others.

Poor Man's Guardian, 17 May 1834.

Robert Owen on Marriage

The following extracts from Mr Owen's writings, place his views on the subject of *Marriage* and *Divorce* in a clear and indisputable light; and furnish a most complete reply and refutation to the misstatements which have been so industriously circulated by means of garbled and disconnected quotations from his various publications, and by the most filthy and unfounded assertions of parties either excessively ignorant of Mr Owen's real views, or determined, in defiance of morality and truth, to distort and misrepresent them. They also prove beyond the possibility of doubt, the total disregard of truth in those parties who have endeavoured to make it appear that Mr Owen's denunciations of the '*Marriages of the Priesthood*', '*Indissoluble Marriage*', '*Marriages without affection*', etc. were applied to *all* Marriage.

FIRST EXTRACTS

From Mr Owen's Six Manchester Lectures, delivered in 1837. Shewing that the proposed arrangements of the New State of Society are formed with a view to promote the PERMANENCE of Marriage, the happiness of the parties united, especially of the Female sex, and the general good order and virtue of Society.[3]

Under this classification and consequent arrangement of society, every individual will be trained and educated, to have all his faculties and powers cultivated in the most superior manner known; cultivated too, under a new combination of external objects, purposely formed, to bring into constant exercise the best and most lovely qualities only of human nature. Each one will be thus well educated, physically, intellectually, and morally. Under this classification and consequent arrangement of these associated families, wealth, unrestrained in its production by any of the artificial absurdities now so common in all countries, will be most easily produced in superfluity; all will be secured in a full supply of the best of it, for all purposes that may be required. They will, therefore, all be equal in their education and condition, and no artificial distinction, or any distinction but that of age, will ever be known among them.

There will be then, no motive or inducement for any parties to unite, except from pure affection arising from the most unreserved knowledge of each other's character, in all respects, as far as it can be known before the union takes place. There will be no artificial obstacles in the way of permanent happy unions of the sexes; for under the arrangements of this new state of human existence, the affections will receive every aid which can be devised to induce them to be permanent; and under these arrangements, there can be no doubt, that, as the parties will be placed as far as possible in the condition of lovers during their lives, the affections will be far more durable, and produce far more pleasure and enjoyment to the parties, and far less injury to society, than has ever yet been experienced, under any of the varied arrangements which have emanated from the imagined free-will agency of the human race.

If however, these superior arrangements to produce happiness between the sexes, should fail in some partial instances, which it is possible may yet occur, measures will be introduced by which, without any severance of friendship between the parties, a separation may be made, the least injurious to them and the most beneficial to the interests of society.

No immorality can exceed that which is sure to arise from society compelling individuals to live continually together, when they have been made, by the laws of their nature, to lose their affections for each other, and to entertain them for another object. How much dreadful misery has been inflicted upon the human race, through all past ages, from this single error! How much demoralization! How many murders! How much secret unspeakable suffering, especially to the female sex! How many evils are experienced over the world, at this moment, arising from this single error of the imaginary free-will system by which men have been so long, so ignorantly, and miserably governed!

This portion of the subject, to do it full justice, would, alone, require a longer course than is now given to the development of the whole system under consideration; but this limited view must suffice at present, for a sketch or outline of what is in contemplation.

(Pages 76, 77)

SECOND EXTRACT

From Mr Owen's Address, delivered at the Charlotte-street Institution, London, in 1833. Shewing the object of the proposed changes in the laws of Marriage and Divorce; and the regulations proposed. (This is divided into paragraphs, with headings, for the sake of perspicuity.)

Many persons grossly mistake our views on the subject of the union of the sexes. Our object is to remove the causes of the immense amount of sexual crime and misery, and consequent physical and mental disease which now exists. It is nature's laws, now disregarded, which we desire to discover and implicitly obey; there being none other which can produce virtue and happiness. In the present absence of real knowledge, derived from experience, and with the existing irregular feelings of the population of the world, created by a false education, we propose that the union and disunion of the sexes should take place under the following regulations:

MARRIAGE

Announcement. Persons having an affection for each other, and being desirous of forming an union, first announce such intention publicly in our Sunday assemblies.

Preliminary Period. If the intention remain at the end of *three months,* they make a second public declaration.

Marriage. Which declarations being registered in the books of the Society will constitute their marriage.

Object of Marriage

Marriages will be solely formed to promote the happiness of the sexes; and if this end be not obtained, the object of the union is defeated.

DIVORCE

First – When Both Parties Desire to Separate

Announcement. Should the parties, after the termination of *twelve months, at the soonest,* discover that their dispositions and habits are unsuited to each other, and that there is little or no prospect of happiness being derived from their union, they are to make a public declaration as before, to that effect.

Preliminary Period. After which they return and live together *six months longer;* at the termination of which, if they still find their qualities discordant, and both parties unite in the declaration, they make a second declaration.

Divorce. Both of which being duly registered and witnessed, will constitute their legal separation.

Second – When One Only Desires a Separation

Preliminary Period. Should one alone come forward upon the last declaration, and the other object to the separation, they would be required to live together *another six months,* to try if their feelings and habits could be made to accord, so as to promote happiness.

Divorce. But if at the end of *the second six months,* the objecting party shall remain of the same mind, the separation is then to be final.

Position of the Parties After Divorce

The parties may, without diminution of public opinion, form new unions more suited to their dispositions.

Provision for the Children

As all the children of the new world will be trained and educated under the superintendence and care of the Society, the separation of the parents will not produce any change in the condition of the rising generation.

Concluding Remarks

Under these arrangements, we have no doubt, a much more virtuous and happy state of society will be enjoyed than any which has existed at any time in any part of the world.

THIRD EXTRACT

From Mr Owen's Address, April 29, 1839 (see New Moral World, *page 443.) Shewing that it is not contemplated that marriage should ever be annulled.*

My present impressions are, that for ever there must be rationally devised Marriage and Divorce, improved as society advances in knowledge and goodness.

FOURTH EXTRACT

From Mr Owen's Preface to his Manifesto, 1840. On the present Laws of Marriage and Divorce in England.

Since the publication of my views upon the old system of 'Marriage by the priesthood,' the *form of marriage,* by the new Marriage Act, has been made exactly to meet my ideas and wishes; and all that I now desire is to see another law enacted, by which *Divorces,* under wise arrangements, and on principles of common sense, may be obtained equally for rich and poor; to remove the chief cause of so much existing deception, prostitution, promiscuous intercourse, and crime, and the dreadful evils which necessarily flow from them to both sexes, but especially to the poor unprotected part of the female sex, whose extremity of suffering is so much hidden from the world. And this change in the law of Divorce is all that is now required to enable me, legally and immediately, to introduce to the world the most splendid practical arrangements, easy of introduction, for the emancipation of man from ignorance, poverty, division, and crime, that have ever yet been conceived, even in the most fervid and sanguine imaginations of poets, philosophers, and reformers, of past and present time.

Appendix to 'The Influence of the Present Marriage System', lecture by Frances Morrison, 2 September 1838.

Margaret Chapellsmith on Marital Relations

To the Editor of the *Dispatch*,[4]

September 23, 1838.

Sir,

In your paper of to-day, in your notice to correspondents, you have given expression to a most lamentable error, by which calumny and pain are inflicted on a large class; and, in the degree that your opinions have effect, their labours for themselves and fellow-creatures will be rendered nugatory.

You say, 'We cannot rank ourselves as admirers of Mr Owen's broad principle – *what we call virtue is vice, and what we call vice is virtue: nor do we think with him that it would be desirable to get rid of jealousy and its attendant crimes, by ABROGATING MATRIMONY, and permitting a PROMIS-CUOUS INTERCOURSE of the sexes; no man singling out and cherishing a female and her offspring, but every man working for the community, and to help to support all the women and all their children – a state in which the relation and duties of father and child would be equally unknown with those of husband and wife. The idea of a community in which there shall be "no disappointment of the affections; both sexes naturally enjoying the rights of their nature" – a sort of general partnership in wives, such as exist among savages, as we read in Mrs Frazer's narrative of the wreck of the Stirling Castle.'*

The case is, that Mr Owen, seeing the vast number of brothels and prostitutes which our own country, and the world in general, produces, is satisfied that the sentiments of veneration for chastity and conjugal fidelity which we everywhere hear, are merely on the tongues and not in the *minds* of the great mass of human beings. He also knows that the character of human beings must be deteriorated by such circumstances. They engender hypocrisy, for men profess to be what they are not; and women, who profess an abhorrence of libertinism in the abstract, are expected to 'love, honour, and obey' the associates of prostitutes. And should any woman in her veneration for virtue, and in her good faith that it is possessed by her lover, venture to assert her belief in his chastity, she would be laughed at as a good-natured fool; for the case would be deemed too rare to be probable. And women, in despair of meeting with any one better, take to their bosoms those whom, under a better system, they would look at with pity or disgust.

An association with prostitutes degrades the mind, because it affords no stimulus to the intelligence or to the sentiments; sources of permanent pleasure and dignity which the propensities never can afford.

Mr Owen cannot look at the unhappy prostitutes themselves, without wishing the system that produces the whole changed. He sees, that by injudicious education, and by vicious association, youth are led into vice before their reason has power to control. They arrive at maturity without the support of previous good conduct – they see our competitive system rendering their hopes of living *well* with a *wife* and *family*, impossible of realisation – they continue their profligate career, or they marry where they can obtain property; or, blinded by passion, they marry those whose character, in its most important points, they have never investigated; and who have been led by their own unhappy circumstances to veil, instinctively, their real selves, whose approbativeness, whose affections being excited – they speak, during courtship, the language of these alone. They marry – learn the unfitness of each to the other – disappointment ensues – they wear out life with altercation – and, too often, both husband and wife live in adultery: man, the privileged libertine, being the most likely to do so.

How frequently, under such a system, the husband and wife separate; and then what is more common than for them to form new attachments and to gratify them?

Mr Owen's system, by its certainty of producing abundant wealth and equal distribution, does away with all restraint upon marriage from pecuniary considerations, and does away with all temptation to form marriages from any other motive than affection.

By his system will be imparted to youth, as a matter of philosophical investigation, information which under any system they will obtain, but which under our system is obtained slyly, and in ways which ruin mind and body; and thus will they be led to perceive the evils of premature indulgence.

By his system of bringing up boys and girls from their infancy together, under the *immediate and continued* superintendence of their parents and of efficient teachers, which Mr Owen's system and no other will afford the means of doing, they will be together engaged in those healthy and intellectual pursuits to which their individual capacities fit them. Under such circumstances, boys and girls who resemble each other in intelligence and sentiments, will become attached, long before passion, except in very rare cases, can exist; and when it does arise, it must be towards those who have excited their kindliest feelings for so long. Mr Owen knows that feelings thus engendered are more binding, more enduring, than any legislative enactment; but, that nothing may be wanting to prevent that desecration of character which he abhors, he has *that* also; and, knowing how much public opinion controls, he calls that to his aid; for, he will have men and women, wishing to live together, come before a meeting of all the persons of a certain age, say from twenty to forty, in the community, and declare that such is their wish; and then, that it may not be done rashly, they must appear *again in three months*, and declare it to be their continued wish, and then they are deemed to be MARRIED.*

Under such circumstances, infidelity or jealousy are not likely to arise. There must be confidence that affection has determined the choice; and those who experience affection, know its intense, its enduring power. But, as it might happen that there would be some one or two so weak in intellect, so vacillating as to what constitutes his or her happiness, as to make an erroneous choice, Mr Owen thinks it better to let such separate, and form new engagements openly, and with persons likely to be virtuous, than that they should be tied together to the end of their days, living a worse than cat and dog life, and each seeking gratification in the society of the profligate; for none but the debased in body and mind will enter into an engagement which is a practical lie, and to which the sentiments, if not the practice of the community, is opposed; or than, that the eminently virtuous should pine away their lives under the conviction that one single error had blighted their comfort for ever.

This plan of separation and re-union is supported by the opinion of our 'seraphic' Milton.[5] Under a system which allows this, a system which teaches that SEPARATION IS A GREAT EVIL; but, that to live together *without affection* is a greater – is actual prostitution! Jealousy and its attendant crimes *cannot* exist. To prevent separation being the result of a mere whim, the parties wishing to separate are required to appear before the community to state their wish, and to appear again at the expiration of three months to reiterate it; which being done, they are deemed to be divorced.

As to 'every man working to support all the women and all their children', both men and women will be required to give a certain amount of labour for the good of all. Because each has peculiar duties to perform, and because each will be healthier in mind and body for having a certain daily exercise of three or four hours; every temptation being offered for a *voluntary* exercise of the faculties in a becoming course during the rest of the day.

As to the 'relation and duties of father and child being unknown,' considerations that the children *of all* are entitled to an equally good education, and that a child's character is formed, as far as external circumstances can affect it, in its *first few years*, cause Mr Owen to

---

* Should any wish to have the sanction of any church or religious sect, they may have it, though it will not be required by the community.

determine that they shall all be brought up from their earliest infancy under the management of philosophical, conscientious, and benevolent men, whom the COMMUNITY shall appoint. The whole of the women between certain ages, to be employed by turns in the important task of anticipating the wants, and promoting the healthy enjoyment of, the young. This the circumstances of co-operation will allow them leisure for; and, as they will not be under that system of competition, which, working on a mother's love of her offspring, causes her to be unjust to the offspring of others, a general love must be generated; though thoughts of the father of the child, if there were no other cause, *will make each mother regard her own child with more interest than any other.* Under such a system all fathers will be engaged in teaching children arts and sciences imperatively necessary, or interesting and amusing; and as their minds would not be harrassed by too much rigidly enforced business; as they would not have their minds occupied by a strife to obtain the means of supporting such a style of living as their connexions expect of them, that love of children, which is inherent in nearly all, must be active; and thoughts of his wife must endear *his* children to every father, as thoughts of him endear them to her; and, as children soon perceive who yield them *especial* regard, they would, while they love all, love their parents in a remarkable degree.

An investigation of Mr Owen's system, and a reflection of the innate affections of human beings, must lead to the conclusion that his is the only system yet offered to us, which excites and regulates the social feelings and the intelligence in the most virtuous degree. I am, sir, yours respectfully,

Margaret Reynolds.[6]

It is important to notice that Mr Owen *will not have his system of marriage and divorce acted upon under the existing state of things*; for he maintains that beings must be much better educated than they now are, before *all* those principles which should lead to virtuous marriages can be excited.

New Moral World, 27 October 1838.

Mrs Chapellsmith's Lecture

London, Jan. 14th, 1840 – Social Institution, 81, High Street, White-chapel.[7]

The evening's lecture was by Mrs Chapellsmith[8] on the 'Marriage System of the New Moral World'; our fair lecturer gave us an excellent treat, delivering her sentiments in a mild though animated and very impressive style, contrasting the marriages of the Old Immoral World with those of the New. The lecture appeared to give general satisfaction to a crowded and respectable audience. After the lecture Mrs Chapellsmith named a fine infant belonging to one of our members and delivered a very appropriate address on the occasion, which gave great delight to all present, showing the power which society possessed over the smiling babe, pointing out the fact that the crude materials which she then held in her arms, could be formed to possess any character and any religion, according to the circumstances and country it might be placed in, without the possibility of its knowledge or consent.

T. Marshall, Secretary.
New Moral World, 25 January 1840.

Marriage at the Social Institution John-Street, Tottenham-Court Road, London[9]

On Tuesday, the 25th of January, J. Mowbray Jackson, Esq., and Miss Maria Grocock were married at the Social Institution, John-street, Tottenham-court-road, London. The ceremony was performed by Mr Owen, in the presence of the Registrar of the district, and many friends of the parties and members and friends of the society. It consisted as required by law, of a solemn declaration made by the parties, each separately repeating the words after Mr Owen, that they knew of no impediment to their being lawfully united in marriage; after which, the gentleman, again repeating the words after Mr Owen said 'I, John Jackson, take thee, Maria Grocock, to be my lawful wife'; the lady afterwards making a similar declaration on her part. The form was completed by the registration being made in the book kept by the Registrar.

Mr Owen then addressed those who were present as follows: 'You have just witnessed the first ceremony of marriage performed under our new arrangements. The Legislature have very properly reduced the ceremony required by law on these occasions, to the smallest amount of error that the false training and prejudices of society would permit. All that is necessary, as you have seen, after the licence has been obtained, or the required notice has been given, is for the parties to declare in the presence of the registrar and the requisite witnesses, that they know of no impediment why they should not be married, and that they take each other as husband and wife. With us, however, these proceedings have a very different character to that which they have with general society. These parties just married understand their own nature very differently from the ordinary notions on the subject. They know the great law of human nature – that human beings are compelled to like that which is agreeable to them, and to dislike that which is disagreeable. Having this knowledge, they possess the strongest inducement to endeavour to promote each other's happiness, and to become as agreeable as possible to each other; being fully conscious that it is only by so doing they can reasonably expect to be beloved. They have the strongest inducement to the acquisition of the best qualities, and when they acquire a knowledge of that which is conducive to each other's happiness, they will be much more likely to preserve their mutual affection than those who are ignorant of the laws of human nature. Our friends, therefore, have a much better prospect of happiness than the ordinary members of old society, when they enter into this legal compact; and unless they are united according to the laws on the subject, they render themselves liable to many inconveniences, and their children also, if they should have any. I trust that these who are the first parties united in our Institution, will be an example of conjugal affection, and will live long and be happy together; and that their children, if they should have any, will be trained under the influence and in the knowledge of those principles of human nature which will form them, physically, mentally, morally, and practically, into superior members of society.'

New Moral World, 5 February 1842.

Notes

1. George Jacob Holyoake, *Sixty Years Of An Agitator's Life*, 2 vols (1892), vol. 1, p. 41.
2. Concordia (Anna Wheeler), *Crisis*, 22 June 1833.
3. The Six Lectures were delivered by Robert Owen in Manchester to the Annual Congress of 'The Association of All Classes of All Nations' held in the Social Institution, Great George Street, Salford in May 1837. They were subsequently published by Abel Heywood as a booklet.
4. The *Weekly Dispatch* was started in 1801 under the title of *Bell's Weekly Dispatch*.
5. John Milton's pamphlet *The Doctrine and Discipline of Divorce* was published in August 1643. In it he contended 'Since marriage is a union

of minds not merely of bodies, it must be freely entered into and freely dissoluble.' *Collected Works*, vol. 1, p. 245.

6. Margaret Reynolds was the maiden name of Mrs Chapellsmith.
7. The Social Institution at 81 High Street, Whitechapel was opened on 5 January 1840. The first lecture, given there to an audience of 400, was by Mrs Chapellsmith on the Principles of Socialism.
8. See biography in Ch. 6.
9. The Social Institution at 23 St John Street, Tottenham Court Road was the headquarters of London Branch A 1. It was described as a Social, Literary and Scientific Institution in which lectures on Geology, Drama and English Humour were given. It was opened by Robert Owen on 23 February 1840.

8
Women in Trade Unions

They will ultimately abolish wages, become their own masters, and work for each other. Labour and capital will no longer be separate but they will be indissolubly joined together in the hands of working men and women.

The Man, 22 December 1833.

Capital eschews no profit, or very small profit, just as Nature was formerly said to abhor vacuum. With adequate profit, capital is very bold. A certain 10 per cent will ensure its employment anywhere; 20 per cent will produce eagerness; 50 per cent positive audacity, 100 per cent will make it ready to trample on all human laws; 300 per cent and there is not a crime at which it will scruple nor a risk it will not run, even to a chance of its owner being hanged.

T.J. Dunning, *Trades' Unions and Strikes*, 1873, p, 42.

Introduction

Between 1799 and 1824, trades unions were illegal under the terms of the Combination Acts.[1] Trades Clubs, mainly of craftsmen, acted as trades unions clandestinely whilst functioning as Friendly Societies. Their sick and burial rules were registered with the Registrar of Friendly Societies while their trade rules were agreed verbally. By 1824 the Combination Acts were proving ineffective because of the growth of the industrial working classes, and when they were repealed limited legal recognition was given to trade union organisation. However severe restrictions were still enforced.

Women and children had been herded into the rapidly developing factories where they worked in degrading conditions for long hours and low pay. Serious accidents were frequent and the insanitary conditions in which they were forced to live and work gave rise to outbreaks of fever and cholera. At that stage in the textile industry, women outnumbered men; the strikes that broke out involved and were often instigated by women.

Women were enslaved twice over: in the factory and in the home.

134

One feminist historian noted that whereas the democratic radicalism of the 1790s had 'opened up the question of women's rights as a citizen, the struggle for the rights of labour opened up the issue of the status of women as workers and her place in class based organisations.'[2]

Robert Owen,[3] who had tried to find ways of alleviating the conditions under which people lived and worked, realised that he would only find the way to a 'new moral world' if the trades unions were involved. At a conference to consider ways of supporting the Derby silk weavers[4] who were on strike, the *Grand National Consolidated Trades' Union*[5] was given its Constitution. Among the clauses was one saying, 'Lodges of Industrious Females shall be instituted in every district wherein may be practicable; such Lodges to be considered in every respect, as part of, and belonging to, the G.N.C.T.U.'[6] James Morrison[7] was given the responsibility of editing the *Pioneer* or *Grand National Consolidated Trades' Union Magazine* to serve the movement.

It was for attempting to form a Lodge of the Grand National that the agricultural labourers in Dorchester[8] were arrested, tried and sentenced to be transported to Australia. Their charge was for administering an illegal oath, but their real 'crime' was organising some of the poorest and most exploited workers in the country in the teeth of opposition from the landed interests.

From the start, the *Pioneer* gave space to women's interests and published a number of articles of a discussion character. It also acted as a focus around which Female Lodges could organise and communicate with each other. There is little doubt that Frances Morrison (1807–98) played a part in assisting her husband to develop this aspect of the paper. Her imprint can be clearly distinguished and her contributions were influential.

Frances was born Frances Cooper, the illegitimate daughter of a Surrey farm worker, and was brought up by her grandmother. When she grew up, she joined her mother in Pershore and there met a house painter, James Morrison, on the tramp for work. Though only 15 years old, Frances went with him to Birmingham where they lived together until she became pregnant four or five years later. They then married.

They had four daughters and Mrs Morrison was fully occupied in looking after them and a small newspaper shop. But with the encouragement of her husband she also tried to educate herself in radical politics, especially in the theories of Robert Owen.

James Morrison, who had been active in the movement for the reform of parliament and also as an activist in the Operative Builders' Union, in 1833 became editor of the *Pioneer*. Under his guidance, the paper became the organ of the Owenite trade union movement. Frances contributed to the paper under the pseudonym 'A Bondswoman' and together with her husband contributed articles on feminist themes, from the inequalities of the marriage law to the demand for equal pay for equal work.

The *Pioneer* started producing a 'Page for the Ladies' in 1834. The first such pages had a somewhat patronising tone and may have been written by James, but after a few weeks, it became 'Woman's Page' and adopted a far more down-to-earth tone. Women's letters were carried regularly and also news items of women's activities. It is possible that Frances undertook to produce the page on her own account although there is no proof of this.

Following James's death c. 1838 Frances became a paid lecturer for the Owenites, travelling through Northern towns speaking on women's rights and marriage reform. Finding that she had insufficient wages to keep her daughters, she obtained a teaching post in Hulme near Manchester and apprenticed her girls to the tape-weaving trade.

She obviously continued to play a part in the Owenite movement because George Jacob Holyoake described her when he visited the Salford Social Institute. 'One Sunday at noon,' he said, 'I found my way to the pretty little Social Institute which I knew existed in Salford, where I should meet with some friends familiar with my name, as it had been mentioned in the *New Moral World*, read there. Not long before, James Morrison had died. His widow, a pleasant little person, was mistress of the tea-parties at the Salford Institute, where I spent the remainder of the day very happily and heard the afternoon and evening lectures.'[9]

Frances Morrison again became a paid Owenite lecturer and she attracted large audiences, especially of women. Among her lecture subjects were the formation of character and also dress reform. In 1844 she is cited in the *Movement* as having promised to expose instances of 'infidel immorality', offering to use George Holyoake as the first example. It is possible that this was a false report because, on the evidence of her daughters, Frances retained her socialist sympathies to the end of her long life.[10]

Female Lodges were formed mostly in the small metal trades and in miscellaneous garment making. Wages in such trades were atrocious and working conditions appalling and often highly dangerous. It was these women, not the women in the textile industry, who raised the questions of pay differentials and the relative position of men and women.

The short-lived Grand National Consolidated Trades' Union provided historians with some insight into the ferment of interest and activity that women entered into when the opportunity presented itself. The *Pioneer* is an invaluable record of a short period of intense organisation which could not be sustained for longer periods. However, what happened in

1834 offers some idea of the way that women seized upon the idea of organisation and combination to alleviate their downtrodden situation.

* * *

Meeting of Women in Glasgow

Female Association – Hurrah! for the Women of Glasgow
On Wednesday night (says a Scotch paper) a meeting of not fewer than *one thousand females*, delegates from public works in and around Glasgow, to the extent of eighteen miles, was held in the Lyceum Rooms, for the purpose of forming themselves into an Association 'for their mutual protection against the encroachments of tyrannical overseers, and the reduction of masters'. A *Chairwoman* having been appointed, the fair assemblage began their deliberations. A female Secretary and a Treasurer were appointed, and a committee of twelve were appointed as a provisional government, for one month, to regulate the proceedings of the Society. This meeting was a representative body, acting for 12,498 power-looms, from each of which one halfpenny is, in the mean time, to be received per week. The Association also contemplates the relief of members when sick, or otherwise out of employment.

Poor Man's Guardian, 16 March 1833.

To the Ladies in Union at Leicester

Dear Sisters,
It was a pleasant breeze which wafted the glad tidings of your sisterhood to Birmingham: we hear that there are a thousand of you, and to your sweet honour be it spoken – you have shewn your self-styled lords and masters, that you can keep a secret as well as they can. It is in this, as it is in every thing appertaining to general improvement; for after all the boasted refinement of higher society, the working classes are the first to cast away long standing prejudices. The scandalous bye word of 'blue stocking', which has been thrown at every intelligent woman who happened to have more sense than her stupid husband, has not deterred the ladies of Leicester from uniting to obtain the advancement of themselves and their kindred.

The life of woman has hitherto been devoted to the pride, the ambition, and the selfishness of man; but now, when he thinks proper to encourage a union of the fair, we hope that they will profit by the lesson, and in due season claim the respect which their gentleness, their talent, and integrity, has a right to.

Your lodges, we understand, consist entirely of women, with the exception of a *protector* and a *secretary*. In our simple view of the matter, we think that you have no need of the one or the other; not that we think there is a shade of impropriety in it, but because it is our opinion, that you are able to fulfil those duties yourselves. Surely among a thousand fair hands there can plenty be found who are accustomed to use the pen; it would be a slander on the country to say it was not so. Then do, we beg of you, feel the pride of your own strength, and lose the habit of leaning so much on the judgment of the other sex. As to protection, if a hundred women, much less a thousand, could not protect themselves against any aggressor who might dare to interrupt their harmony, then we have no faith in anything that exists – why the rascal would be skinned alive – he would *literally* be brought up to the *scratch*. Good heaven! His fate is too horrid to contemplate. But to dispense for a moment with badinage, we would recommend that the women of Leicester do assert their own dignity, and have a secretary of their own sex, and be self-protected. Do not let us for ever see woman looking up to man for anything which needs so small acquirement. The very habit of doing a little duty like this for themselves, will create a spirit of independence which will rise to things of greater magnitude, and when women acquire freedom their children will never more be slaves.

It is much to be regretted, that you have so long succumbed to the insolent despotism of man. Is it because woman has less intelligence; or that man is more strong? Alas, we fear that strength of muscle gives a tone to his thoughts and his actions which bears too hard on woman's gentleness; and though many a noble woman by her mind's power can turn the savage eye which dares to scowl upon her, yet there are too many who only know their heart's own bitterness. But the law of custom must be torn to shreds; the partial laws of senators erased; and sturdy ignorance laid low, ere lovely woman can achieve her rights.

To return to our fair sisters of Leicester, in the fulness of our heart we invite them to write to us; which doubtless our readers would relish. There is poetry in a woman's pen; their veriest prose is poetry to us. We hope then to hear from the sisterhood: but now ladies, mind and write it yourselves, and indite it yourselves; for if you employ a scribbler it will be sure to lose its pathos; we do not know how to write like you; our thoughts are not your thoughts, nor our ways your ways. A man cannot feign a woman's feelings; he does not know her wrongs; he wrongs her most himself. He is the tyrant, she the slave. How can *he* pourtray *her* smothered thought, or write *her* anxious wish? Write yourselves, then, write yourselves. The Pioneer is far away; he cannot see your modest blush, nor know your doubting mind and nervous fear. He cannot tell from whose fair hand the little treasure cometh. Hail, then, the first 'brave wench' who sends the Pioneer a valentine. Hail! Pretty *Pioneera*!

Alas, we are becoming pathetic; we must sober down a little, and conclude, with all the tenderness our heart possesses,

Your loving scribe, God bless us!

The Pioneer

Pioneer, 26 October 1833.

To the Editor of the *Pioneer*

Sir,

It was with heartfelt pleasure I perused the contents of the *Pioneer* of the 26th of October. Most heartily do I rejoice in the expectation of having a Ladies' Union formed in every part of the United Kingdom. Surely, if it is good for nations to be in friendly union, it must be good for individuals to be the same; and I am glad to find that you acknowledge that even females can do something, as well as men. For instance, what would have become of Bible associations, missionary subscriptions, and many other noble institutions this country can boast of, if female influence and female interest had been withheld? Unions of females (more particularly married women) are, in my humble opinion, of the greatest importance to ourselves, our husbands, our children, and our posterity; they will be of vast importance to generations yet unborn, and to the world at large. I should be glad to hear of a Ladies' Union in London, as I feel confident the beneficial results would soon be felt by every class of society, especially in that of which I am a member (namely, the vulgar mob), as it would tend greatly to the improvement and advantage of our too-often neglected families; becoming pride would, by degrees, begin to display itself; we should vie with each other in every stage of gradual improvement, until the vulgar mob became one general mass of *civilized* society. The ladies of Leicester have set a noble example in commencing so good a cause, in defiance of good or evil report, as I *know* that *women's opinions*, generally speaking, are treated with contemptuous ridicule by many men who think themselves infallible. But how miserably are they mistaken! May they soon discover their error, and be compelled for the future to confine their sneers to a very limited number of our sex.

Waiting the arrival of some account of the Leicester Ladies' Union, I am, Sir, with the greatest respect, a sincere well-wisher to *Unionists*,

A Mechanic's Wife in London.

To the Mechanic's Wife

Dear Madam,

In the tough warfare of labour against the claims of capitalists, the mind is hardened into a forgetfulness of those finer sympathies which pervade the circles where women are the presiding influences. At this moment, when a recollection of all that is amiable in woman's character ought to sweeten our pen, we have a thousand calls upon our exertions. It is like taking a nap in the midst of combat; we admire the spirit which dictated your encouraging letter, and, in a softer moment, could have responded to it with the kindliness and promptitude it so well merits. But the drum of moral warfare is challenging us to fiercer duty. Give us another week to build the fabric of a female lodge: but at this most anxious moment forgive our want of courtesy, and be assured that woman's aid and woman's council are valued much, yea very much, by all who know her worth. Your's, Madam, with the greatest respect,

The Pioneer.
Pioneer, 11 January 1834.

To the People of Derby

Brothers and Sisters of Derby,

You still shall live; and the time is not far distant, when your labour shall have that respect which is its undoubted right. Yes! It shall be supplied *first* with what it produces, and *none* shall have the power to take away that privilege which is yours, but which the juggling hand of tyranny has so long withheld. But the spell is broke; an everlasting eclipse is thrown upon its bloated countenance; oblivion shall be its portion – death its end; it shall go down to the grave with the forgiveness of the productive class; but the stripes it has inflicted, when in its vigour, are too severe to be forgot.

Fellow-labourers of the United Kingdom, hasten to assist its dissolution; it grows faint; its eyes are become dim; seize it in its weakness. Unite together, and one grand effort will terminate its existence. This done, prepare yourselves for its last rites; dig a grave to the very centre of the earth; bid the world to its funeral, and, for fear it should ever raise its head again, erect a ponderous monument to reach the skies, to face the four winds, and, in characters of gold, (large enough, when brightened by the radiant sons of union) let there be written 'Tyranny is dead', with the following epitaph:

Beneath this monument doth lie,
As much tyranny as could die;
Which, when alive, did vigour give,
To as much tyranny as could live.

In consequence of an unexpected call upon our funds, we are not able
to send you more than ...   £6 16 11
Geo.Owram, of Ardsley, near Barnsley, butcher, a *sticker* to the Derby
cause ...   0 2 6
Margaret Parrington, of Barnsley, poor in pocket, but rich in principle,
sends her mite ...   0 0 6
                                                                  £6 19 11

Joseph Ray

Pioneer, 25 January 1834.

To the Females of the Working Class

To the Editor of the *Pioneer*

Sir,

I have been anxiously looking, for this week or two past, for some
friend to respond to the letter of the mechanic's wife, in London. It is
time the working females of England began to demand their long-
suppressed rights. Let us, in the first place, endeavour to throw off the
trammels that have so long enshackled our minds, and get knowledge,
when all are making their way to the temple of truth and justice. Let
not woman – patient, suffering, long neglected woman – stay behind
on the road to improvement. Not but I know the time will come, ere
long, when men will see the necessity of educating their wives, in all
matters that concern themselves, equally as all men see the necessity
of their knowing how our government act as regards them. May be the
time is not distant when the superiority of educated females will be
acknowledged over those that are kept in blind and stupid ignorance.
No wonder at the present state of affairs, when the mothers of the
most able, most useful of England's sons, have been denied the acquisition of truth of every kind. The mother is the first to sow the seed of
instruction in the youthful mind; and if the seed is bad, what can we
expect from the fruits? Sisters, bondswomen, arise! And let us unite to
gain our rights. Let us unite and teach the oppressors, our employers,
their duty.

In manufacturing towns, look at the value that is set on woman's
labour, whether it be skilful, whether it be laborious, so that woman
can do it. The contemptible expression is, it is made by woman, and

therefore cheap? Why, I ask, should woman's labour be thus under-valued? Why should the time and the ingenuity of the sex, that could be so usefully employed otherwise, be monopolized by cruel and greedy oppressors, being in the likeness of man, and calling themselves masters? Sisters, let us submit to it no longer; let us once get to the knowledge of our wrongs, and our cause is won; once entered on the path to improvement, the flowers that are strewed on the road will invite us to travel on. Then will we cast the foul aspersions that have been heaped on our sex into oblivion. The itch for scandal, tattling, and other vices, which we are said to possess, placed in the scale of truth, with affection, sincerity, perseverance, ingenuity, and many other virtues; these, properly cultivated, will ever outweigh the vices that have been forced into our naturally noble minds. Then will woman do justice to the fair form nature has given her. Men, in general, tremble at the idea of a reading wife, being taught to believe it an evil by designing tyrants. Woman's rights, like man's, have been withheld from motives purely political, by deep concerted plans of early oppressors. The sage priests of olden time well knew, if woman's penetrative and inquisitive mind was allowed its liberty, their well-laid schemes of bigotry and superstition would soon have come to light. But, to return to our immediate interest: let our class generally unite; let us make a beginning in Birmingham; there are great numbers of females employed in this town. If our first efforts are feeble, let us fear not; a change must come, and that speedily. The women of Derby have entered the bonds of union; let us, in compliment to these noble but oppressed women, plant the standard of female union in Birmingham. Women of Birmingham, your children's, your own, your country's interest demand it. Be slaves no longer, but unite and assert your just rights! With the anxious hope that we may soon establish a union that will be a shield from oppression of every kind,

I subscribe myself, fellow countrywomen,

An earnest assistant in our cause,

A Bondswoman

Birmingham, Feb. 2, 1834.

P.S. As our friend, perhaps you will have no objection to permit a book to be left at your shop to receive names? By stating your approval, you will oblige.

Proud of the honour – *Pioneer*.

Pioneer, 8 February 1834.

Women's Strike at Broadford, Scotland

Strike among the Females at Broadford – In consequence of an intimation having been made to some of the reelers and spinners on Thursday night their weekly wages would be reduced 6*d*. after next week, a 'turn out' took place. About 140 of them paraded the streets during the day with a flag, and accompanied by a blind fiddler. They halted near Elm-hill, and were then addressed by some of the males, who stated the object of the meeting, and read a resolution to the effect that their proceedings were legitimate; that the standard of liberty was now unfurled; that they would no longer submit to oppression and low wages; that they were only following the example of others in similar circumstances throughout the three kingdoms; and that they then called upon their sisters from the Poyernook to Grandholm to co-operate with them. They were then drawn up two and two, and numbered, when it appeared there were 156 females, who contributed 1*d*. to defray the expense of printing and circulating hand-bills to the above effect. The collection amounted to 15*s*. 8*d*., some of the bystanders (who numbered upwards of 400) having contributed. They were then exhorted to retire peaceably to their homes, and the crowd immediately dispersed. *Aberdeen Herald*.

Poor Man's Guardian, 22 February 1834.

To the Bondswoman of Birmingham

Most happy am I to see the animated address from a sister in Birmingham; it cheers my almost desponding and despairing mind. May our as yet single-handed exertions stimulate the long-neglected and much-degraded daughters of Britain to rise from their long slumber, and assert their claims to honour and to justice! For, until they do bestir themselves for a fair distribution of the productions of labour first, and then for an equal diffusion of knowledge, there can be no hope for redemption. It is an important task to arouse women to a sense of their long-neglected state. If they assumed their proper position in the progressive march of reform, it would, ere this, have gained a more useful elevation. Our persuasions and perseverance when encouraged, our natural and ardent attachment to our tender young, would prompt us to use all our powers to obtain a far better state for the enslaved and degraded children of labour. Shall the idiot-like, the stupid and usurious capitalists, tell us to look to our domestic affairs, and say, '*these we understand best?*' we will retort on them, and tell them that thousands of us have *scarce any domestic affairs to look after*, when the want of employment on the one hand, or ill-requited toil on the other, have left our habitations almost destitute, either a sacrifice to the pawn-shop, or worn to the most slender fragments; when we see abundance of employment, that ought to occupy our time, to make garments for our almost naked children and ourselves, and cannot get the materials to work on. Then is it of the first importance that we should know how to acquire those materials; and that is, by making ourselves acquainted with the rights of labour; and on the other hand, with the all-absorbing and all-destroying principle of capital, as it has hitherto worked against labour. Ah! Fellow-bondswoman and sister in suffering, let us use all our energies to arouse our sex to consider the all-important truth that labour ought to stand paramount above all subjects; that only for it the lazy and useless would not have the chance to hurl their ridicule and contempt towards our sex, for seeking their rights, so long neglected. Millions of our sex have they deluded from virtuous paths, and then left them to pine out a miserable existence; there are many honourable exceptions in the other sex; but the time is arrived when truth must out. It has hitherto been considered almost treason for a woman to write or speak on what are deemed public subjects. These seven years have I exerted my powers (in my private sphere) to arouse my countrywomen to a sense of duty, and am now determined to raise my voice in public to arouse them to seek equal rights, as I hope you will in the spirited town of Birmingham: and may you find many to strengthen your hands and encourage your noble spirit, and may we live to see the whole of our sex exert themselves for their own, their children's, and their country's emancipation from the cruel bondage of physical and mental taskmasters! Your admirer,

A London Mechanic's Wife
Pioneer, 22 February 1834.

Response to the London Mechanic's Wife

Sir,

In perusing your little work, No. 19, of the *Pioneer*, Jan 11, it was with heartfelt joy I read over the letter of a Mechanic's Wife in London. I hope you will not refuse the insertion of a few remarks of a sister in union at Derby. Be it known to the world that a female union is begun in Derby, and that the tyrants have taken fright at it, and have brought forth a document for the females to sign or *leave their employment*, not only to those who are employed in the factory, but *to the servants in their own houses also*. Here is a specimen of knavish tyranny; but, be it known that we have refused to comply with their request, with heroic fortitude. In consequence of this, there is a great number more added to the turn-out. Ha! Ha! Ha! The knaves thought of taking advantage of our weakness, by endeavouring to persuade us to sign, saying – '*Do, God bless you, sign it, for its a thing of no significa-tion to you*'. Aye, thought we, in the simplicity of our hearts, if its a thing of no signification to *us, its of none to you.* So we unanimously agreed not to sign any thing. Sisters! Awake, arise, arouse yourselves from your lethargy throughout the whole United Kingdom. Why sleep ye now in the time of danger? One grand movement on your part, and the victory is ours. The tyrants' heads are already in the dust; one of them again assailing us, while the crystal tears stole down his haggard face, saying, '*Do, God bless you, sign it*'. Ah! I shall never forget his looks; allow me the expression, *I am big with it,* it must out, 'he looked as blue as a sick monkey'. I hope he will forgive me the joke. A word to the females *not* in union: arouse yourselves at this important crisis, and sympathise with us; form lodges in every town and hamlet. Mothers of families, and maidens, come forward and join in this our glorious cause, and we will defy the power of our adversaries; and let the first lispings of your innocent offsprings be *Union! Union!* I apolo-gise, Sir, for trespassing upon your time; but if you think it worth inserting in your little work, you will much oblige a sister in union.

I am, Sir, yours respectfully,

An Everlasting Enemy to All Tyranny.

Derby, Feb. 3, 1834.

Pioneer, 22 February 1834.

The Grand Lodge of the Women of Great Britain and Ireland

A meeting of the members of the Grand Lodge of the Women of Great Britain and Ireland, instituted for the purpose of emancipating them-selves and their fellow countrywomen from the individual dependence and thraldom in which they have been hitherto involved, will be held at number 14 Charlotte Street,[11] on Friday, 21st instant, at seven o'clock in the evening, for the purpose of initiating new members. All persons disposed to join this Lodge may obtain informa-tion and register their names by application to Mrs Brooks at the Institution 14 Charlotte Street, Fitzroy Square.

Pioneer, 15 March 1834.

Letter from an Initiated Weaver's Wife

Dear Sir,

In the ardour of my heart, I return you my sincere and hearty thanks for nobly espousing the cause of insulted women, and so will any thinking man or woman do the same; but allow me, Sir, to inform you, that there is a great number of men that cannot bear the idea of women's union, and yet they are unionists themselves. Now, Sir, I will just ask those men one simple question; 'do you know the fundamental principles of the noble cause you have embarked in?' You will surely say 'yes'; well then, I say, act up to your profession, and if you see that women stand in need of reform; extend your charity towards them, and do them justice. Women, who in your sorrows, drink the very dregs of the bitter cup, deny them not also to participate in your joys; and if they are helpmates in trouble, why do you *cowardly* stand aloof and not accept their assistance? You say that 'women will not keep their own counsel, they tittle tattle', well then I am very glad that I can inform you that women have not been the concoctors of the tattling job, that requires a select committee from among the public purse-jobbers at the west-end of the city. But thanks to our noble Pioneer, that will not let our talents be buried in oblivion, you might as well think of hewing blocks of marble with a razor, as think of preventing women from forming themselves in union. And now, Mr Editor, as our staunch friend, we look for all the assistance that you can give us; a great deal you have done, and yet there is a great deal to do. If a house is divided against itself, it cannot stand; just so, if women were in union, I am positive that it would establish a power, that tyranny would never be able to stand against; as the only thing that is wanted now is to establish family harmony, and to bring both parties to a true sense of their worth in society; and this, Sir, you are able to accomplish if you put forth your strength; for what is it that you cannot do? Therefore, as our friend, you will oblige us very much with your advice in your paper, as we are only waiting for the signal to form our lodges; and we will let them know, that woman, by her own exertions and intelligence will be free, and the very essence of freedom exhibit to the world; and her dastardly tyrants shall yet fall at her feet never more to triumph over her; therefore, they that are not for us are against us. I hope, Mr Editor, that you will use your utmost exertions to convince them of their errors, that none may mourn on their way like a dove that mourns for the loss of her mate. Have the goodness to insert this in your valuable paper of this week, and you will oblige yours truly,

An Initiated Weaver's Wife

Foleshill.

Pioneer, 15 March 1834.

Some Problems Among the Tailors

Sir,

An Initiated Tailor has to complain of your having acted a very unfair part towards him, in publishing a few isolated sentences of a private letter. You well knew the advantage of so publishing them without their connexion, because you could then twist them any way to answer your own purpose, without your readers knowing whether your correspondent was right or wrong, Whig or Tory, St Simonian[12] or Englishman. As you have thought proper to dissect my letter in that style, I ask you now, as an act of justice (for you are an advocate of rights and privileges), to publish the whole of it, so that your readers may judge for themselves. You have told them in No. 29, that I scout the idea of women's rights and privileges. Now, Sir, I said that it was the duty of women in trade to form Unions, and thus protect their rights, and be paid for their labour; but to call wives and matrons away from domestic affairs is the idea I 'scout'. But you deny that you recommend them to do so. You say you do not advise them to spout at meetings, or make themselves public in any way. To see that this is a contradiction, allow me to advise the perusal of No. 27 again.

You told your readers that I said, though not a profligate myself, yet if my wife went to legislate, it would be a certain way to make me one. It would have been better if you had told them why I said so. I said so, because you said 'none but profligates would object to woman's legislation'. I am one who objects to it, though no profligate; but that would be the way to make me one; and this will be clear to any one, who wishes things to go on well at home, so as to make it 'an object of attraction, and not a place of aversion'; and the only way to make it attractive is to have the wife's company in the evening, when man has done his day's labour; for if she goes out to spout, he will go to the public-house. Men's business, in a general way, is done away from home; but 'wives' and matrons' business is at home; and, in my opinion, none but lazy, gossiping, drunken wives will wish to go to meetings. If you do me the justice to insert these remarks, I will thank you for the indulgence, and not trouble you further.

March 24.

Sir,

Having heard it generally professed that the 'general good' was the object of the Trades' Unions, I shall feel obliged if you will allow me, through the medium of your paper, to ask a couple of questions of the Tailors' Union.

1. Do you intend to prevent all women from working in future at

waistcoat making? Should this question be answered in the affirmative, and I have good reasons for believing it will, I would ask –

2. What is to become of the numerous women now working at the business, many of whom are tailors' widows, who have no other means of providing for themselves and families, and between whom and the workhouse this is the only bar? I admit some alteration to be necessary; but surely the men might think of a better method of benefiting themselves than that of driving so many industrious women out of employment. Surely, while they loudly complain of oppression, they will not turn oppressors themselves. Surely, they will not give their enemies cause to say, when a woman and her offspring are seen begging in the streets, 'This is the work of union; this is the justice and humanity of union; this is the remedy proposed by the *men* of Great Britain to relieve them from their present distress.' Surely, this will not be the case: I cannot believe it. But having been informed that such is their intention, I have thought it necessary to ask the above questions.

Thanking you for the interest you have taken in behalf of our injured sex, I am, Sir, yours respectfully,

A Woman

London, March 24th, 1834.

Pioneer, 29 March 1834.

The Dorchester Labourers' Campaign of Support

At a meeting of females in the Nottingham Trades' Union, it was resolved: 'That a Memorial be now prepared, representing the injustice of the sentence passed upon the six men at Dorchester, for belonging to the Trades' Union; and after it has been signed by the Female Members, and Friends of the Union, to be presented to the Commons House of Parliament.'

Memorial
Of the Females of Nottingham and Vicinity, to the Honourable the House of Commons of the United Kingdom of Great Britain and Ireland, in Parliament assembled.

We, your Memorialists, do most respectfully beg leave to draw the attention of your Honourable House, to the harsh, and (in our opinion), unconstitutional sentence, which has been passed by *Baron Williams*[13] one of his Majesty's Judges, upon six of our fellow subjects at the late Dorchester Assizes, for the alleged offence of administering an unlawful oath.

From the Trial, as reported in the Papers, it does not appear to your Memorialists that any evidence was produced to prove that any oath had been administered by James Loveless, George Loveless, Thomas Stanfield, John Stanfield, James Hammett, and James Brine, the prisoners in question, at the time and place charged in the indictment; but if such a case had been clearly made out, still your Memorialists respectfully contend, that their (the prisoners') conviction was obtained under the sanction of an Act of Parliament which was never intended by its framers to be used for such cases as the one now referred to; therefore your memorialists do now hope, and expect, that your honourable house will immediately cause an inquiry to be made into this circumstance, and if it can be ascertained to the satisfaction of your Honourable House that the conviction in this case has been procured wrongfully, through the application of a wrong law, we, your Memorialists, do hope and expect that your Honourable House will immediately address his Majesty on this subject, desiring his Majesty to order the immediate liberation of the prisoners; and we also hope that your honourable house will impeach Baron Williams, as a punishment for the arbitrary and unconstitutional manner in which Baron Williams, has tried with, and trampled upon the liberty of the subject on this occasion.

But if it should be decided by your Honourable House, that the law has not been wrongfully applied in this case, we, your Memorialists, do hope that your honourable house will repeal it, or, otherwise take such measures as shall ensure a general application of it to all, both employers and employed, so that the same law which punishes the working men for combining against their masters in Dorsetshire, may also punish the masters for combining against the workmen in Derbyshire, and other places; and we, your Memorialists, do most respectively assure your honourable house that until an equal measure of justice be dealt to both Masters and Men, and other secret Societies, such as Free Masons, Odd Fellows, etc., as well as Trades' Unions, no solid or permanent satisfaction can be given to the people in general. Hoping that your Honourable House will take this matter into your immediate and serious consideration, and cause equal justice to be done to all, is the fervent desire of your Memorialists.

N.B. All Females ought to sign this Memorial.
Nottingham, March 24, 1834.

Pioneer, 29 March 1834.

We beg to remind our readers that two of the Widows of the Dorchester victims have on sale at the Institution, 14 Charlotte Street, a quantity of earthenware, which has been sent up from Staffordshire to be disposed of for their benefit.

New Moral World, 27 June 1835.

Pages for the Ladies from the *Pioneer* with Correspondence

A Page for the Ladies

We do not despair of very soon arousing the public spirit of the other sex, which has almost lain dormant since old Time first flapped his wings. Women have always been divided; always secluded from the world, and from each other. Their sphere has been greatly more limited than the sphere of man. It has been chiefly confined to the domestic circle; and if, at any time, they have enjoyed a change of scene, it has not afforded them a better opportunity of associating with each other, and acting in concert for the good of 'woman'. Does man think, or does woman think, that women are free, because they can go out to church or market, lecture-room, assembly-room, theatre, or ball-room, at pleasure? They are as much domesticated in all these places as they are at home. What do they hear at church? A *man* haranguing the two sexes; and though he did address himself to woman only, what does he know about woman, of whose feelings he has no experience? If woman go to market, a theatre, a ball-room, a lecture-room, these everlasting men are for ever around her. They are her teachers, her counsellors, her politicians, her pastors, her agents, her every thing. In fine, the whole business of society is so evidently in the hands of man, that a queen is almost necessitated even to look upon her own footman as her superior, merely because he is a man; and man is enabled, merely by the deceitful spell of this nominal supremacy, to exercise a species of control over woman, which does not result from real superiority of intellect or morals, but, like the spiritual authority of ancient priests, from some fancied excellence, which is supposed to be peculiarly and exclusively the inheritance of the male.

Divided as men are – and we vow it grieves us much to see their scattered situation – women are infinitely more so. Men have their public meetings, their social meetings, their newspapers, their magazines, their male speakers, and their male editors, and men with men correspond in all quarters of the world, upon the most extensive scale; but woman knows nothing of woman, except through the medium of man – a dense medium, which distorts her native character, and bedaubs it with the false colouring of the sex, whose feelings, on a thousand delicate subjects, must be the very reverse of her own. How can woman redeem herself from such shackles of ignorance and mental slavery? By application to man? Fool she must be, if she apply to man to get a knowledge of herself, and the interests of her own sex. By taking counsel in part with man? This nominal reputation of man for practical skill and experience will ruin her cause, if she let him have any thing to do with it; for if ever a man is introduced amongst the other sex, they will stick to him like feathers on a tarred seamen, and he will carry the whole union on his back. Men having nothing to do with women; they are two distinct animals altogether; they have each a sphere of their own, with which the other cannot, without creating mischief, interfere. Therefore, we say, let woman look to herself, consult with woman on her own affairs; allow no male to enter her meetings, until she has obtained sufficient skill and experience to act in public, and then let her assembly rooms be thrown open.

And what are women to consult about, say some? Why, their own affairs, to be sure; their own rights and privileges. Let them make rules and regulations for managing domestic matters, morals, etc., or any other matters which peculiarly interest them, as women; and let these be submitted to the General Union of both sexes; and, if approved, let them be acknowledged as obligatory, both at home and abroad; and let him that will not submit be degraded, as unworthy the name of man. By this means the women may, in a few months, do an immensity of good; they may reform drunken husbands, procure clean and comfortable homes, get good clothes and education for their children, etc. etc. Who are afraid of female legislation but profligates? Woman will only interfere where woman finds herself aggrieved; and has she not a right to interfere? He who denies the right of woman, declares himself a rebel.

We are glad to find that a General Union of the Female Shoe-binders and Closers is to take place on Monday, the 10th of March, at the Assembly Rooms, 59, Poland-street, Oxford street, to enlist themselves under the banner of their brothers, and form themselves into a Lodge on the principle of the National Consolidated Union. Such a meeting, of course, can only interfere with its own department of industry. It is only when matrons unite, as we hope they soon shall, that domestic affairs will be turned over the coals, and profligacy put to shame, and for ever annihilated in our land, by the moral legislation of *woman*.

Pioneer, 8 March 1834.

A Page for the Ladies

An Initiated Tailor has been rebuking us very severely for our preposterous absurdities about the women, and seems to think that we are
greatly mistaken in our opinion respecting the feelings of women in
general upon the benefits derivable from female Unions. Perhaps we
are; but, notwithstanding, we are not disposed to yield until we are
convinced by plain reasoning, and we should like it fully as well
without any abusive epithets. We shall publish any reasons of men or
women, for the prevention or discouragement of female Unions,
provided they be temperate in expression. This initiated unionist scouts
the idea of women's rights and privileges, and of their associating
together to demand them of the male, and he says, that though not a
profligate himself, if his wife were to go to legislate, it would be a very
likely, nay, a certain way of making him a profligate. It is out at last.
This is the spirit of the male. We wanted to draw it out, in order that it
might be exposed. The working-men complain that the masters exercise
authority over them; and they maintain their right to associate, and
prescribe laws for their own protection. There is no high treason here;
no; for the men are gaining authority, and not losing it. But speak of
any project which shall diminish the authority of the male, or give him
an equal, where once he found an inferior, and then the spirit of
Toryism awakes that has long been dormant. All men are Tories by
nature. Even the unionists themselves, who rail against tyrants and
oppressors, have the blood of the aristocrat flowing in their veins.

The rights and privileges of women, says our correspondent, may be
found in the *oldest* book in the world, 'that they be *discreet*, chaste,
and keepers at home, not gadding about or busy bodies; and how can
this be exemplified if they go out to *legislate*'. This is the opinion of a
male unionist. It only belongs to men to *gad about and be busy bodies*.
Women have nothing to do but to keep at home, and remain in ignorance of every thing but cooking, washing, scrubbing pots, etc. Men
alone are busy bodies; men alone should go to meetings, etc; for men
alone have rights and privileges: all the rights and privileges of women
are absorbed in the male, and he will protect woman, provided she
only be obedient and keep at home. Now, this oldest book in the
world, which has been quoted against the women by a master, may be
quoted with equal authority against the men. It says, 'Servants, be
subject to your masters with all fear, not only to the good and
merciful, but also to the perverse; for this is thankworthy, if a man for
conscience-sake endure grief, suffering wrongfully'. Again, 'Let as
many *as are under the yoke* count their masters worthy of *all* honour'.
Then, if men are going to bring the oldest book in the world against

the women, we hope the women will bring it against the men, and 'down with the unions'. But we want no partial quotations; if our opponents quote from the master's page, let them quote from the servant's page also, or we shall do it for them.

But we are pretty sure that our correspondent misunderstands us. We do not want to set women agadding, but to prevent their gadding and their tattling. What is it that makes woman a tattler and a busy body, but the confined sphere in which she moves? She is individualised by the narrowness of her knowledge and experience. What is it that makes a villager less liberal than an inhabitant of the city? His confinement certainly; the little variety of character and circumstances which present themselves; and, therefore, we find that, in small villages, the tittle tattle of private families is much more prevalent than in large cities; the only way to cure women of tattling and gadding is the way by which men are cured, enlarging their views and widening their sphere of activity. It is a physical and metaphysical absurdity, to suppose that the mind can be liberalised by the confinement of the body.

But what do we recommend for women, that can annoy any one but a Tory? We do not recommend politics or trade to matrons. If they are not traders, why should they interfere with trade? Neither do we advise them to go and spout at meetings, or make themselves public in any way. We only advise them to associate with each other, and commune with each other upon subjects connected with woman alone; and if they find themselves aggrieved in any respect by the *mal*-administration of the male, to express in clear and determined language their opinion and resolutions upon the subject. It is to create peace, that we make the proposal; it is to prevent individual quarrels at home, by forming regulations, and for the proper management of families, that we recommend the social intercourse of women.

But our correspondent would have women utterly scattered; each woman subject to her own husband; so that if a working man should make thirty shillings a-week. He may drink tea if he pleases; go to a coffee-house every night, and read the papers, and bring in fifteen shillings a-week to keep home and pay the rent withal. *He has a right to do this*, for he makes the money. But what is the woman doing? She is working from morning till night at house-keeping; she is bearing children, and suffering all the pangs of labour, and all the exhaustion of suckling; she is cooking, and washing, and cleaning; soothing one child, cleaning another, and feeding a third. And all this is nothing; for she gets no wages. Her wages come from her husband; they are optional; he can give her either twenty shillings to keep house with, or he can give her only ten. If she complain, he can damn and swear, and say, like the Duke of Newcastle, 'Have I not a right to do as I please with my own?' And it is high treason in women to resist such authority, and claim the privilege of a fair reward of their labour! Good! Good! If we thought that the sex *woman* could patiently endure such a yoke of bondage, we should hate her most heartily? But how is she to prevent it? Why, by the very same means by which the men will prevent the tyranny of the master. Women will save themselves abundance of labour by association. We shall give an idea of what might be done by union.

Our matrons at present are burdened with labour; and this labour is increased by the want of system or method. If a woman, with a family, is washing, she leaves her young ones to roll on the floor, and puts her baby on the knee of a larger baby, which is seated squat on the ground. By and by they are both tired, and the two babies begin a screaming; the mother stops her work, takes up the little baby, and gives the great baby a thrashing. Then perhaps it is time for cooking; the husband will soon be home, and what a storm there will be if there is no dinner! The washing must be suspended, and suspended perhaps it is till the children go to bed, and then the poor mother is obliged to scour and rub when her children and her husband are all fast asleep. Might not some remedy be applied for this evil? Supposing, merely, ten matrons were in friendly union, might not one take charge of ten families of children for a day, and relieve all the other nine, who would each take the office in her turn, and thus be released for nine days out of ten, of the greatest proportion of her labour? Might not infant schools be instituted, *not* for teaching children to read; for amusing infants, and affording a comfortable opportunity for mothers, not only for improving their minds, but adding to the comforts of their husbands, and making home a place of attraction, instead of an object of aversion, as it is at present. What an agreeable change would this be both for parents and children! How gladly would the little creatures walk off to school in a morning, with their clean hands and faces, and laughing countenances, if, instead of drilling them there, like a parcel of mutes, forcing them to sit all day on a bench, with a little book in their hands, and two big tears rolling on their cheeks, they were amused and entertained by a variety of innocent plays: drawing their little horses, rolling their little wheelbarrows, whipping their wooden donkeys, jumping, and dancing, and singing; their little hearts distended with joy, and as happy to return on a morning to their amusement, as now they are loath! All this might be done by women, if they would merely commune with each other on the subject; and who better qualified than women for such legislation as this? Might not washing establishments be instituted, where each, in her turn, might assist in person, or by proxy, as she pleased, and thus divest the workman's fire-side, or his kitchen, of many of the disagreeable inconveniences which so often drive him to the public-house. Perhaps our correspondent is happy in his wife and his home. We rejoice in it if it be so; but we know, from personal observation, that we have not drawn an extravagant picture of a working man's home, nor written 'preposterous absurdities' respecting the method of procuring additional comforts to the poor man, by the union of women. Nay, we are certain that homes will never be comfortable till this union be accomplished, and such projects as these, and many others, to which we shall allude, shall be carried into effect. It is for the happiness of man and woman that we write.

Pioneer, 22 March 1834.

A Page for the Ladies

We are happy to hear from A Mechanic's Wife, *and to find that she and other females are encouraging our efforts in the cause of woman. We hope they will consider well the subject of female emancipation, and forward us plans of amelioration, to give us a list of their grievances. Woman only can tell her own grievances; and it is necessary that we, as the advocates of woman, should know them.*

We must, for the sake of justice, answer our 'Censor' of last week once more; and for the satisfaction of himself and others, we publish a reply which he has sent to our last Ladies' Page. Let our readers judge for themselves; we do not fear the result. He does not understand us. Because we advocate the cause of female associations, do we therefore advise woman to cast off her feminine character, and assume the effrontery of man? Can women not associate without becoming impudent? Without becoming gossips, gadders, busy bodies, spouters, and every other contemptible thing? If union is to produce such a corrupting effect, then, for heaven's sake, let the men beware of it; for man and woman are one nature, and are refined or corrupted by the same means. Why may women not attend female associations, as well as go to church on a Sunday? And why may not all the women of England be free to speak their mind in public, and yet preserve their characteristic softness and peacefulness of manner, as well as the Quakeresses, who, for aught we hear or know, are as intelligent, as amiable, as social, prudent, and domestic, as any class of women in England. Our friend is too hasty. He has not properly investigated the subject; and the reason we did not publish his last letter was, that we were sufficiently aware of this, and wanted him to reconsider it. But since he persists, we comply with his request this week, at the same time assuring him that we are more and more convinced, that he has too much of the spirit of the *master* in him; a spirit which we are determined to resist, wherever we find it, unless it be the mastership of pure moral worth, which we shall always be ready to acknowledge. But it is degrading to human nature to admit the superiority of one being over another, merely because the *gender* is different. What is this but aristocracy? If we admit the right of man to rule over woman, merely because he is *man*, then we may, upon the same principle, admit the authority of one man to tyrannize over another, merely because he is of noble blood, *high born*. We are now making a bold stand against all these artificial aristocracies of birth, and are determined to acknowledge only moral and intellectual superiority. This will always attain its own place, if not kept down by artificial laws and tyrannical customs. Certainly, nothing can be more unjust than that law of public opinion and of political jurisprudence which gives a fool (merely because he is a man) a political and domestic authority over a woman, who may, in every other respect except the circumstance of sex, be his decided superior. We say, most decidedly, it is a tyrant's law; and we hope to demonstrate to our fair readers that it is destined in the counsels of heaven, for the good of both sexes, to be for ever annulled. Now is the day of general redemption for all. Black slaves and white slaves, male slaves and female slaves, must all be freed, and the curse of the first man and woman be taken off – *he* no more to eat in the sweat of his brow, and *she* no more to trust for individual happiness to his capricious smile; to laugh when he laughs, and fear when he frowns.

Let our doctrine not be misunderstood, and you will find that it is the doctrine of liberty, of modesty, of chastity, of every species of purity, and, at the same time, of enjoyment to both sexes; a doctrine, which shall teach you how to disencumber yourselves of the greatest burthens of social and domestic life; which shall refine all your pleasures, develop all the characteristic features of the two sexes, and clothe them with everlasting beauty; which shall not only put an end to gadding and gossiping amongst the women, but also amongst the men; and so far from making the women a parcel of spouters, shall put a stop to the evils of male spouting, and substitute the social converse and cheerful meetings of *both* sexes, in room of the roaring and drunken clubs of the male.

Our friend says that our doctrine might do very well for the women of the continent, but not for the modest dames of England, who are more domestic in their character. But what good effect has this domesticity of the English women produced upon the English husbands? They are the most drunken husbands in Europe, perhaps in the world! Hear it, O, heavens! In this very island there are 61,231 publicans, and only 27,942 bakers. Who support these publicans? Not the modest dames of England, surely; the patterns for all the world to follow? No; it is their lordly husbands, whose corrupt taste for male associations, to the exclusion of women, has produced a depravity of habit in this country, which makes it a by-word among neighbouring nations. We know the cause of this evil, and we shall not fail to assail it most stoutly. We shall brave the wrath of man, and the suspicion of woman for a time; and a short time only is necessary; for a little reflection will demonstrate to both that our views are conducive to good morals, and must be adopted in practice before mankind can be moralized, and secure to themselves every species of social and domestic comfort.

Woman must not be individualized. We warn all our sisters against every attempt in the male to scatter them, and prevent their communion. Men will attempt it under every guise – the guise of love, of modesty, of religion, of chastity; in fine, every guise under which the male contrives to woo the female. But what is the consequence of your yielding to their insinuations? Why, you see the consequences already. The practice has had a fair trial. Woman is a slave, a servant to man; and when not supported by man, the most helpless creature in the world, and subject to the most piteous fate. We burn, we weep to see her, as she appears to us daily, in a hundred shapes. We know how to cure the evil; but man, man, and *she herself, deceived by man*, resist our endeavours, and cry out, like the landowners and the clergy, against all innovations.

Pioneer, 29 March 1834.

A Page for the Ladies

In our last number we published the letter of 'A Woman', (we like this word better than *lady*,) who requested an answer to a simple query, which we left entirely to the tailors to reply to; but, like his most gracious majesty, they have answered nothing. One of our male correspondents, however, feeling intensely the hardships with which the female tailors seem to be threatened, has written us very feelingly upon the subject, and say it were better that Unions had never been formed, than that they should proceed at once to act the part of tyranny over their fellow-labourers. True! But we hope the matter will be amicably settled; and as the subject is not generally understood, we shall state it in such a way as to enable our readers to form a judgment on it.

The women have always been worse paid for their labour than the men; and, by long habit and patient acquiescence, they have been taught to regard this inequality as justice. They are, therefore, content with merely a portion of a man's wages, even when their work is equally valuable. The consequence of this is, that men are either obliged to work for women's wages, or lose their work. If a woman makes a waistcoat for two-thirds of the sum which is charged by a man, she will, without doubt, monopolize the waistcoat trade to herself, or compel him to lower his charges. It is to prevent this diminution of wages that the male tailors have declared war against the female tailors. They do not want to deprive the women of their means of living, provided they do not prove prejudicial to the trade at large; they would have a woman's work to be valued by the same standard as that of a man's, and equally well paid. This at least is the professed reason which the tailors give for their proposed system of exclusion. Were this to have the effect of raising the wages of the women, and still preserving to them their employment, we should give the tailors our hearty support; but where they wantonly throw out of employment a number of females, merely because they were women, we think this an encroachment on the liberties of humanity, which is too much to be tolerated.

This question divides itself into two:

1. Has one man a right to reduce the wages of his fellow-workman, by lowering his own? Our aristocratical opponents, in their great zeal for the liberty of the workingman, say, 'Yes, a man has a right to work for as little as he pleases'; or, in other words, he has a right to tyrannize over his fellows by bringing their resources down to the starving point. This is quite the doctrine of legislators, and when carried to a certain extent, it becomes an argument for the divine right of kings, and the duty of passive obedience and abject submission. We say decidedly, that no man has a right to reduce the wages of labour by lowering his own charges; for by doing so he compels his brother to do the same.

2. Has woman a right to reduce the wages of man, by working for less than man? Certainly not, were woman considered equal to man, and did she enjoy the same rights and privileges; but since man has doomed her to inferiority, and stamped an inferior value upon all the productions of her industry, the low wages of woman are not so much the voluntary price she sets upon her labour, as the price which is fixed by the tyrannical influence of male supremacy; therefore any attempt to deprive her of labour, because she works at a reduced price, is merely punishing woman for the cruel and pernicious effects of male supremacy. To make the two sexes equal, and to reward them equally, would settle the matter amicably; but any attempt to settle it otherwise will prove an act of gross tyranny.

Pioneer, 5 April 1834.

A Page for the Ladies

Man is stronger than woman by nature; his bones are larger, and his body is taller. We suspect that few will be so hardy as to deny this. There are some, we know, who do; but it is easy to find individuals who pass in the world for being quite as sane as their neighbours, who deny the most self-evident axioms. There are not only many who doubt that they have souls, but many who doubt that their bodies are real. We have met with genuine sceptics who doubted their own existence. Then it cannot be thought very singular that there are some who doubt if woman is bodily weaker than man, and attribute the present difference between the two sexes to education and habits of life. We have nothing to do but to refer such sceptics to the brute creation, and they will find that the male is always stouter in body than the female.

But granting all this, what is the conclusion to be deduced? Is man thereby demonstrated superior to woman? Then, by a parity of reasoning, a black bear or a wild buffalo is superior to man, for it is much stronger. But it is by this argument of the strongest alone that the doctrine of male superiority is defended, for man can never have the hardihood to maintain that his frame is more delicate, either in shape, features, or complexion, than that of woman, his feelings more acute and sensitive, his moral sympathies more refined, or his love more fervid. He must admit that, if superior to woman in physical strength, there is a delicacy about the female character to which the male can never attain: in fine, that there is a characteristic difference between the two sexes, so peculiar to each that the one would suffer deterioration by being invested with the character of the other.

Now the query is, which of the two characters is the most valuable? This question has been hitherto answered by the male in his own favour, and for six thousand years it has scarcely ever been disputed. This is not at all to be wondered at, considering the habits of mankind, and the condition of society during that period when strength has always been considered the standard of worth. This principle has been long acted upon, but it is now gradually being abandoned; but man always begins reformation with himself, and leaves his fair helpmate to the last. Men are not now valued, as formerly, by their physical strength, so much as by the nicety and delicacy of their workmanship. A fine artist is much more highly rewarded than a sturdy artizan; but the selfish male has not yet learned to apply the principle of action to his treatment of the female. A woman's wage is not reckoned at an average more than two-thirds of a male, and we believe in reality it seldom amounts to more than a third (and wives have no wages at all). Yet, is not the produce of female labour as useful? Is not a shirt as great a luxury as a coat, and is it not regarded as equally ornamental in the list of male habiliments? But the coat requires more strength than the shirt or the gown, and upon this account it becomes a task for the male, and is paid accordingly. There are many departments of the arts which are peculiarly suited to the female hand, which is much lighter in execution; and by the skilful combination of the properties of each sex, the finest results in the department of human industry may be accomplished. We may take the art of music as an example of what may be done by united action, and as a proof of the decided natural difference between the two sexes; yet the male and female voices are not rivals in the musical concerto – the melody is enhanced by the contrast. The one sex cannot personate the other; the attempt is either a caricature, or disgusting to the feelings of refined taste. The same sexual difference characterises all the respective productions of the sexes; but the superficial minds of former generations have not brought these differences to light. That discovery remains yet to be made; and when it is made, it will divide every species of labour, like music itself, into male and female – not, however, to prevent the effeminate male from prosecuting a female employment, nor the masculine female from a male employment. There are many pursuits in which both may engage. Both the male and the female voice may sing the common air, but the woman cannot with dignity descend to bass, nor a man ascend to the treble, even though his lungs could permit.

But the discovery of this sexual difference of handicraft will only tend to bring the two sexes to an equality. This is the grand conclusion to which we must finally attain – that the two sexes are each distinct in their kind; and by the proper application, or blending of male and female skill and labour, the arts may be brought to perfection; that an equal proportion of both is necessary for the perfection of social happiness, and that the industrious female is consequently well entitled to the same amount of remuneration as the industrious male.

To the Editor of the *Pioneer*

Second letter to the Tailors

Sir,

There is an old saying, that 'a friend in need, is a friend indeed,' and never was its truth more agreeably proved than it was last week, by the very kind manner in which you were pleased to notice my appeal to the Tailors' Union. To you, Sir, are due the thanks, not only of myself and the other females of my class in the metropolis, but also of every working female in the kingdom, for the zeal and ability with which you have pressed, and are continuing to press, the record of our various wrongs upon the notice of our 'lords and masters'.

An ingenious commentator has observed that woman was made of a rib taken out of the side of a man – not out of his head, to *rule* him, nor out of his feet, to be *trampled upon by him*; but out of his side, to be his *equal* – under his arm, to be protected; near his heart, to be beloved. Alas! Alas! That poverty and oppression should so have hardened the hearts and blunted the feelings of *man*kind, that, instead of regarding woman in the light it was intended by their Maker they should do; instead of extending to her that protection, which, as the weaker party, she can in justice claim; instead of acting, in fact, as *man* ought to act towards *woman*, they should be found amongst her worst oppressors! Nay, that they should have united themselves together to deprive her of the means of subsistence! And this, if they persevere in their present course, they certainly will do. I told you, in my former letter, that I had 'good reason' for believing they would answer my first question in the affirmative; and to prove to you, Sir, who have so kindly espoused our cause, and to the public, who are not, I think, *uninterested* spectators of the matter, that I am not needlessly alarmed, I will state that reason. I have worked for a house at the West-end for the last eighteen years, and a short time ago was told by my employer that he feared he should not be able to employ me much longer, as the men intended to prevent the women from working in future at the trade. 'If,' said he, 'they should insist on this measure, harsh and unfeeling as it is, I shall be forced to comply with it.' This, of course, alarmed me very much, and induced me to apply, through the *Pioneer*, to the Tailors' Union, to know if such really was their intention. Their silence on the matter is, I think, a proof of their guilt; they cannot deny it; and knowing they cannot exculpate themselves from the charge of unfeeling brutality in the eyes of the public, they are ashamed even to *attempt* a defence of their conduct.

One reason why this odious measure has not yet been enforced is, that it has been opposed by many among themselves, from various motives. Some of them, for instance, have married, solely because their wives have been able to do *so much* work, and to earn *so much* per week, so that, instead of working themselves, they can loiter away half the week in a pot-house; while the poor woman sits slaving at home, and gets only scorn and abuse for her self-devotedness. These have opposed the measure. There are others, again, who are perhaps afflicted, or constantly suffering from illness, and are therefore incapable of doing much work, and whose chief dependance is on their wives' earnings. These have opposed the measure. I myself know a woman, whose husband was ill, and unable to work for four months, and during that time, by unremitting exertion, and almost unceasing labour, she supported him, herself, and three children, by the work of her own hands. That husband is now dead; and if the men succeed in their present diabolical purpose, this honest, worthy, and industrious woman and her children must starve, or *go to the workhouse*. This is but one solitary instance out of hundreds of similar cases. Again; there are other men, who, from a naturally idle disposition, while their wives are willing to work and slave, actually will not work themselves; and yet, when they come home, after having spent the day at a gin-shop, they complain that the place is dirty, their shirt is ragged, and their children neglected! And how can it be otherwise? Is not this misery actually caused by *themselves?* Did the man so complaining do his duty as a husband and a father – make the most of his time, and procure the means wherewith to support his family – would not his wife take a pride in rendering his home as comfortable, and his children as cleanly as possible? But while she is obliged to work, not only for herself, but for him, she actually has not the time to do this; and finding, after all her exertions, instead of being thanked, she is abused, she becomes reckless; her home, instead of being resorted to as a blessing, is avoided and hated as a curse. She seeks refuge from reflection (I regret to say too often) in the bottle; and thus the misery and degradation of the unfortunate pair are completed!

There are some good men, who, from humanity and a fellow-feeling with the female labourer, instead of wishing to banish her from the trade, would gladly join in raising the price of her labour to the male standard: to these men, I present my heartfelt thanks; the consciousness of having done a good action is its own reward.

There is one part of the remarks in the last *Pioneer* which I most particularly wish to impress upon the minds of the men; it is this: 'the low wages of woman are not so much the voluntary price she sets upon her labour, as the price which is fixed by the tyrannical influence of *male supremacy*.' Hear this, ye men! And when next you meet to proceed against the rights and liberties of the weaker part of the creation, may the still small voice of conscience whisper in your ears the words of the *Pioneer*, and before you presume to judge, be sure that *you yourselves are guiltless!*

I could say much more on the subject, but as I fear I have already trespassed too much on your valuable columns, I will, Sir, with your permission, defer it to another communication.

Your obliged and humble servant,

A Woman.

London, April 7.

P.S. I have enclosed half-a-crown for the wives of the six unfortunate men of Dorchester, and were it in my power would gladly send five times as much. I think, Sir, if you were to call upon the females of the metropolis for a penny weekly subscription in their behalf, the call would not be made in vain.

The Dorchester Victims

Female Petition

A petition for *justice* (for mercy it *is not*, the spirit cannot brook the satire to petition for *common justice*, and call it *mercy*); a petition for *justice* in this land of liberty is now in course of signature by the females of Birmingham, to our most gracious Adelaide, the acknowl-edged queen of these realms, praying her most gracious majesty to intercede with his most gracious majesty on behalf of these six guilt-less men, who are torn from their families and their friends, merely as an experiment for the base, cowardly, witless Whigs, who now hold the reins of government over us. Can the women of England remain unmoved, when they behold such deeds as these? No; the mildest spirit must rebel against such tyranny as this! But hope brightens when we remember that our petition is dedicated to a woman, and to one holding a station in which she ought to be the paragon of womankind; and believing she must possess those virtues which so eminently adorn the female character, we think her good sense must lead her to sympathise with these victims of an unwise government, and use her utmost influence in justice to the nearest and dearest ties of nature, and restore these good and useful members of society to their disconsolate wives and families. This would be an act worthy the queen of England, and an act that would gain her a nation's blessing. My object in writing these few lines is to make known, through your extensively circulated paper, the inten-tion and spirit of the women of Birmingham, hoping it will be acted upon throughout the country. If this is done, we think, in woman's unsuspecting confidence, that the appeal cannot be made in vain provided the petition be fairly presented to her majesty. As for Baron Williams, his name is in high repute among the people. I *could tell you* to what height some of our Birmingham sisters would elevate him for his unflinching service to the Whigs! We should vastly like to hear a lecture from his learned Whighship on law and equity; we fancy his text would be something to this effect: The English law comes upon us like a thief in the night; there shall be a million persons grinding at the mill; six shall be taken, and the others left. We can only divine this equable poise of the scales of justice in this manner. Arise then, females arise, and let us see whether England may boast of a just and virtuous queen!

Yours, Sir, in the earnest cause of right,

A Bondswoman.

To the Editor of the *Pioneer*

Sir,

Although I have been a constant reader of the unstamped publications, yet the *Pioneer* did not come into my hands before the 22nd of March. The contents of that book have made a very deep impression on my mind. Having long been advocate for the emancipation of women, I therefore, offer myself as a volunteer to join a union of women, which, in my weak opinion, will be the means of finishing the work the men have begun, as they cannot do without us; and the oldest book in the world declares, as God saw it was not good for man to be alone, he made woman; but, I am certain, for a much better purpose than that insolent tailor understands; as God is a good master, a merciful master, and has set an example for man to follow. And why not man set the same example for woman to follow? Because he does not know the value of her; if he did, he would remember who gave him birth, and from whom he received his first instruction. A woman! The oldest book says women should adorn themselves with a meek and quiet spirit, which in the sight of God is a pearl of great price. What a misfortune it is to see those pearls so often cast before swine, to be trampled upon until their weakness is turned into violence; then down goes the poor woman; it is all her fault; the man never does wrong! Possibly this is the tailor's reason his wife should not go to meetings, for fear she should hear that he is in the wrong, and herself entitled to demand of him that which he demands of others. But I am afraid that he is a hard master, and such a man I never would obey. I am neither a lazy, gossiping, drunken, nor tattling wife; and yet I have been at meetings alone, likewise with my husband, not to speak, but to hear. Very likely this would alarm the tailor. However, as long as my own eyes are open, I will never be led by a blind man; for fear we should both fall into a ditch; and great would be the fall of many prudent, discreet women, if they suffered themselves to be dictated to by husbands; as I am persuaded a good wife knows when to go out and when to stay at home: she will not neglect business to seek that which is useless. Again; the oldest book says, 'Husbands love your wives, and be not bitter against them.' But how often is that pretended love converted into hatred by his own misconduct, as he would rather pay for those dandy caps the publicans' wives wear, than give to his own that which the oldest book recommends – modest apparel! But she must work, or go without. But that is not enough; she must be insulted with all the diabolical language that man can utter. What a bitter mixture for a poor woman to take! And if she offers the least resistance, it is thrust down her throat with his fist, possibly with the loss of a tooth or the spilling of a little of that blood which he thinks so inferior to his own. As he is lord of his castle, he is master and will be obeyed. But what does he suppose women must be? Surely, he must think we are either stocks or stones; I was ready to say, like himself. But I hope he will find himself mistaken, as I do not believe we were made for the abuse, but for the use, of man; not to be slaves to the passions of either body or mind, but co-equal with him; and if we are to share his troubles, why not his pleasures also? If not, then down with the Union that now is amongst men! As I believe it is but a shadow, and never will be completed until the women bring forth the substance.

An English Woman.

April 7th, 1834.

P.S. Good *Pioneer*, as you appear to be a friend to the women, if you do not approve of the above I hope you will not expose a woman nearly sixty years old, who has not had a pen in her hand the last seven years; therefore you will find many errors; however, if there is but one observation that you think would be of service to the women, I should be happy to see it in print.

To the Bonnet Makers of London, Hartford, and Bedford

Whilst with pleasure I have been watching the glorious progress the men of England are making towards their emancipation, I regret to find so few of my own sex attempt to raise their heads out of the degraded situation we are placed in. Who produce more wealth for our employers, who accumulate princely fortunes from our labour? And who more oppressed than we bonnet-makers? And from whence can we trace the evil? Not so much from our employers as ourselves. Are there not, even at the present time, some among ourselves who are reducing the prices on purpose to get the bulk of the work in their own hand; and will, if not stopped, starve the rest? We cannot blame our employers for getting their work done cheap, if we do not know the value of our own labour enough to protect ourselves. We feel the effect, and it is time to seek a remedy; and that can only be effected in union. Do not say they are only for men; 'tis a wrong impression, forced on our minds to keep us slaves! When men can do our work they shall legislate for us. I do not wish to take any power from man that he can with justice claim; only let us, who bear an equal share of the evils of circumstances, unite to defend our own; the men will not think us less amiable for knowing our own value, or the value of our labour, if kept within the bounds of reason. We have been foolishly taught to think it preposterous for woman to make herself in any way public; and even now, whilst knowledge is taking rapid strides over the world, we are told unions of women would make us idlers; and some have the audacity to say, drunkards. Let us, sisters, banish the idea, and prove to the men what they have proved to the aristocracy; it may make us intelligent, and will set us free. I entreat fathers to teach their daughters the nature and value of union; brothers to lead their sisters into the midst of them; and you, husbands, who have seen your wives, when you have been out of employ, toiling early and late to get a bare existence for her children and you, rouse her from the lethargy her sorrows have sunk her into. A word from you will do wonders; it will animate her when she feels assured it is the wish and example of the friend of her bosom. I am induced to plead to the men, from hearing so many say they do not like women from home. Are we not forced from home to labour, and may we not go from home to endeavour to lighten that labour, without the fear of an angry husband when we return? Every feeling manly heart answers we have. Then let us, sister workwomen, make a beginning in our own business; our number is great, our power equal, the time of year in our favour; we may better our condition, but cannot make it worse, for that is impossible.

P.A.S.
Pioneer, 12 April 1834.

Women's Pages from the *Pioneer* with Correspondence

To Correspondents
A Woman *is rather too severe this week*

Woman's Page

We have adopted a new title for the female department of our little Journal. This we always preferred from the first, but the other happened inadvertently to introduce the cause of our sisterhood into our columns, and we thought proper to continue it for a season. Woman is an endearing, social name; but lady has something shockingly aristocratic and unequal about it; it conveys the idea of superiority and control; it is the counterpart of lord; but how the term lady happened to be applied to the female sex so generally, whilst lord has always been an exclusive title conferred only by a patent of nobility, is difficult to say. Surely, it did not originate from any sovereign domination exercised by the women over the men? But it may have arisen from the slander of the male respecting their government properties. They have been abundantly bantered and stigmatised for their talents and ambition for petticoat control, their curtain lecturing, and all the other dictatorships of the political economy of home; but all this has been mere twaddle on the part of the male, who, whenever woman pretends to dictate to, or even to advise, her robust helpmate, brands the presumption by the name of petticoat rule.

It is a common opinion that lady derives its origin from loaf-day, or laaf-day, contracted la-dy. The loaf day was a yearly festival in ancient times, when the barons' wives used to distribute a portion of bread and ale to their vassals; and, in process of time, the day and the baron's wife became synonymous. But, whatever was its original meaning, it implied the same kind of inequality which is included in the counter-title 'lord', and it almost looks as if it was bestowed upon woman as a kind of soothing, flattering title, to atone for the deprivation of the real authority which the name implies. Man is the lord, without assuming the title. Woman has got the title, but wants the authority. The time shall come, however, when the influence of woman on society will be greatly superior to that which she at present exercises. Her moral influence, even now, acts as a powerful check upon the brutish character of the other sex; the greater proportion of whatever refinement in manners the age can boast of, comes originally from her. But were she properly educated, were she placed in such circumstances as would make her independent, and remove the humiliating necessity of assuming a mercenary character, and becoming an outcast upon society, miserable in herself, and the source of corruption to all of the other sex who associate with her, the reaction upon the male which would thereby take place would regenerate the whole morality of love, which is the leading passion in the great social intercourse of mankind, and the source either of good or bad morals, according as it is invested with a pure and honourable character. The consequence of this regeneration we need not describe, our fair readers can well imagine it.

Since I wrote my last letter addressed to the Bonnet Makers of London, etc. etc., I am delighted to hear some spirited men are about to call a public meeting of the women of our trade, to take into consideration the best method of forming a Union for the protection of our labour. 'Tis time we began to look around us, or our slave drivers will find some despotic means of counteracting our designs. If we intend to do any thing, we must do it quickly and resolutely, and prove to our oppressors we are worthy the characters of British women. It may be asked by some women what can we do. I answer, all that is necessary for our happiness and preservation, if we will but put our shoulder to the wheel; at least we can but attempt it; if we fail in our first endeavour, we may not in the second. Many a brave general has been driven from the field the first time, and has returned again to the charge and made his victory more perfect. I do not complain of our circumstances without cause, for we are paid so low for our work, that if we pay others honestly, we are half-starved ourselves, besides being treated like beggars, and kept at the greatest distance by the counter-skippers that take in our work. And a more daring act of tyranny was ever practised on individuals than was performed in the house I work for. A woman took in twenty-six hats, two the warehouseman thought fit to send back to have a few stitches altered, and took off twopence in every other hat, though the other twenty-four was made in the first style; thus eight women were robbed for the fault of two. This is not a singular case, for it is the practice to find fault with work when they wish to get it done cheap. In the year of 1800, sixty yards of plat was paid for sewing five and six shillings, now in 1834, I was paid 1s. 9d for ninety yards. In 1800 Devon plat was paid five shillings per score for only platting, now in 1835 you may buy the same kind in the markets for tenpence and a shilling. How much of that can be paid for labour? Our employers want the luxuries of life out of the profit of the goods they sell, and they certainly have a right to it, as well as princes and peers, for under present circumstances they run great risk; ruin stares them in the face; they will find soon they had better unite their force to ours, but we who suffer most must make the first movement, time will teach them to follow. Some designing knaves will tell you the Union is illegal, and will be put down; do not believe it. Lord Howick was compelled to say the other night in the House, man had a right to set what value he thought proper on his labour, but he strongly reprobated secrecy. His Lordship thought where there was any secrecy, there must be some evil design intended. I agree with his lordship's opinion, for I suppose that was the reason his lordship would not discuss the policy his Majesty's government intended to pursue with respect to the Trades' Union. For the satisfaction of Lord Howick, I beg to state, we women will have no secret, what we do will be in the face of the whole world; we will break no laws, do no injuries to any one, but all the good we can; with these determinations what earthly power can crush us? And for the information of Lord Howick and other curious persons, I will state our object. First, the protection of our labour; secondly, the support of our sick, and to bury our dead, that we may not be driven to ask relief from merciless parish officers; thirdly, to instruct each other's minds in true and moral knowledge; fourthly, to form an infant school for both sexes, under the tuition of the most intelligent men, so that liberty and truth may be the first seed cast into the infant mould; and, lastly, for the protection of our noble brothers in Union. The last article may seem to some contempt-ible, but ask the princes and peers of any nation if they think so. No. Their secret amours have taught them a better lesson; they well know, and have often felt the effects of the inventive genius of woman when they have any favorite object in view. If woman can defeat in a bad cause, she may be sure she will in a good one, backed by fathers, brothers, husbands, and lovers. Come to the Union, sisters, old and young, rich and poor, if you love liberty, study to deserve it. Let us set our wits to work, 'tis right against might. Children yet unborn must have to remember, there was woman as well as man in the Union.

P.A.S.

P.S. Any woman wishing to become a member, will apply to Mr Austin, Charlotte-street, Rathbone-place.

Pioneer, 26 April 1834.

Woman's Page

There is a strife to come between man and woman, the one has rights to claim, the other concessions to make. Great as the love may be which the one feels for the other, that love is of an insulated private character, and is indulged and gratified independent of the war of individual interest, which often annihilates domestic comfort, and must soon exhibit itself on a larger scale in the great domestic family of society. Love is altogether selfish, and when it longs for the society of the other sex, and sacrifices its own personal comforts in behalf of the object beloved, it is only because these comforts afford no pleasure unless they are shared with the object of the all-subduing passion. But what a man or a woman will sacrifice for an individual mistress or lover, men or women in the aggregate will not sacrifice for each other. The individual is very different from the sex collectively. The indi-vidual is a lover, the sexes collectively are not lovers; they are merely political parties, who eye one another with jealousy, and whenever an opportunity is afforded of a fair encounter, they will separate from each other like master and slave, the one to insist upon her rights to equality, the other to insist upon her obligation to obey.

There is much less pure moral love in the world than appears to the superficial eye. Love is like piety, a kind of traffic, in which there are a great many dealers, but they are double-dealers, and assume the sacred garb of passion for sinister purposes. The holy flame is desecrated and defiled by the unhallowed lust of power and money, and all the other grovelling selfish motives which take the precedence of purer springs of action. Woman is made a hireling; she is not so by nature or by feeling. In heart she is a lover, a fond lover, and one that is capable of making the most generous sacrifices for him she loves. But when does woman meet the man she loves? More frequently she finds a purchaser. She is sent to market like a calf, and appropriated by the highest bidder. She is not equal to her wooer, either in political or pecuniary influence; she also is a perishable article; and past a certain age, when men are still a prize, she becomes the butt of unfeeling waggery and heartless disrespect. The fear of the reproach, the love of settlement, the envied honours of the name of matron, oft hurry women into married life without the moving principle of love to stir them. Thus this very circumstance of woman's inferiority destroys true love in her, and robs the other sex of all its confidence. Who can count the tortures that have rent the hearts of the best and fairest of Nature's sons and daughters, amid such cruel obstacles to social sympathy and generous intercourse?

At present woman's chief support is sensual love. Were man not powerfully actuated by this passion, woman would be almost treated as an outcast from society. This is the source of all the kindness that man condescends to show her. But, as already said, this passion is individual, and will not influence the male in his general treatment of the other sex. The man who in private will yield himself up to the tender tyranny of a favourite mistress, and ruin himself merely to humour her caprices, may still be a merciless tyrant to the sex at large. There are men who hate the sex with one solitary exception; and there are women also who have similar feelings. The strength of passion, then, in man is no resource for woman; the sense of justice only in her rival, or her bold demand for justice from him, with a firm position of resistance to farther inroads on her natural rights, these are her only hopes. 'Tis a war of reason, not of mere feeling, and each party will derobe itself of sensual feeling in the contest. Nor can resistance in the woman be decried by those who now occupy the place of women as servants to their masters.

If the principle of resistance be justifiable in the male, it cannot be reprobated in the female. If women are compelled by want to leave their homes, and give their services for money we cannot see that any law of sound morality or legislature can put an interdict upon them. Such an interdict is a war against liberty itself, and though it may do partial good to some, the general good can amount to nothing. Arbitrary laws will never save us. The last smuggler will survive the last exciseman, and if the women be prohibited from producing wealth, they will speedily become outlaws, and raise a sexual war. If women be prevented from making clothes, binding shoes, spinning, weaving, etc., what shall they do? They must haunt the street and prowl for prey, and then be reprobated by pious magistrates and other godly censurers of public morals, who devour their own children in punishing the crimes which they themselves create.

To the Female Straw-workers of London

Fellow Workwomen,

The necessity of some determined steps to prevent the mad competition among the warehouse and shopkeepers must be obvious to every thinking mind; and all who will give themselves the trouble to look into the cause, will find it to emanate more from themselves than those that employ them. We women, who should have protected our labour, have, in many instances, been the first to reduce it for the gain of the moment, without considering what ruin we were bringing on ourselves and posterity. We have among us widows and orphans, whose only support depends of the produce of their labour; I ask those, does the present price you receive support you in those things necessary for your health and comfort all through the year? No! And does the reduction of our labour benefit the majority of our employers? I am quite certain it does not. I remember hearing a gentleman say in the workroom – if the girls would come to a determination to work for no less than a shilling per score, they would be doing their masters more good than by any other act they could ever do. That is the price he gives, and when, from the ruinous proceedings of other houses, he has been compelled to lower his price, I am certain he has felt really sorry. His workwomen honour him – his goods are of the best, and finished in the first style, without half the trouble of other masters; his hands grow old in his employ. The cause is evident – his interest is in the hearts of those he employs, for they feel it is their own. Now look on another picture. There is a house in Holborn that gives threepence per score, and gets its work done for that price. There is another house near Blackfriars-bridge, that gave twopence per score last winter, and had a large stock of goods made up by some of the best hands. Another low-priced master in Newgate-street says he has no occasion to lower the price himself, for the women will come and offer to take it at any price. I beg our employers to look into this, and to ask themselves if protecting our labour will not preserve them?

When, gentlemen, our labour is reduced to the lowest, the struggle must begin among yourselves; then, like us, the weakest will go to the wall. Let not the gain of the present devour the prospect of the future, lest your children be compelled to toil as we do. If we cast a look on Hartford, Bedford, or Essex, it presents a sight most painful to a humane bosom. Little children are sent to school to learn to read and spell; and instead of being taught to work at the needle, are kept at straw plaiting; their work is sold cheap, to supply those houses that undersell the others, to the ruin of the trade. In the winter, when there is not so great a call for plait, the great dealers go to the markets and buy the plait at their own prices; then those who have capital reap a rich harvest, to the ruin of those that have none. I again ask our employers if this is not madness, and if some of them do not now, and will still more, feel the effect? Cannot this be prevented, your interest be promoted, and we rendered more healthy, intelligent, and happy? You, gentlemen, know it can, and we women are gaining wisdom enough to be certain of it; but not by dividing our interest from yours, but by steadfastly clinging to those among you who have ever shown a disposition to give us the reward of our daily toil. I am happy to say that we have still some wise masters, and have authority to say we shall be sure of protection if we will be firm and true to each other; and as we gain strength we will use it for the interest of our employers and the glory of our native land. It is doubtful to me if the people of England are aware of the immense capital we women raise for our country in the course of a year, or the men would take some trouble to inform us better, and not look with such contempt on our feeble efforts to assist the cause of freedom. The men educate us to think ourselves bound to obey them, and then make us slaves: we are placed by them in the same position as they are placed by their rulers, and we find that we shall have to struggle as hard for our freedom as they are struggling now for theirs. But I am sanguine in my expectations. I am sure in time we shall gain our freedom, for the men will find it necessary for the preservation of their own.

P.A.S.

Pioneer, 12 May 1834.

Woman's Page

If men were openly to acknowledge the instruction and assistance they receive from women, it would soon appear that, after all their boasted superiority the women have the principal guidance in the common affairs of life. There is a nominal respect paid to the women of this country, but it is in most instances only nominal. How often have we been disgusted with the hacknied, common-place 'compliments', as they are called, which are *thrown* at the 'ladies', the clumsy 'attentions' which are *vouchsafed* to them, and the high precedence which is given to them at feasts, till the men have filled their bellies, and then the delicate creatures expect the ladies to retire to the drawing-room! The reform of these abuses must begin with the women themselves; they ought to train their little male brats to think properly of their mothers, and sisters, and aunts, and the whole of their feminine acquaintance, and to instruct the little Pollys and Sallys at the same time not to be quite so afraid of masters Jackey and Tommy. However loudly the men may bellow out for their own liberties, they will never bestow what they obtain upon woman until she demands it from her masters, as they were done for theirs; and whenever that struggle arrives, the men will be as tenacious of giving up their absurd domination as is any other power which exists of relinquishing its authority.

It is fortunate, however, that the male part of the population cannot progress in real civilization without imparting the value of independence to those whom they at present consider their inferiors. A writer on the Rights of Women observes, that marriage seems ordained exclusively for the comfort of the man, that of the woman being disregarded; she must follow all his counsels, without having any veto on his determination; she must change her abode to suit his convenience, must break all the friendships of her youth to flatter his caprice, and bear his absence whenever he is pleased to quit her. Yes, and he has taken care to make the law as well as custom support him in his tyranny; for an operative may thrash his wife with impunity, and be in little danger of punishment for his brutality. Indeed, if the law were to punish him, the poor woman would become a victim for want of the means of his support.

In making these remarks, we do not wish a thought to be entertained that we desire to set the sexes at variance with each other; we only hope that, for the mutual happiness of both, the women will endeavour to create a public opinion among themselves sufficiently strong to command fair play, and the respect and kindness which is due to them, and which they will never obtain but by their own exertions and determination. Women would be no less amiable for being more independent, and mankind would be none the worse for a little of their gruffness being rubbed off to give place to the natural rights and privileges of woman.

Man has his particular sphere, and so ought women; nevertheless, owing to his superior physical strength, he has filched a great deal more from her than what belongs to him; and the sooner and with the better grace he renders it back again the happier for us all.

We are happy to inform our readers that the Miscellaneous Lodge of Females have resolved to devote one hour each Lodge-night to the imparting of domestic and other information to each other. This looks well, and as great ends mostly arise from small beginnings, we wish them God-speed with all our heart and soul.

Women's Grand Lodge of Operative Bonnet-makers

We understand the members of the above lodge will meet on Monday evening, at seven o'clock, at the Griffin, Eagle-street, Red Lion-square. Sisters are requested to be punctual to time. Women wishing to be members must leave their names and address in writing with P.A.S., 50, Zoar-street, Southwark. Men-pressers hold their lodge at the same place, at half-past eight o'clock.

Grand Lodge of Miscellaneous Female Operatives, 14, Charlotte-street, Fitzroy-square

At a meeting of the above lodge, held 27th May, it was proposed and carried unanimously 'that the thanks of this lodge are due, and are hereby presented, to the editor of the *Pioneer*, for his kind support in the cause of woman, and that he be requested to insert the same in his valuable publication.

Pioneer, 31 May 1834.

Woman's Page

[We shall beautify our Woman's Page this week by an extract from the 'Rights of Woman', by Mary Wollstonecraft.[14] It breathes the spirit of one who was deeply sensible of the degradation which is imposed by education upon the whole female world, and the contagion which infects the opposite sex, by the resistless moral influence which woman exercises upon the species. Whatever refinement of mind the male possesses, whatever suavity of manner, elegance of deportment, or gentleness of demeanour, all has been cultivated by the fair preceptor, the first and the kindest friend of man; his cradle in infancy, his tutor in youth, and his companion in riper years. How important then the subject of female education, when woman herself is the first and the most impressive teacher of the whole human race!]

Contending for the rights of woman, my main argument is built on this simple principle, that if she be not prepared by education to become the companion of man, she will stop the progress of knowledge; for truth must be common to all, or it will be inefficacious with respect to its influence on general practice. And how can woman be expected to co-operate, unless she know why she ought to be virtuous? Unless freedom strengthen her reason till she comprehend her duty, and see in what manner it is connected with her real good? If children are to be educated to understand the true principle of patriotism, their mother must be a patriot; and the love of mankind, from which an orderly train of virtues spring, can only be produced by considering the moral and civil interest of mankind; but the education and situation of woman, at present, shuts her out from such investigations.

To the Editor of the *Pioneer*

Sir,

I thank you, in the name of that sex, too long confined to their views by false maxims, and the present artificial state of society, for the service you have already rendered them by your able pen. I have been induced, by reading your papers, to seek into the causes of our unhappy lot, and the unfortunate effects of our degenerate condition upon society at large. I am aware my bounded capacity and attainments will not command the whole view of the question as to the means that will lead woman to a better knowledge of herself, what is for her interest, and what will place her in the position to win respect from the other sex, and love, with all good offices, from her sisters. My sentiments, humbly and sincerely given, may induce others, more highly gifted, to come forward and do justice to our cause.

Instead of, in youth, moulding all our thoughts and actions to obtain attentions from mortals like ourselves, let us first consider what may eventually be for our happiness, certainly not notice that which has not respect for its first actuating principle. Let us set our minds in order, and have faith in ourselves. Above all things to eschew the feelings of pride and vanity, that cumber too often our best qualities, and make them unfruitful. We shall then also be free from much of male dominion, unkindly exercised over us to the destruction of our weaker sisterhood. We have been ruled by the masculine ideas of what is our right, what is our duty, without the opinion we entertain upon these matters being asked, or wished for. We have been ruled by men, or through them for ages; and what benefit has our yoke presented either to them (if they must always be first) or to us? Our talents and duties are very properly to be exercised in making domestic life easy and comfortable; and that we are greatest then in our homes, I will not deny, if perfect in these pleasing feminine occupations; while man, from his stronger frame, can better buffet the stormy world without. Yet surely there are neutral grounds, if I may so express my sentiments, where both parties can meet; and will feel this truth, that there is no sex in the mind, or in conversation, instruction, advice, and other operations of the intellect. That we should each in our turn be merely spectators of each other, and even at times be necessarily divided, by 'man going forth to his labour'; and we, as Milton so sweetly tells us of our first father, and mother Eve, remain at home to do our tasks. Still, is there in these two several allotments of Providence any thing that degrades woman as an inferior creature to man? Woman now dreads every thing that is unusual, if it will lead her into a path not yet taken by the many; in this state of uncertainty she will follow the multitude to do evil, as she fears to act from her own responsibility. Her faults are frequently spoken of as impossible to be amended, and as if they were a part of her nature!

By the reform, which is in some state of progress, the social scheme of society will be renewed. The school of adults, whose teachers shall instruct them for their great and permanent benefit, shall accomplish this great change.

I have the honour to be, Sir, your obedient servant

Gertrude.

London, June 2, 1834.

The Women's Grand Lodge of Operative Straw Platters, Sewers, Bleachers, and Blockers, we understand, hold a Meeting every Monday evening, at seven o'clock, at the Griffin, Eagle-street, Red Lion-square, till a more eligible situation can be obtained; and the Sisters most earnestly request their Brother Unionists to make the lodge known to their wives and daughters, in order to forward the grand object for which all are now uniting.

Grand Lodge of Female Miscellaneous Operatives – A Special General Meeting of the above Lodge is appointed to take place on Wednesday, June 11, at eight o'clock in the Evening, on the most important business, when all the members are earnestly requested to attend.

Pioneer, 7 June 1834.

Meetings of the Female Miscellaneous Lodge

On Tuesday evening next, a meeting of the Female Miscellaneous Lodge will be held at the Institution, Charlotte Street, Rathbone Place when all the members and persons wishing to be initiated are requested to attend.

Pioneer, 19 April 1834.

Female Grand Lodge of Miscellaneous Operatives
This Lodge will meet every Tuesday evening, at seven o'clock, at number 14 Charlotte Street, Fitzroy Square. Persons desirous of becoming members must send their names addressed to the Secretary, on or before Monday in each week.

C. Dempsey Grand Secretary.
Pioneer, 3 May 1834.

Straw Bonnet Makers Organise

To the Straw-Bonnet Makers

Fellow-Workwomen,
I am happy to inform you we are on a straight road towards our emancipation; but it is necessary that we take a right position, and most resolutely keep it. Let no man laugh you out of your claims to liberty; nor let flattery deter you from the hope you have now of gaining your freedom. At the same time, let the woman of the Union be known by her modesty, virtue, sobriety, and cleanliness – not usurping the man's power, but wisely defending her own.

I have seen in the *Pioneer* a notice from the Blockers and others, calling a meeting of the trade. As we hope for support and protection from our brothers in union, and their wives (for we do not mean to let our money lie idle), it is but just they should know what right we have to demand the whole management of our own affairs. A titled lady in Essex, nearly a century since, wishing to employ her own sex, ingeniously invented the platting and sewing of straw bonnets. In the reign of George the Third, his queen, Charlotte, seeing the number of industrious women supported by that one article, and most likely being wise enough to know the capital it would raise for the British realm, patronized it, seldom the queen or her daughters were seen in public without a straw bonnet. Under these circumstances, the business was brought to the highest perfection; and there are those, whose fathers were mere beggars, now in the city, who keep carriages from the produce of women's labour. When the war ceased, in the year 1815, many useful men were thrown out of employment, their wives having to support them. The men, not wishing to be idle, were taught by the women to block; and in a very short time these men went round to all the principal houses in London, and offered to take home the work, and finish it for less money than the masters gave in-doors, the latter finding every thing for the girls' use. It was soon discovered by the women that these men were more tyrannical than their former masters; and, to get the business out of their hands, they offered to take it for less still. This mad competition has sunk the business from one of the best to one of the worst a woman can have. The men will, perhaps, attempt to deny the charge; but was it not against the principles I hold sacred to throw public odium on any individual, I would give the names of the first men, and those who have been actively engaged this spring in lowering the price of our labour. Yet these men we will forgive, if they are willing to take their proper place; and we will be proud to own them as our brothers, and to promote their interest: we will go hand in hand together with them to attain the full reward for our labour, without contention or fear.

My next letter will inform you where to find our Grand Lodge, to give you publicly our intentions and laws, and to show you the advantage of being a member.

P.A.S.

Operative Shoe-Binders and Closers of the Metropolis – We understand that a meeting of the above branches will take place at the Burton Rooms, on Tuesday, the 17th instant, at six o'clock, when business of great importance will be considered. Every sister should attend.

Pioneer, 24 May 1834.

We understand that the Woman's Grand Lodge of Operative Straw Platters, Sewers etc. will hold a meeting at the Griffin, Eagle Street, Red Lion Square, on Monday evening next, at seven o'clock; and the United Sisters most earnestly request their Brother Unionists to make the Lodge known to the women in their employ in order to facilitate the great object for which they are all united.

Pioneer, 28 June 1834.

Woman's Grand Lodge of Operative Straw Workers
At a meeting of the above Lodge, held on Monday June 23rd, it was proposed and carried unanimously, 'that the thanks of this Lodge are due and are presented to the Editor of the *Pioneer* for the kind and manly way he ever comes forward to advocate the cause of woman; and that the sisters of this Lodge feel bound in gratitude to give him their utmost support; and that he be requested to insert the same in his valuable columns'.

Pioneer, 5 July 1834.

Frances Morrison Lectures

On Friday evening, the 9th instant, Mrs Morrison delivered a lecture here on the subject of education.

A female philosopher, with moral courage and confidence in the truth of our principles sufficient to induce her to 'hold forth' those doctrines to the public which are yet subjects of so much dispute, being a novelty here, much excitement was created; and, although no notice was given by placards, a full audience attended, and listened to the sublime truths, as sublimely communicated, with the most solemn attention and stillness. There was a good attendance of females, who, it may be anticipated, benefited much from being present.

We have had a glorious day to-day. Mrs Morrison lectured in the afternoon on the Rights of Woman, and named a child (the third over whom she has performed that ceremony) which ceremony appropriately introduced the 128th hymn. In the evening she lectured on the marriage question. On both occasions the Institute was densely crowded, and from 200 to 300 most respectable females attended each lecture. The institution on both occasions contained, I think, above 600 individuals, and some hundreds must have returned, disappointed, being unable to obtain admittance.

We are now the centre of an extensive and extending sphere of operations. The villages and hamlets, generally, around us (and they are many) within a circle of the extent on all sides, of a 'Sabbath' morning's 'journey', are up and doing in the great and glorious work of disseminating the benign principles of truth and humanising charity. Several have obtained institutions or lecture-rooms, and the strong demands for instruction which are made by the inhabitants are being supplied weekly by us to the utmost of our ability, with the limited means (compared to the demands) which we can command. The harvest augurs well, but the labourers are few. Our lecturers, about five in number, have 'full' Sabbath 'employ', and their zeal and the bright prospect before them enable them cheerfully to persevere in the work.

Mrs Morrison lectures to-morrow evening at Lepton, a hamlet three miles distant, where many of our Huddersfield friends intend to follow her; on Tuesday evening she will lecture again in our institution; and on Wednesday she proceeds to Leeds.

Truly yours,

L. Pitkethley, jun.

Social Institution, Huddersfield,
Nov. 11th, 1838.

New Moral World, 17 November 1838.

Hymn Number 128 from the Rational Society's Hymn Book

Dear Infant, are thy tender powers
  Then sinful, vile and base;
Or dwells there evil in that smile
  Which decks thy lovely face.

No, smiling innocent, 'tis false,
  No natural vice hast thou;
Thy mind expanding free shall be,
  Broad, placid as thy brow.

For circumstances pure and bright
  Thy progress shall surround;
A mother's care, a father's love
  In fulness shall abound.

Social Hymns for the Use of the Rational System of Society,
2nd edn Leeds, J. Hobbson, 1840.

Lace-runners Organise

To the Lace-Runners of Nottingham and its Vicinity[15]

Sisters, On Monday last, a meeting was held, in the Democratic Chapel, Rice's-place, Nottingham, to consider the best means of putting an end to the present injustice practised towards you, by those who call themselves mistresses; you are well aware, that they are in the constant habit of going round to the warehouses taking out nearly all the work, and dealing it out to you, at what price they think proper to give; that you are not only obliged to take work from what are called 'second-handed mistresses,' but also from 'third-handed ones'; that in consequence of this method of giving out work, the lace-runners in many cases receive for their work not more than one-half the original price, the mistresses reserving to themselves the remainder for that most useful of all purposes, walking with your work to the warehouse! Are you thus to be robbed of your hard-earned pittance to maintain these cormorants in idleness, and many of their husbands in drunkenness and profligacy; no wonder that misery enters our dwellings – that we are in the depth of poverty, that our children are crying for bread, while there is a swarm of locusts hovering between us and the manufacturers, ready to devour one-half of our hire, it is not enough that we have to compete with machines which, in many cases, superseded needlework; but are also robbed in the manner described above; is this state of things to exist? Remember the Scripture saith, 'they that won't work, neither shall they eat'. Lace-runners of Nottingham, be determined, that this passage of scripture shall be verified, as far as you are concerned. The Committee whom you appointed to manage your affairs, have agreed that there shall be a turn out on Monday next, against this most unjust of all practices, and we trust that the lace-runners will be at their post and show their oppressors, 'that their occupation is gone'.

We respectfully request, that the manufacturers will condescend to assist us in this just undertaking; we also trust that the male portion of society will assist us, as it is the cause of the working man as much as the females.

Committee

Mary Smith
Hannah Weatherbed
Mary Chapman
Ann Davis
Sarah Hargreave, Secretary.

1840. Women in the Trade Union Movement,
Trade Union Congress 1955, pp. 41–2.

Mrs Morrison Attacks G.J. Holyoake?

Mrs Morrison – This lady, the widow of the much respected editor of the *Pioneer*, has lately been lecturing in Manchester, in answer to Mrs Martin. Mrs Morrison formerly lectured to the Socialists. In a recent lecture she promised her audience to display cases of Infidel immorality, and cited Mr Holyoake[16] as a first example. She declared that his conduct when in Gloucester Gaol, in refusing to go to chapel, was highly *discourteous* and improper. Gravely, this was the charge – well it was too bad. Seeing that the state so kindly provided for him – Christians giving him his daily bread and keeping him out of harm's way – refusing to go to chapel where there was a nice parson kept to preach to him – was ungrateful. He must behave better next time.

Movement, 27 November 1844.

Notes

1. The Combination Acts were severe restrictions on trade union activity passed in 1799–1800. They applied to all industries. The acts remained in force until 1824–5 when they were repealed.
2. Barbara Taylor, *Eve and the New Jerusalem*, Virago, 1983, p. 89.
3. Robert Owen worked on the principle that 'man's character is made for him and not by him'. He therefore aimed to provide an environment in

which people could develop in a cooperative and socialistic way. His opposition to formal religion made enemies among the wealthy so he sought friends and allies among the workers.

4. In the winter of 1833, silk weavers in Derby were locked out by their employers. The ensuing agitation around the country in their support helped the Grand National Consolidated Trades' Union to grow. Women played a prominent part in Derby.

5. The Grand National Consolidated Trades' Union was established in 1834 under the inspiration of Robert Owen. It aimed to involve all trades and women as well as men. It grew rapidly but survived for only a year.

6. G.D.H. Cole, *Attempts at General Union*, 1953, p. 197.

7. James Morrison was a tinsmith by trade who was influenced by Owenism. He was active in his union and played a prominent part in the unstamped agitation. He helped in the formation of the Birmingham Labour Exchange in 1833, and edited the *Pioneer* from September 1833 until it ended in July 1834.

8. The six Dorchester farm labourers, who were tried and transported to Australia in 1834, were accused of swearing an illegal oath, but their case was intended to deter further growth of the Grand National Consolidated Trades' Union. They later became known as the 'Tolpuddle Martyrs'.

9. George Jacob Holyoake, *Sixty Years of an Agitator's Life*, vol. 1, 1892, pp. 71–2.

10. Taylor, *Eve and the New Jerusalem*, p. 304, n. 78.

11. See Chapter 6, n. 14.

12. Saint-Simon was a French utopian socialist who subscribed to the views of tne materialists. He believed in the study of nature and had a small following in England.

13. Baron Williams was the judge who sentenced the Dorchester labourers to transportation. He was made a Baron of the Exchequer in 1834.

14. See Chapter 1, n. 6.

15. The lace-runners embroidered the lace and were frequently young women or girls. They were considered to be the most skilful, the hardest worked and the worst paid of all the operatives connected with the lace trade. They worked 15 or 16 hours daily.

16. George Jacob Holyoake, writer and reformer (1817–1906), was active in nearly all the reforming campaigns of the second half of the century. He wrote about 160 pamphlets on various subjects covering the whole field of human progress.

9

The People's Charter

Ought women to interfere in the political affairs of the country?
Yes! And for the following reasons.
First: Because she has a natural right.
Second: Because she has a civil right.
Third: Because she has a political right.
Fourth: Because it is a duty imperative upon her.
Fifth: Because it is derogatory to the divine will to neglect so imperative a duty.

R.J. Richardson, *The Rights of Woman*, 1840.

Introduction

It soon became clear that the 1832 Reform Act[1] had ignored the claims of workers to enfranchisement. In their frustration, many activists took part in other campaigns and, for a time, abandoned the cause of parliamentary reform. But towards the end of the 1830s, there was a renewal of the campaign for an extension of the franchise and the exercise of political rights by all. This determination manifested itself in support for the People's Charter based on six points, all of which, except the demand for annual parliaments, have now been incorporated into law. Secret ballots, the payment of MPs, equal electoral districts, adult suffrage and the end of property qualifications have been accepted for many years.

The first draft of the Charter included 'adult suffrage', but it was quickly changed to 'adult male suffrage' when it was pointed out in discussion that if women were included, men might have to wait much longer before achieving the vote.

The four stages by which the Chartist movement developed were distinctive in character and women played a significant part in each. The first stage included mass demonstrations of workers and middle-class reformers who were dissatisfied with the results of the 1832 Reform Act. The second stage was dominated by the formation of the National Charter Association, the first working-class political party, and by the General Strike of 1842 under the leadership of the Chartist rank and file.

The third phase reached a peak in 1848, the year of revolutions in Europe and the final stage saw the mass movement decline into a sect in the 1850s. But although the mass basis became eroded, the ideas of the Chartists became absorbed into the ideas and objectives of the socialists. Feargus O'Connor,[2] the charismatic Chartist leader in the movement's early stages, attempted to direct Chartism through his land schemes, but Ernest Jones,[3] in the 1850s, under the influence of Karl Marx and Frederick Engels and their *Communist Manifesto*,[4] looked forward to scientific socialism as the solution.

Because Chartism was a community campaign in which whole families took part, women were deeply involved. There is some evidence that a few women expected enfranchisement, but the majority participated on the basis that enfranchisement of their husbands would affect the bread-and-butter issues which were at the heart of their willingness to become active. However, the working-class women involved, although many in number, were rarely identified as individuals and there are few names as prominently known as the Owenite missionaries or the women imprisoned in the fight for the freedom of the press.

A further reason why women have not been identified individually in the Chartist movement is that histories have until recently tended to concentrate on the national scene. When the local situation is researched and written women appear more frequently. The participation of women in any aspect of the struggle has been seen by historians as reducing its importance or validity. In order to raise the status of Chartism, they have therefore tended to minimise the part played by women. They have also ignored the essentially feminine contributions to the campaign, such as the concentration on schools, social events and processions in which women were prominently active.

Chartism was the manifestation of working-class recognition of its potential as a class. Women saw themselves as part of that class and recognised their responsibility to join in the activities planned as part of the campaign. Perhaps because the activity was class based rather than feminist in outlook – as much of the Owenite philosophy was interpreted as being – modern historians have not given women in the Chartist movement the same credence as those who supported the Owenites. There were some women, of course, who became involved in both campaigns. Emma Martin,[5] the Owenite missionary, chaired a meeting of the female inhabitants of London at Millbank in support of the imprisoned Chartists, Frost, Williams, and Jones[6] in January 1840.

Women's participation in the movement started even before the Charter was published in London in May 1838. Ever since the Poor Law Amendment Act had been passed in July 1834, there had been growing opposition to its draconian terms. The female inhabitants of Elland met together in February 1838 to launch a petition addressed to the young Queen Victoria asking for the repeal of the act. Mrs Grasby in moving the resolution said that the New Poor Law had not been concocted by men, but 'by fiends in the shape of men'. She pointed out that women would suffer more from the act than men because separation from their families was bitter medicine to take.

Once the charter was published, the Poor Law agitation became submerged in the campaign and identified with the same political ends. The Chartist movement was an amalgam of several radical strands that had been gathering momentum since the Reform Bill, in which working-class aspirations had been largely ignored, was published. Government attacks on trade unionists such as those at Tolpuddle[7] were seen by working-class radicals as part of the same oppressive regime as the imposition of the hated Poor Law. The disparate strands became a cohesive force in the recognised need for workers to have a say in the decisions that affected their lives and which increasingly became seen as the right to vote.

The first goal after the six points had been made public was to spread the word. Mass meetings were held throughout the country to present the charter and elect delegates to the proposed National Convention. Women were fully involved in those meetings.

In Birmingham, Thomas Clutton Salt[8] addressed a meeting of women at which he estimated that 12,000 were present. He reported that 'iron had entered their souls'[9] and commented that the movement could not afford their neutrality; it needed their enthusiastic friendship.

He mentioned that a meeting had been planned in Manchester later in the year. That was the first of the Kersall Moor meetings at which women were present in numbers.

At Whitsun, the following year, there were again huge demonstrations in the main population centres, and Kersall Moor was the scene on Whit Monday, 25 May 1839. Among the contingents representing different trades were a number of carts in which women travelled carrying green banners with slogans such as 'Remember the foul deeds of Peterloo', 'Universal Suffrage', 'Vote by Ballot' and 'For a nation to be free, sufficient that she wills it'.

The *Annual Register*, in a typical reference said, 'The only novelty worth noticing was the presence of several female political associations. It was observed by an eye-witness that the appearance of some of the fair sex who figured on this occasion, both as to person and apparel, furnished a stronger argument than any adduced by their orators, of the necessity of adopting immediate legislative enactments for improving the condition of the mass of the people.'[10] Dr Taylor from Scotland said he 'gloried in seeing around them so numerous an assembly of Englishmen, and witnessing so many Englishwomen present on the occasion. It was a sure proof that they had felt the wrongs under which they had so long laboured; that, in the first place, they knew they were slaves – in the second place, that they were resolved not to be so much longer – and in the third place, that they intended to try the best means of obtaining their liberty.'[11]

When it became clear that the signatures to the petitions that had been circulated at the mass meetings were getting nowhere, the Chartists changed tactics by regrouping and uniting into a more powerful organisation. The government retaliated by arresting prominent leaders and sentencing many to death or transportation. Among those sentenced to nine months in prison was the Salford delegate to the Convention, R.J. Richardson.[12] Whilst in Lancaster Castle he wrote a pamphlet *The Rights of Woman* in which he argued the case for the full political enfranchisement of women, quoting the Bible in support of his case. But he reasoned that married women, having voluntarily given themselves to the marriage state, forfeited their rights as individuals.

When the National Charter Association was formed in 1840 and the working class acquired a formal identity in a class-based political party for the first time, women were accepted as full members on the same terms as men. But evidence suggests that in a number of cases the male member of a Chartist household was deemed to be the representative. More than one subscription would be a strain on many household budgets. Women tended to shy away from structured formal organisations, possibly because meetings were often held in public houses at times when women could not attend.

In 1842, the cotton manufacturers tried to impose a wage cut of 25 per cent in Ashton-under-Lyne and Stalybridge. This was the final straw that triggered a General Strike. The concept of a strike had been well publicised by William Benbow[13] in his pamphlet, *Grand National Holiday and Congress of the Productive Classes*. The unprecedented depression in the cotton industry coincided with a meeting of the Chartist leadership in Manchester. The cotton workers appealed to other workers to support them in their refusal to accept the wage cut and they took their message around Lancashire and further afield by walking from one factory to the next, pulling the boiler plugs. This effectively stopped the factory from working. The slogan was for 'A Fair day's wage for a fair day's work' and almost immediately it was extended to include the People's Charter. What had begun as an economic strike rapidly became political in character. The Chartist leadership left Manchester to return to their homes, putting the strike in the hands of two groups of working people – the representatives of the metal trades, who met at the Carpenters' Hall in Manchester, and the representatives of the textile workers, who met at the Fustian Cutters' Room in Tib Street. Similar organising conferences soon set themselves up elsewhere in the country, principally in Lancashire and Yorkshire. As the strike developed, the two Manchester conferences joined and met in the Owenite Hall of Science. Among the resolutions passed was one to continue striking until the People's Charter became the law of the land.

It was a measure of the wholehearted support that the strike had from the working class that women played a considerable role in it. Among the unformulated demands was a recognition of the need for change in the working and living conditions under which women were expected to exist.

On the second day of the strike in Manchester, a crowd of women assembled in Great Ancoats Street at 5.30 a.m. and marched through the streets attracting others as they went. At the first mill they came to in Mill Street, the workpeople acceded to their request to turn out. They went on towards Kennedy's Mill. There their request was refused so they were about to invade the building when a posse of police arrived on the scene. The *Northern Star* described what happened. 'The police charged the people sparing neither age nor sex, but laying about them right and left with their bludgeons and cutlasses; many were knocked down and beaten till they were unable to rise from the ground.' The women fought back with volleys of stones and the police took off in all directions 'amidst the curses and execrations of the immense assemblage'.[14] It was only when a detachment of the Dragoons and another of the Rifle Brigade arrived on the scene that the women dispersed.

The following morning in Granby Row fields, the *Manchester Guardian* reported, 'Notwithstanding the wetness of the weather, probably upwards of ten thousand persons of both sexes (the number of women was large) congregated there.'[15] While there is little evidence that women played any part in the leadership of the strike, there is sufficient comment in press reports to indicate that they played a full part in the activity. For instance, on the march from Rochdale to Bacup, Todmorden and back, the Manchester *Guardian* reported, 'Girls, not more than twelve or fourteen years of age, wearing heavy clogs, went along with this party – a distance of at least twenty-one miles, without the least refreshment. It was distressing to see them come down Yorkshire Street haggard, tired and lame, after having walked from Rochdale to Bacup, from Bacup to Todmorden and from Todmorden to Rochdale.'[16]

A group of women from Stockport marched to Greg's mill at Styal, where they burned down the female apprentice house and in the potteries they attacked the pawnshops. A number of women were among those arrested: of 39 arrested and taken to Stafford nine were women, who were described as 'all young and all assuming a sort of dare-devil manner'. Several were 'of delicate and decent appearance'.[17]

One young woman, Alice Kershaw, arrested in Ancoats, Manchester for hooting after a number of women whilst waiting for her strike pay of four pence, was called 'of rather interesting appearance'.[18] She said in court that she was a weaver and lived at home with her parents. Another striker, Elizabeth Taylor, was accused of having called Ellen Gowan a 'knobstick' but Ellen could not be found to give witness against her. Elizabeth McQuin, a 13-year-old-weaver, was hit on the head by a piece of tile thrown from the roof of Birley's mill by members of the factory management on to the massed pickets below.

There are numerous references to women taking action in the newspaper reports of the month-long strike. On one occasion in Halifax, the *Manchester Guardian* reported 'perhaps the women were at this encounter the more valiant of the two; approaching to the very necks of the horses they declared they would rather die than starve.'[19]

At a mass meeting on Skircoat Moor in Leeds a resolution was passed demanding the release of prisoners who had been arrested previously. The women were vociferous in their demands and urged the men to attack the prisons. A comment was made that the 'well disposed inhabitants looked on the women with commiseration' as 'many were poorly clad and not a few marching barefoot'.[20] When the Riot Act was read and the people ordered to disperse to their homes, a large crowd of women stood in front of the magistrates and the military, 'loudly declaring they had no homes, and dared them to kill them if they liked'.[21] They then defiantly sang the union hymn: [22]

Oh! worthy is the glorious cause,
   Ye patriots of the union;
Our fathers' rights, our fathers' laws
   Demand a faithful union.
A crouching dastard sure is he
   Who would not strive for liberty,
And die to make old England free
   From all her load of tyranny.
     Up, brave men of the union!

Our little ones shall learn to bless
   Their fathers of the union,
And every mother shall caress
   Her hero of the union.
Our plains with plenty shall be crowned,
The sword shall till the fruitful ground,
The spear shall prune our trees around,
     To bless a nation's union.

A plate fired in commemoration of the strike shows the scene at Preston where soldiers fired on the strikers. Women are shown falling to the ground. Another plate shows women at Stockport workhouse taking loaves of bread and handing them on to children. The authorities took troops from areas such as London and redeployed them in the worst-hit industrial towns. But this gave rise to a strong solidarity movement in London where the departing troops were subjected to protest demonstrations as they left by train on their journey north.

While women did not apparently participate in the organising conferences of trades unionists who controlled and directed the strike, there are reports of women meeting to discuss their activity and to pass resolutions saying that they would 'neither go to work themselves, nor allow their husbands to do so'. [23]

After four harrowing and hard-fought weeks, the strike ended. The workers had to return to their original wages and the Charter had to wait some years before it became law. But during the strike, women had demonstrated conclusively that they saw themselves as part of the working class and considered that they had a responsibility to participate in action taken by their class in support of their just demands.

In December 1842, the *Annual Register* noted that Miss Mary Anne Walker, the head of the Female Chartists, pronounced an address on the points of the Charter at the National Association Hall High Holborn.

The lady lecturer, who was dressed in a mourning suit, is about middle height, slightly formed with pleasing features, dark eyes and hair and a cast of countenance decidedly intellectual. Her natural powers are of no slight order, but her acquirements have evidently been narrowed to a very limited range, as her only reading appears to have lain among the crude political tracts which form the staple of a Chartist library. Her voice is low and sweet in many of its intonations, but probably from the want of practice, deficient in modulation. Miss Walker's oratorical powers and style of ratiocination will sufficiently serve the purpose of confirming Chartist faith in those who make the Six Points their creed; but it is by no means calculated to make new converts from the thinking and intelligent. [24]

Such a description certainly tells much about Miss Walker and possibly more about the male writer.

As the Chartist organisation became formalised and the more intense activity declined, women settled into the routine organising jobs and, no doubt, helped to keep the flame alive. New evidence may indicate that women played a more significant role in the years after Chartism's greatest days. Certainly there is evidence that as late as 1851 organisations such as the Sheffield Female Political Association were still being formed. It is more than probable that many of the women who took part as young girls in the heady days of the General Strike in 1842 became active in the suffrage movement as it developed from the mid-1860s.

What is certain is that at peaks of working-class activity, women and men were equally active and involved. Working-class history can no longer be accepted as a one-sided interpretation of events. Women's participation was a fact and must be recorded.

* * *

Female Public Meeting

The Female inhabitants of Elland held a public meeting in the Radical Association Room of the town, on Monday last, for the purpose of addressing Her Majesty for the repeal of the Poor Law Amendments Act.

Mrs Susanna Fearnley having been voted into the chair, opened the business of the meeting, by exhorting the females present to take their affairs into their own hands and not to rely on the exertions of others, least of all, in the House of Commons; but, at once to assert the dignity and equality of the sex, and, as the chief magistrate in the realm was now a female, to approach her respectfully and lay their grievances before her; and should their application be successful, she would then call upon them to resist the enforcement of this cruel law even unto the death. (Loud cheers.)

Mrs Grasby then moved the following resolution, 'That this meeting considers the New Poor Law Amendment Act an infringement on our rights.'

'Because it considers it to be unmercifully oppressive and tyrannical, sparing neither sex nor age.

'Because it takes all power out of the hands of those who pay and who have the best right of knowledge and means of disposing of the rates.

'Because it places the sole power in the hands of the three Commissioners who are utter strangers to the circumstances of the poor.

'We therefore as part of the community consider it a duty incumbent upon us to come forward in heart and mind, to solicit its total repeal.'

She said her heart responded to these resolutions. The New Poor Law was not concocted by men but by fiends in the shape of men. It had been hatched and bred in the bottomless pit. (Cheers.) The Word of God was filled with denunciations against those who oppressed the poor, and she was sure that God never influenced these men to pass that most unchristian law. They might be asked why women should interfere in public matters. She should answer at once, it was a woman's duty to be there; for women had more to fear from the bill than men. (Cheers.) Could she, the mother, be brought to forget the suckling child? No. No mother could, therefore, under the influence of the Word of God, she would oppose that law and she called upon her sisters now before her to follow her example. (Tremendous cheering.) Women have still more to do with this cruel measure than men. Their feelings were more susceptible and the pangs of being separated from those to whom they had been used to look to for support, and from their children of their own bearing were more severe, she believed, than it was possible for men to feel. (Loud cheers.) They ought also to resist it from a sense of duty. It was their duty to be, each one, a help-mate to her husband, to soothe his sorrows, but this law prevented her from being able to do so. The law was iniquitous and she exhorted them to act with firmness, and she was quite sure they would ulti-mately succeed. She could wish the authors of the law to be sent to St Helena, where Napoleon[25] was sent to, and remain till their bodies were wet with the dew of Heaven, and their hair as long as eagle's feathers. She attributed all their sufferings to misgovernment and exhorted them fearlessly to address the Queen, and if they should do so unsuccessfully still not to be desponding, but boldly and patiently persevere in their opposition, and all obstacles would ultimately be overcome. (Great cheering.)

Mrs Hanson, in seconding the resolution, described the distress existing in the neighbourhood of her residence; she knew families who had not one penny a day per head to live on. Thus, then, they were preparing them for the Bastille[26] diet before they put them in. Mrs H. then read and commented on a Poor Law dietary table, observing that food like that was calculated not to do them good, but to hasten them into eternity, and prepare subjects for the dissecting knife. In speaking of the hardships of this law, as peculiarly applicable to females, Mrs H. alluded to the personal disfiguration of the hair cutting off, which excited much disapprobation; this was followed by a description of the grogram gowns of shoddy and paste in which the inmates of the Bastille are attired. The speaker then drew a touching picture of the circumstances under which a sick child might be bereft of the attentions of its mother, and concluded her speech amid the tears, cheers, and execrations of the audience.

An address to the Queen was then agreed to be sent to Earl Stanhope[27] for presentation. After which, thanks were voted to Mrs Fearnley for her valuable services in the chair; to Mrs Grasby and Mrs

Hanson for their eloquent and able speeches; and to the other females who had assisted in getting up and managing the meeting; to Mr Oastler[28] for his constant and unremitting exertions in defence of labour in the cause of the poor, and more particularly for his opposition to the three Bastille tyrants and their emissaries. To Feargus O'Connor Esq. and the Editors of the *Northern Star*, for their opposition to the Poor Law Amendment Act and their able defence of the masses. To Earl Stanhope, John Fielden Esq.[29] and the Rev. Mr Stephens,[30] for their unwearied opposition to the Bastille tyrants.

Northern Star, 17 February 1838.

Important Meeting of Women At Birmingham

(From the Sheffield Iris)[31]

The following letter to Mr Elliott[32] will be read with great interest:
Birmingham April 16th, 1838.

Dear Sir,

I sent you, last week, a Birmingham journal with a very much curtailed account of a meeting of women. I alone of Birmingham reformers, dared convene or attend it. The experiment was triumphant. Not only was the vast hall full, but even its spacious lobbies were crowded. There could not have been less than 12,000 women there. A more beautiful and moving sight was never seen; a meeting more enthusiastic and orderly was never assembled. It was evident that the iron had entered their souls; that they felt deeply, and resolved religiously, that their children's children should not be trampled upon as they had been. I mention this meeting to you because it forms part of my general plan. I believe (I might say I know) that hitherto, the women have thought so little upon politics, and being so utterly ignorant of the connection of our system with their poverty and degradation, that they have either not interfered, or persuaded their husbands from meddling with politics, as a thing of no profit. We cannot afford their neutrality or hostility; they must be our enthusiastic friends.

I intend to have these meetings repeated throughout England. I am happy to inform you, that our Missionary in Glasgow has completely lifted up the whole population there.

The Reformers are also making preparations to receive us at Dundee, Edinburgh, Sunderland, Manchester and neighbourhood. They are preparing to hold a great meeting here, to sanction and give dignity to our mission, and to pass our national petition. We shall then break ground at Glasgow on the 19th May, and obtain the sanction of the people there; and from thence roll up the masses southward to London; where I should like to see 700,000 meet us on Hampstead Heath. But to effect any good object – to acquire any power for the people – we must exhibit, on the whole of our course, an unfailing, nay, a growing and increasing enthusiasm. May we depend on your potent aid to prepare the people at Sheffield, and some information as to their disposition towards us? From the middle classes, I expect nothing until virtue becomes with them a necessity, and they see the people strong in their union; then they will begin to seek shelter in their ranks.

You are aware I intend the national petition to be two-fold; the one to be signed by the millions of men, the other to be signed by the millions of women; and to be the first great evidence of a national simultaneous action; a simultaneous action which, well-directed, will have a moral omnipotence.

Time prevents my giving you more than this hasty sketch, and asking you what will Sheffield do?

With every good wish and sincere respect, I am, dear Sir, yours sincerely,

Thomas Clutton Salt

To Mr Ebenezer Elliott.

At the meeting referred to in the above letter, Mr Salt delivered a very spirited address in the course of which he gave a melancholy picture of the state of Birmingham.

Northern Star, 5 May 1838.

Meeting of Females

A very large meeting of females was held on Tuesday evening last, for the purpose of adopting a memorial to Her Majesty, praying her to use her influence to repeal the Poor Law Amendment Act. The meeting was called for eight o'clock, but long before that hour a considerable number of ladies were in attendance. At the time appointed, Mrs Moore was called to the chair. In addressing the meeting, she stated that when God made man, he made him with an help mate also, and ordained that they should live together as man and wife; and in that book, which she hoped all present read as the guide of their life, it was written, 'that what God had joined together, let no man put asunder'. But, said the speaker, in contradiction of this wise ordinance, our rulers have passed a law to separate man from his wife, and children from their parents; and because we are poor, we are to be confined in workhouses, more like prisons, as unworthy that liberty which ought to be the privilege of every honest individual. She said there never was a law in existence compared to it; except in the days of Pharaoh, when the young children were torn from their mothers and put to death. After pointing out various parts of the Poor Law Bill as, in her opinion, exceedingly objectionable, she called on her hearers to unite their influence to endeavour to obtain its repeal. The following memorial was then read, and, having been proposed and seconded for the adoption of the meeting, was carried unanimously:

To her most gracious Majesty, Victoria, by the Grace of God, of the United Kingdom of Great Britain and Ireland, Queen, Defender of the Faith.

The Petition of the loyal Females of the Ancient City of Carlisle, in the County of Cumberland.

May it please your Majesty –

We, your Majesty's faithful and loyal subjects, of Carlisle, have assembled for the purpose of addressing your Majesty on a subject which seems to us of paramount importance. But while we address your Majesty, in hopes that you will use your powerful influence to abolish the grievance of which we more immediately complain, we beg leave to state, that we feel the utmost respect for your Majesty's person, that we offer you our sincere congratulations on your accession to the Throne of your ancestors, and that we hope you will wear the Crown and wield the sceptre of these realms in peace and happiness, for many years to come. That you may be better enabled to do this, we would pray your Majesty graciously to recommend to your Ministers the speedy abolition of that most iniquitous measure called the Poor Law Amendment Act; an Act most infamous in its details – most cruel in its operations, which has converted our workhouses into prisons, which separates those whom God has joined together and whom no man ought to be able to put asunder; which tears the babe from its mother, and punishes helpless poverty as the worst of crimes. Your Petitioners also beg leave to state, that this Act gives power to three Commissioners which they ought not to possess, and which they have, in many instances, grossly abused; particularly by giving food to many of your Majesty's subjects insufficient in quantity and pernicious in quality, which has caused, in many instances, disease, and in several, death.

Your Petitioners therefore feel assured that if this Bill is not speedily abolished, great and universal discontent must spread through all ranks and classes of your Majesty's subjects, and, in the end, the stability of the Throne itself will be endangered.

It is long since the Females of England had an opportunity of

addressing a ruler of their own sex, they humbly hope, therefore, their petition will not be disregarded.
And your Petitioners, as in duty bound, will ever pray.

After the passing of the memorial, a discussion took place on the subject of purchasing a flag, £3 having been collected for that purpose, and what would be the most suitable motto to inscribe on it. It was at length agreed to have a white flag with a green fringe, and a committee was appointed [to consider] what would be the most suitable motto.

Northern Star, 1 September 1838.

Birmingham Women's Political Union

On Wednesday evening week, the Women's Union met at the Public-office; the large room was crowded. A chairwoman having been appointed, it was announced that upwards of thirteen hundred tickets had been disposed of. The announcement was received with applause. One of the females present briefly addressed the meeting. She said she had lately been very violently attacked by some of her Tory acquaintances, who had demanded to know what right she had to busy herself about politics! She replied, that she would not have done so, had she not suffered by politics; and had she not found that, by leaving politics entirely to the men, her condition, and that of her neighbours, was getting worse. She considered the women had a right to interfere for the purpose of procuring such changes as would improve their situation. The lords and ladies of the land enjoyed all the good things of the creation, while those who procured them could not touch them. She had long since given up the practice of repeating that part of the grace before meals which thanked the Almighty for his 'good creatures' because seldom or never did it happen that good creatures came to her humble table (Hear! Hear!). She hoped the women would persevere now that they had begun, and if they did so, things would soon be altered.

Mr Salt and Mr Collins[33] addressed the meeting, and were loudly cheered.

Each of the members of the committee was supplied with copies of Mr Salt's last address to the women, for distribution. The ticket money, amounting to some pounds, was handed in very freely, and there was no lack of spirit. It was ruled that only those having tickets would, in future, be admitted to these meetings.

Northern Star, 1 September 1830.

Address of the Female Political Union of Newcastle upon Tyne to their Fellow Countrywomen

Well ye know
What woman is, for none of woman born
Can chose but drain the bitter dregs of woe
Which ever to the oppressed from the oppressors flow.

                                                    Shelley[34]

Fellow-countrywomen,

We call upon you to join us and help our fathers, husbands, and brothers, to free themselves and us from political, physical, and mental bondage, and urge the following reasons as an answer to our enemies and an inducement to our friends.

We have been told that the province of woman is her home, and that the field of politics should be left to men; this we deny; the nature of things renders it impossible, and the conduct of those who give the advice is at variance with the principles they assert. Is it not true that the interests of our fathers, husbands, and brothers, ought to be ours? If they are oppressed and impoverished, do we not share those evils with them? If so, ought we not to resent the infliction of those wrongs upon them? We have read the records of the past, and our hearts have responded to the historian's praise of those women, who struggled against tyranny and urged their countrymen to be free or die.

Acting from those feelings when told of the oppression exercised upon the enslaved negroes in our colonies, we raised our voices in denunciation of their tyrants, and never rested until the dealers in human blood were compelled to abandon their hell-born traffic; but we have learned by bitter experience that slavery is not confined to colour or clime, and that even in England cruel oppression reigns – and we are compelled by our love of God and hatred of wrong to join our countrywomen in their demand for liberty and justice.

We have seen that because the husband's earnings could not support his family, the wife has been compelled to leave her home neglected and, with her infant children, work at a soul and body degrading toil. We have seen the father dragged from his home by a ruffian press-gang, compelled to fight against those that never injured him, paid only 34s per month, while he ought to have had £6; his wife and children left to starve or subsist on the scanty fare doled out by hired charity. We have seen the poor robbed of their inheritance and a law enacted to treat poverty as a crime, to deny misery consolation, to take from the unfortunate their freedom, to drive the poor from their homes and their fatherland, to separate those whom God has joined together, and tear the children from their parents care – this law was passed by men and supported by men, who avow the doctrine that the poor have no right to live, and that an all wise and beneficent Creator has left the wants of his children unprovided for.

For years we have struggled to maintain our homes in comfort, such as our hearts told us should greet our husbands after their fatiguing labours. Year after year has passed away, and even now our wishes have no prospect of being realised, our husbands are over wrought, our houses half furnished, our families ill-fed, and our children uneducated – the fear of want hangs over our heads; the scorn of the rich is pointed towards us; the brand of slavery is on our kindred, and we feel the degradation. We are a despised caste; our oppressors are not content with despising our feelings, but demand the control of our thoughts and wants! Want's bitter bondage binds us to their feet, we are oppressed because we are poor – the joys of life, the gladness of plenty, and the sympathies of nature, are not for us; the solace of our homes, the endearments of our children, and the sympathies of our kindred are denied us – and even in the grave our ashes are laid with disrespect.

We have searched and found that the cause of these evils is the Government of the country being in the hands of a few of the upper and middle classes, while the working men who form the millions, the strength and wealth of the country, are left without the pale of the Constitution, their wishes never consulted, and their interests sacrificed by the ruling factions, who have created useless officers and enormous salaries for their own aggrandisement – burthened the country with a debt of eighteen hundred millions sterling, and an enormous taxation of fifty-four millions sterling annually, which ought not to be more than eight millions; for these evils there is no remedy but the just measure of allowing every citizen of the United Kingdom, the right of voting in the election of the members of Parliaments, who have to make the laws that he has to be governed by, and grant the taxes he has to pay; or, in other words, to pass the people's Charter into a law and emancipate the white slaves of England. This is what the working men of England, Ireland, and Scotland, are struggling for, and we have banded ourselves together in union to assist them; and we call on all our fellow country-women to join us.

We tell the wealthy, the high and mighty ones of the land, our kindred shall be free. We tell their lordly dames we love our husbands as well as they love theirs, that our homes shall be no longer destitute of comfort, that in sickness, want, and old age, we will not be separated from them, that our children are near and dear to us and shall not be torn from us.

We harbour no evil wishes against any one, and ask for nought but justice; therefore, we call on all persons to assist us in this good work, but especially those shopkeepers which the Reform Bill enfranchised. We call on them to remember it was the unrepresented working men that procured them their rights, and that they ought now to fulfil the pledge they gave to assist them to get theirs – they ought to remember that our pennies make their pounds, and that we cannot in justice spend the hard earnings of our husbands with those that are opposed to their rights and interests.

Fellow-Countrywomen, in conclusion, we entreat you to join us to help the cause of freedom, justice, honesty, and truth, to drive poverty and ignorance from our land, and establish happy homes, true religion, righteous government, and good laws.

Northern Star, 2 February 1839.

The Address of the Female Chartists of Manchester to their Sisters of England, Ireland, Scotland and Wales

Passed at a Public Meeting of their Sex, holden in the Chartist Room, Tib Street, on Wednesday, July 21st, 1841.

Sisters in Bondage,

We, the females of Manchester, feel it our duty, at this important crisis, thus to address you, from a conviction that our principles and motives need only to be known to gain your assistance, appreciation, and co-operation, in gaining our object.

Our principles are justice to all, and injustice to none; a right to subsistence in the land of our birth. It may be asked by those who wish for things to remain as they are – by those who are not actuated by a desire to save their country from impending ruin, why we engage in and concern ourselves about politics! In reply to which we say we have an interest in the prosperity of the country. We all sprang from one common parent – are the children of one all-wise Creator, who has provided for all; therefore we have the same right to subsistence, though dwelling in a cot, a cellar, or a garret, where forced by circumstances over which we have had no control, as the lady in the drawing room, or the ballroom, or the Queen upon the throne.

A love for ourselves, our husbands, our children, our country, and everything valuable in existence, stimulates us to take a part in a struggle which we conceive calculated to end in success, and thus avert the awful calamity that has been for some time, and is now, pending over us; and which will certainly overtake us if not thus averted.

We take our stand, also, as a matter of right; as fully and fairly illustrated by circumstances before our eyes. Surely, if by our labour we are compelled to maintain two Queens at the expence of £570,000 a year; and if a female is allowed to take the highest seat in the state, and give directions for the government of the country, we have a right to struggle to gain for ourselves, our husbands, brothers and children, suitable houses, proper clothing and good food. Then, Sisters, we call upon you in behalf of upwards of four hundred females who had their husbands torn from them at the instigation of class-made law in 1839, and placed in dungeons for merely wishing to redress the grievances which press upon both you and us; left without their guardians and protectors at the mercy of the public, with a forlorn, sorrowful and agitated mind by day, weeping and mourning and sighing over their husband's sufferings; and dreary, restless, and sleepless hours by night, their children bereft of kind and affectionate fathers, and the long affection and concord which existed betwixt them cut asunder by the tyrants. We call upon you on behalf of the wives of those unfortunate men, Frost, Williams and Jones, who are left disconsolate, heart broken, and in a state of anxiety for their husbands, who are sent across the seas; subject to insult, torture, and slavery; on behalf of the widow, Mrs Clayton, whose husband died in Northallerton prison; and on behalf of the good, true, and virtuous men who have suffered, and are now suffering, imprisonment.

Sisters, if ever there was a time when it was our duty to shake off our lethargy and engage in a grand struggle for liberty, surely it is now. Does not the sword of persecution draw nearer and nearer every day, tyrannising over us in various ways! Thousands of both males and females are walking the streets for want of employment, compelled to pledge and sell their clothes and furniture to purchase food to supply their physical wants, until their houses and clothes boxes are nearly empty, while the pawn-brokers and furniture brokers shops are wedged and crammed with the furniture and clothes of the industrious poor. Our granaries are full of the food which providence has sent, and the warehouses are full of clothing, while thousands are starving. How grievous must it be to see our husbands wandering the streets, willing to work but unable to procure it, thrown out in consequence of the improvements which have been made in machinery! What can be more piercing and heart-rending to a woman than to hear her off-spring crying for food to satisfy the cravings of hunger, and she none to give to them! And after pledging and selling all they have, driven to begging from their neighbours, who are in the same condition as themselves, or nearly so!

What prospect is there for us, when our husbands are supplanted by machinery, except to emigrate to a foreign land, or be inmates of a Poor Law Bastille, which will be inevitably the lot of a large number of our fellow creatures without a speedy change!

Sisters, suffering humanity cries for your assistance at this most important crisis, to endeavour to alleviate the miseries which every where abound amongst the industrious yet starving millions.

We ask for nothing but what is consistent with the laws which God has laid down in the unerring standard of divine truth – the Scriptures, and exemplified in the laws of nature.

The fowls of the air, the fishes of the sea, the beasts of the field, and every other living agent, have enough, without either toiling or spinning, while we can scarcely get sufficient to keep body and soul together, for working twelve or thirteen hours per day. Should such a state of things exist, when there is sufficient for every man, woman, and child in existence? Justice and common sense say no! Then why is it that, in the midst of plenty, we are in such a condition? Why is it that those who are willing to work, that those who have produced everything valuable in society, without whom the factories would not have been built, the machinery made, the railroads constructed, the canals cut, who build and man the ships, who fight the battles, make their hats, shoes and coats, and till the land – cannot get enough to quell the ravings of hunger? Why, because they have no power to make laws that influence the distribution of such wealth.

It rests with the industrious people whether they will any longer submit to a system so wicked, fraught with injustice and misrule.

Up, then, brave women of England, Ireland, Scotland, and Wales, and join us in the cry for the Charter, which will protect labour, and secure plenty, comfort, and happiness to all! Give us your support in paying due respect to our champions who are about to be released from their dungeons, and lead us on to victory, namely O'Connor, O'Brien, and Benbow.

Sisters, in the cause of democracy, we remain,

Yours, in the bonds of affection,

The Female Chartists of Manchester.
Hannah Leggeth, Treasurer.
Sarah Cowle, Secretary.
Northern Star, 24 July 1841.

Woman's Rights

[Though we abstain from inserting anything eugolistic of our own writings, we think ourselves authorised to break through the rule in the case of our fair friends; but, especially, because the voice of woman is not sufficiently heard, and not sufficiently respected, in this country. The greatest test of enlightenment and civilisation among a people is the estimation in which woman is held, and her influence in society. Woman has an important mission in this country, and our fair friends in Sheffield shew themselves worthy of the task.]

Women's Rights' Association
84, Pond-street, Sheffield, Dec. 17, 1851.

Respected Sir,

A recent number of your 'Notes to the People' was brought to our last meeting by one of our members, to consider that ably-written letter on 'Raising the Charter from the Pot-house', and it was unanimously carried that a vote of thanks be given to you, and reply sent to that effect, for your advocacy of woman's influence; also to solicit your continued support; and in doing so, sir, we beg to state, or rather confirm your statements, that did our brothers but admit our rights to the enjoyment of those political privileges they are striving for, they would find an accession of advocates in the female sex, who would not only raise the Charter from those dens of infamy and vice from which so many of us have to suffer, but would with womanly pride strive to erase that stigma, which by the folly of our brothers has been cast on Chartism, not only by exercising their influence out of doors, but by teaching their children a good sound political education. This, sir, will never be done while men continue to advocate or meet in pot-houses, spending their money, and debarring us from a share in their political freedom.

Signed on behalf of the meeting,
Abiah Higginbotham, Cor. Sec.
Notes to the People, vol. II, 1852, p. 709.

Universal Suffrage

To the Editor of the Friend of the People

Honoured and Excellent Friend,

The noble thoughts breathing through thy 'Friend of the People', in No. 9, its first article, embolden me to address these few lines and papers on the immense blessing of Universal Suffrage, and its crying want among us, to send to the right about the Greys and Russells,[35] that they may no more harass the world by their insolent defiance of the People's claims. But my friend, let us see what is the people, what is universal? Is it only half and that the smallest half, or is it the entire human family, all the adult burden-bearers, tax payers? Is it or is it not? You ought with your strong pen to declare the truth, the whole truth, and demand the right of all; with this motto the rights of all human beings are equal. Will you do this, or not? Will you still remain in the half-way house, still do as the poor French have done, and failed in the old revolution and perhaps as bad now? Leave the Charter; it is now a dead letter; the poor, superannuated upholders of it have gone to sleep or almost as bad, or in almost twenty years their doings would have told for something, never mind the points one, two, three, four, five, or six, possessing the first in its true logic, in its real meaning, the others would be at our beck and fell like nine-pins every refuge of lies, our taxes, seven-eights for war, would soon melt away with the expelled 300 slaughter-men from our houses of law making, and the People would breathe from their nightmare. Insert this in thy 'Friend' if it please thee and, conform with thy views of justice and give me at early leisure thy sympathies with the views of thy sincere and cordial friend.

Anne Knight.[36]

Chelmsford.

Friend of the People, 8 March 1851.

Rights of Women

To the Editor of the Friend of the People

Esteemed Friend,

Thy name in *La République* is come to me with several other names, showing the Chartists are just waking out of their sleep, and are meeting for a good many things – but still persisting in their infatuation of calling that universal which is only half, in spite of the suggestions of common sense and the appeals of the injured majority of your species. Some have united to demand the right, but it is futile to expect that slaves can break their bands. It is hardly likely any other town will rouse in the sense of wrong, and ask for redress; and it is no trouble to you just to add the name of Woman to your demands, and will cost you nothing – but rather confer on you glory for overcoming the selfishness which has too long warped the minds of many of the race. A simultaneous demand will, my good brother, cost you nothing, and rejoice the hearts of many with that of thy sincere friend,

Ann Knight.

Paris: Avenue Sante Moneda Rouie 8, 5 mo., 12 1851.

Friend of the People, 31 May 1851.

Notes

1. See Chapter 3, n. 2.
2. Feargus O'Connor (1796–1855). Irish barrister who founded the *Northern Star* newspaper and gave leadership to the Chartists. He was a noted orator.
3. Ernest Jones, 1819–69. An outstanding leader of the later Chartist period. Editor of *Notes to the People*. Influenced by Karl Marx and Frederick Engels. Practised as a barrister in Manchester.
4. The *Communist Manifesto* was first published in German in London in 1848. The English translation by Helen Mcfarlane appeared in the *Red Republican* on 9 November 1850 and the three subsequent issues.
5. See biography in Chapter 6.
6. John Frost, Zephaniah Williams and William Jones were the organisers of the Newport rising in 1839. They were arrested and sentenced to death and later sent for transportation for life.
7. See Chapter 8, n. 8.
8. Thomas Clutton Salt was a lamp manufacturer, one of the leading Birmingham Chartists.
9. *Northern Star*, 5 May 1838.
10. *Annual Register Chronicle*, May 1839.
11. *Full Report of the Grand Moral Demonstration of the Working Classes of South Lancashire*, 1839, p. 9.
12. Reginald John Richardson, 1808–61. See Introduction by Edmund and Ruth Frow to the Limited Facsimile Reprint, 1986.
13. William Benbow, 1784–? A leading radical who was active from 1816 until the General Strike of 1842. He formulated the policy of the general strike and wrote a pamphlet in which he outlined how it could be organised.
14. *Northern Star*, 13 August 1842.
15. *Manchester Guardian*, 13 August 1842.
16. Ibid.
17. *Manchester Guardian*, 24 August 1842.
18. Ibid.
19. *Manchester Guardian*, 17 August 1842.
20. Frank Peel, *The Risings of the Luddites*, Brighouse, 1895, p. 333.
21. Ibid.
22. Samuel Bamford, *Homely Rhymes, Poems and Reminiscences*, Manchester, 1864, pp. 179–80.
23. *Manchester Guardian*, 3 September 1842.
24. *Annual Register*, 3 December 1842.
25. Napoleon I (1769–1821). Emperor of France exiled to St Helena.
26. The prison fortress built in Paris in the fourteenth century and destroyed during the French Revolution.

27. Charles Stanhope, Lord Mahon, 1753–1816. Author of several scientific papers, he constructed successful calculating machines. He was a radical Member of Parliament where he was known for his energy and volubility. He was interested in the reform of Parliament from the 1770s.

28. Richard Oastler (1789–1861). Prominent Tory radical who campaigned for the Ten Hour Bill and became known as the King of the Factory Children.

29. John Fielden (1784–1849). Radical manufacturer at Todmorden. Supporter of the factory movement and Member of Parliament for Oldham.

30. Joseph Rayner Stephens (1805–79). Non-conformist Minister at Stalybridge who campaigned vigorously against the New Poor Law. Advocated physical force Chartism.

31. Started as the *Sheffield Register* in 1787. Became the *Sheffield Iris* and continued publication until 1856.

32. Ebenezer Elliott (1781–1849). Known as the Corn Law Rhymer. Active in the Anti-Corn Law movement and supporter of the Chartists.

33. John Collins, a journeyman pen-maker sent as an emissary from Birmingham to Scotland to campaign for the People's Charter in 1838. Collins was especially popular with women who applauded him at meetings.

34. P.B. Shelley, *The Revolt of Islam*, VIII, verse XV.

35. Charles Grey Earl (1764–1845). Whig leader and Prime Minister 1830–4. John Russell (1792–1878). Whig party leader and Prime Minister 1846–52 and 1865–6.

36. Anne Knight (1786–1862). A Quaker campaigner against slavery and friend of the Barmbys and other Owenites, she supported the Chartists.

10
Ireland

> In Ireland the plundering and even extermination of the tenant
> farmer and his family by the landlord is called the property right,
> whereas the desperate farmer's revolt against his ruthless executioner
> is called an agrarian outrage ... This regime of terror makes it possible
> for the landowners to redouble their oppression with impunity.
>
> Jenny Marx on Agrarian Outrages in Ireland,
> *Marx/Engels Collected Works,* vol. 21, 1985, p. 434.

Introduction

Events in Ireland and the atrocities committed there by the British were
exposed in the radical press throughout the first half of the nineteenth
century. Irish women suffered greatly at the hands of the occupying British
and they were occasionally the reporter and commentator on Irish matters.

Anna Wheeler was 13 years old when the events described in her article
in Feargus O'Connor's journal, the *Political Instructor,* took place. In all
probability she had regarded the United Irishmen as heroes from an early
age and the British as the villains. Frederick Engels appreciated the value of
the tradition of passing folk history on through the family when he
commented that the infamous episode in which three young Irishmen
were hanged in Manchester would be 'sung to every Irish babe in the
cradle in Ireland, England and America'.[1]

Irish women were exceptionally ill-treated. They suffered at the hands of
the clergy and the British government, in addition to the 'normal'
restraints of a woman's life in terms of restricted access to the law, gross
exploitation at work and no rights in marriage or civic life.

Anna Doyle Wheeler (1785–?)
Anna Doyle was born in Limerick where her father was a radical Protestant
Archbishop. Her godfather was Henry Gratton, one of the leading Irish
nationalists. Her upbringing was typically middle class and at the early age
of 15 she married a neighbour from a nearby estate, Francis Massey
Wheeler. The marriage was a disaster.

Francis Wheeler was a drunkard and a fool while his wife was an intelligent and lively young woman. For the first years of their life together she found herself constantly either pregnant or nursing one of her six children, of whom only two survived. As her husband's behaviour became more and more intolerable, Anna spent her time in reading and self-education. She sent to London for parcels of books and became familiar with French and German philosophy as well as the classics.

In one bundle of books she was sent a copy of Mary Wollstonecraft's *Vindication of the Rights of Women* which was a revelation to her. Her discontent with her situation deepened and in 1812 she had had enough. With her two daughters, she left home and sought sanctuary with her uncle, the Governor of Guernsey. After spending time recuperating there, she went to France where she became involved with the St Simon socialists. For the next 20 years she spent her time in contact with radical groups in England, France and Ireland and became an important contact between them.

Anna Wheeler met and was familiar with many of the leading radicals – Charles Fourier and Flora Tristan in France, Robert Owen and William Thompson in England. She collaborated with Thompson in writing *The Appeal of One Half of the Human Race, Women, Against the Pretensions of the Other Half, Men* which was published in 1825.

By the late 1820s she was writing and speaking for the Owenites, always on the theme of women's rights and their unequal position in society.

Anna Wheeler bridged the gap between the middle-class reform-minded elite and the radical thinkers in the Owenite movement. She was convinced that woman's subservient position in society stemmed from her lack of education and she strongly advocated knowledge as a means of power. Her own unhappy marriage gave her plenty of experience on which to base an assessment of women's unsatisfactory state in relation to men and in addition she studied the laws which governed the situation. Her lectures were well received by large audiences.

Anna Wheeler often wrote under pseudonyms and published in the radical press as 'Concordia'. There is still much research needed to establish which was her writing, but the references to classical works and philosophy offer some clues. Anna Wheeler was an unusually well-educated woman in her day and her writing reflects it. However, she did not only write on an abstract level. In 1833, she criticised Robert Owen's intention to publish a code of laws on which marriage in the new moral world could be based. She warned Owen that, as a man, he was not fully competent to frame laws binding women and called for women to be allowed a say in their own destiny. Benjamin Disraeli described her as 'very clever, but awfully revolutionary', a label of which she would almost certainly have approved.

* * *

Closing Scenes of the Irish Rebellion of 1798[2]

By Concordia[3]

On the 3rd of October, 1798, the inhabitants of the small town of Newtownards, County Down, Ireland, were put into a painful state of excitement, by a rumour of the Rev. Archibald Warick having been arrested on a charge of high treason. Not that such an occurrence was by any means infrequent, for there had been many an unfortunate person sacrificed during the three previous months, to satisfy royal vengeance; but Mr Warick was widely known and beloved, and his apprehension was felt like a public calamity. Through the kindness of his neighbours he had been able, up till this period, to elude the vigilance of the local yeomanry. But, one of this corps having learned that Mr Warick was under hidence at his brother's, Mr John Warick's residence, carried the glad tidings to his ruthless leader, Captain Cleaveland, who lost no time in bringing to punishment the fallen and defenceless clergyman.

This Captain Cleaveland belonged to the cadet branch of some English aristocratic family, but who had left his country for the purpose of courting the good will of an old gentleman, to whom, through his mother, he was distantly related, and to whose property he had some hopes of becoming heir. Like all other fortune-hunters he was proud, yet mean; and it is said of him that he took much pains to prove that his ancestors had, since the reign of Henry II, never produced a single farthing's worth of wealth, but, on the contrary, that they had always been very liberal consumers.

His ancient, but ignoble, blood,
Had crept through scoundrels ever since the flood.

Such was the man that the aristocracy of the country thought a proper tool to entrust the command of a company of yeomanry to, and it must be confessed that he played his part well, after all danger was over, in hunting out and becoming the general hang-man of all the unfortunate rebels he could lay his hands upon; while the cries of the widow and the orphan were borne by the flames of their burning habitations to Heaven, there to be marked in the book of justice against him.

Before this scourge of mankind Mr Warick was tried – at least, he had the mockery of a trial under the form of court martial. He was charged, and soon convicted, of having appeared in arms against his sovereign and country. When asked if he had anything to say why sentence of death should not be passed upon him, he replied;

I will not plead before them who have no right to try me, nor for a life that they have the power to spare; for, dear as life is to every living creature, I would not purchase it at such a price. But, it is false to say that I bore arms against my sovereign, *for I acknowledge no sovereign but God*; and, as to my country, it was not against her that I bore arms, but against her enemies – it was because I loved her that I now suffer – because I could not suffer to see her trampled beneath the heel of a merciless foreign tyrant – because I could not behold, without concern, my countrymen 'beg for leave to toil' at the gates of those men who had robbed them of their common birthright, and God's free gift to all – *the land* – because I saw religion made the means of supporting tyranny – in a word, it was because I loved my country, and would have given to her 'liberty' that I now must die; but take my life, and I know you will; and if I had a hundred lives I would stake them all for the same glorious cause. Yes, take away my life, and mangle this poor body, and let ascend to Heaven, there to enjoy freedom, this soul that scorned to be a slave on earth.

This reply was hailed as a confession, and he was condemned to be executed on the following morning.

It was about nine o'clock in the evening of the day on which Mr Warick received his sentence, that Captain Cleaveland was sitting alone in his parlour before a clear burning fire, enjoying his glass of punch. A savage like smile played about his features, as no doubt he thought of the noble deed he had that day performed. No doubt but he thought that such actions would draw on him the notice of the aristocracy, at whose feet, notwithstanding all his pride and arrogance to those below him, he would crouch and fawn like a spaniel. Probably he foresaw what did come to pass – namely, that those bloody actions would find him a place at the table of my Lord this and my Lord that, the Marquis of Londonderry's, etc. Such were his hopes and thoughts, when he heard a gentle knock at the door. On the servant opening the door a female entered, who carried in her arms a child about two years old – she would be about twenty-five years of age. She was about the middle size, and extremely handsome, yet her pale but beautiful countenance contrasted strongly, even somewhat disagreeably, with her black dress. Her fine arched forehead showed she was intellectual, and her dark hazel eye bespoke intelligence as it glanced rapidly round the hall, or pensively fell on the smiling face of her innocent child. It was the soon to be made widow of Mr Warick.

'Is Captain Cleaveland at home?' she inquired, addressing the servant.

'Yes, madam.'

'Is he at present disengaged?'

'Yes, I believe he is.'

'Tell him, then, that a person wishes to speak to him on urgent business.'

The servant obeyed, and soon returning, told her that she might walk into the parlour.

Trembling with hope and fear, she entered the presence of the man of whom she was about to beg in vain the life of her husband.

After eyeing her for a moment as if to ascertain if he knew her, he carelessly said, 'Well, good woman, what is your business?'

Mrs Warick, advancing towards him, laid down her child, and, kneeling beside it, said, 'I come, sir, to beg the life of this child's father and my husband, the Rev. Archibald Warick, who was this day condemned to death.'

'Foolish woman,' replied the captain, 'You know not what you ask; I have it not in my power to grant your request.'

'Oh, sir! I know thou canst not pardon him, but thou canst put back the execution for three days; in the meantime, I will go, with my child, to the Lord-Lieutenant, and there beg his life, and I feel confident it will not be denied me.'

'I cannot even grant you that – my duty to my sovereign, and the safety of the country, alike forbid it.'

'Dost thy duty to thy sovereign forbid thee to be merciful? If so, thou wouldst be better wanting one; and dost the safety of the country demand that an innocent man should die?'

'No; but the safety of the country – nay, justice itself – demands that a hypocritical rebel should die.'

'Is the justice more just than God's, since he forgives his rebels.'

'Madam, I am not to be questioned thus, and I have only to add, that I will do nothing in the matter.'

'Oh, sir! Look upon this innocent child.' and she parted the golden curls that clustered on his brow; 'he has no protector but his father – no hope, save in him; for his sake, for the sake of the Almighty God, put back the execution but three days, and we will all live to bless thee. Oh, do! I will not leave thee till thou hast granted it to me.' Here her sobs stifled her voice, the tears ran down her lovely cheeks, her child beheld her emotion, and, as if by instinct, became alarmed; it twined its little arms around its mother's neck, their tears mingled together, and thus the mother and her infant pleaded and wept for mercy at the tyrant's feet.

Even he was moved, but it was only for a minute, for he said, 'These tears are all in vain. Nothing under Heaven can alter my determination, and I am determined that Warick shall die.' This he uttered in a tone of voice that left no hope.

At these words Mrs Warick arose, and dashing the tears from her eyes, said: 'Had I taken my husband's advice I would not have been here, but without his knowledge I came to thee, hoping that there might yet be a spot of feeling in thy hardened heart. But I am disappointed; and, oh, how I loathe myself for having kneeled to such a wretch.'

'Will you dare to insult me in my own house? I will have you punished for it!' And the savage put forth his hand to lay hold of her.

'Hold! Thou scion of a base aristocracy – thou tool by which they have deluged this country with blood, and hold our lands by the same right that the robber holds his booty – hold off, sir, and pollute not with thy bloody touch the wife of him who is *not a monster, but a man.'*

With this she hurried from the house, leaving Cleaveland stupefied, nor did the servant dare to stop her. But she had not gone far before her passion subsided into grief, and her strength failing her, she sank to the ground, and raising her eyes towards Heaven, the pale moon shining on her yet paler face, exclaimed, 'Oh, God, have mercy on us.' The cries of the child brought some persons to her help, who carried her to the nearest house, when she was found to be in a state of insensibility, but was soon, through the efforts of the inmates, restored to consciousness.

The next morning, before daylight, she visited, for the last time, her husband. The scene was too touching to detail, and too short for her to mention her encounter with Cleaveland. And when they parted none there beheld it without emotion. She never saw him again, for in the afternoon he was taken from his cell and hanged, then beheaded, and his head stuck upon a pike, when it was exposed to the public as the head of a traitor. It was taken down by his friends at night, who buried it with the trunk in the family burying ground, at Newtownards, where visitors may yet see, on a plain slab, the following epitaph:

Sacred to the Memory
of
Archibald Warick,
who suffered for the Cause of
FREEDOM
on the 5th October, A.D. 1798.
Also
his wife Elizabeth, who died
March the 4th, A.D. 1799.
And also
their son William, who died
August the 20th, A.D. 1800.

National Instructor, 8 February 1851.

Notes

1. The 'infamous episode' was the hanging of Alan, Larkin and O'Brien after a police sergeant had been shot in the rescue of two Fenians from a van taking them from the court to prison in Manchester in 1867. Frederick Engels made the comment in a letter to Karl Marx (24 November 1867). Marx/Engels *Ireland and the Irish Question*, Moscow 1978, p. 155.
2. For a fuller account see Charles Hamilton Teeling, *History of the Irish Rebellion of 1798*, 1828.
3. Anna Wheeler.

Bibliography

Periodicals

Black Dwarf: 29 January 1817–December 1824. Edited, printed and published by J.T. Wooler. An important unstamped periodical which advocated universal suffrage.

Bonnet Rouge: the Republican Magazine: 16 February–13 April 1833. Edited by Benjamin Franklin and James Henry Lorrimer.

Cap of Liberty: a London Weekly Political Publication: 8 September 1819–5 January 1820. Edited by James Griffin. A radical unstamped paper supporting Henry Hunt and universal suffrage.

Cobbett's Weekly Political Register: January 1802–February 1836. Long-running and influential journal.

Crisis and National Co-operative Trades' Union and Equitable Labour Exchange Gazette: 14 April 1832–23 August 1834. Edited by Robert Owen, Robert Dale Owen and Rev. James E. 'Shepherd' Smith.

Friend of the People: 14 December 1850–24 April 1852. Edited by George Julian Harney. Called for 'the Charter and Something More' and the abolition of classes in favour of the sovereignty of Labour.

Gauntlet: 10 February 1833–30 March 1834. Edited by Richard Carlile. Expressed Carlile's republican views. Includes letter section with reports of working-class action.

Isis: a London Weekly Publication: 11 February 1832–15 December 1832. Edited by Eliza Sharples Carlile ('the Lady of the Rotunda') while Richard Carlile and Robert Taylor were in prison. The first journal produced by a woman in support of sex equality and political and religious freedom.

Manchester Observer or Literary, Commercial and Political Register: 3 January 1818–14 September 1822; Edited by Thomas Rogerson and then by James Wroe. Aimed to 'revive the people's press and to restore the Rights of Man'.

Movement and Anti-persecution Gazette: 16 December 1843–2 April 1845. Edited by G.J. Holyoake – motto 'Maximise morals, minimise religion'.

National Instructor: 25 May 1850–3 May 1851. Conducted by Feargus O'Connor and others in support of the Charter.

New Moral World: a London Weekly Publication, Developing the Principles of the Rational System of Society: 1 November 1834–8 November 1845. Edited by Robert Owen and his followers.

Northern Star and Leeds General Advertiser: 18 November 1837–27 November 1852. The leading newspaper of Chartism with a national circulation. Organ of the National Charter Association.

Notes to the People: May 1851–May 1852. Edited by Ernest Jones, it represented the left-wing of Chartism.

Oracle of Reason; or, Philosophy Vindicated: 6 November 1841–2 December 1843. Edited by Charles Southwell, G.J. Holyoake, Thomas Paterson and William Chilton. Articles on religion, atheism and socialism.

Pioneer; or, Trades' Union Magazine: 7 September 1833–5 July 1834. Edited by James Morrison, organ of the Grand National Consolidated Trades' Union.

Poor Man's Guardian; a weekly Newspaper for the People Established Contrary to the Law to Try the Power of 'Might' Against 'Right': 9 July 1831–26 December 1835. Edited by Bronterre O'Brien and Thomas P. Mayhew. The best-known and most popular of the unstamped press.

Republican: 27 August 1819–29 December 1826. Edited by Richard Carlile in the interest of radicalism and freethought.

Sherwin's (Weekly) Political Register: 1817–21 August 1819. Edited by W.T. Sherwin for a reform of parliament.

Working Man's Friend, and Political Magazine: 22 December 1832–3 August 1833. Edited by John Cleave. Attacked factory abuses and called for universal suffrage.

Further Reading

The following three works are particularly relevant and valuable:

Bellamy, J. and Saville, J., *Dictionary of Labour Biography*, vols 1–8, 1972–87.

Taylor, Barbara, *Eve and the New Jerusalem, Socialism and Feminism in the Nineteenth Century*, London, 1983.

Thompson, Dorothy, *The Chartists*, 1984.

Bamford, Samuel, *Passages in the Life of a Radical*, London, reprinted 1967.

Banks, Mrs G. Linnaeus , *The Manchester Man*, Manchester, 1896.

Belchem, John, *'Orator' Hunt. Henry Hunt and English Working-class Radicalism*, Oxford, 1985

Chadwick, Stanley, *'A Bold and Faithful Journalist'. Joshua Hobson 1810–1876*, Kirklees Libraries and Museums Service, 1976.

Frow, Edmund and Ruth, *The New Moral World. Robert Owen and Owenism in Manchester and Salford*, Working Class Movement Library, Salford, 1986.

—— 'Women in the Early Radical and Labour Movement', *Marxism Today*, April 1968.

Gaskell, Mrs, *Mary Barton*, London, 1906.

Hollis, Patricia, *The Pauper Press. A Study in Working-class Radicalism of the 1830s*, Oxford, 1970.

Holyoake, George Jacob, *The History of Co-operation*, London, 1908.

Lewenhak, Sheila, *Women and Trade Unions. An Outline History of Women in the British Trade Union Movement*, London, 1977.

Marlow, Joyce, *The Peterloo Massacre*, London, 1969.

Marx, Karl, *Capital. A Critical Analysis of Capitalist Production*, vol. 1, Moscow, 1959.

Pinchbeck, Ivy, *Women Workers and the Industrial Revolution 1750–1850*, London, 1930.

Richardson, R.J., *The Rights of Woman* (1840). Working Class Movement Library, Salford, reprinted 1986.

Royle, Edward, *Victorian Infidels. The Origins of the British Secularist Movement 1791–1866*, Manchester, 1974.

Thomis, Malcolm I. and Grimmett, Jennifer, *Women in Protest 1800–1850*, London, 1982.

Thompson, Dorothy, 'Women and Nineteenth-century Radical Politics: A Lost Dimension' in Juliet Mitchell and Ann Oakley (eds), *The Rights and Wrongs of Women*, London, 1976.

Thompson, E.P., *The Making of the English Working Class*, London, 1963.

Wiener, Joel H., *Radicalism and Freethought in Nineteenth-century Britain*, Connecticut, 1983.

The authors would like to acknowledge the value of the following unpublished thesis:

Morgan, Carol Edyth, 'Working-class Women and Labour and Social Movements of Mid-Nineteenth-century England', University of Iowa, May 1979.

Books, pamphlets and periodicals consulted can be seen at the Working Class Movement Library, Jubilee House, The Crescent, Salford, M5 4WX, with the exception of *Isis*, which is at Manchester Central Reference Library.

Index